Put more fun, adventure & scenery
in your next getaway or vacation —
without spending a lot of money

Best Low Cost Things To See & Do

*Top attractions in the U.S. & Canada
that are inexpensive — or free!*

Loris G. Bree

ML MarLor Press

Saint Paul, Minnesota

Copyright 1988 by Loris Bree

ISBN: 0-943400-25-2

Distributed to the book trade by **Contemporary Books** / 180 North Michigan Av./ Chicago, Illinois 60601/ Telephone (312) 782-9181

Printed in the United States of America

First Edition April 1988

ML

MarLor Press/ 4304 Brigadoon Drive/ Saint Paul, MN 55126

Contents:

Introduction

You can plan a fun-filled, affordable vacation with this value-minded guide to thousands of attractions throughout the U.S. and Canada that charge no more than $5 admission. Some of the best may even be *free*.

You can choose from landmarks, museums, historic sites, scenic wonders, architectural landmarks, factory tours, live performances, regional happenings---and much more.

You can explore:

*An atomic submarine
*A gold mine with Gold Rush prospecting gear
*The sightseeing hot spots in major cities
*Unusual museums
*Scenic wonders
*Beautiful gardens
*Living history forts, houses or industries

Every state is included, as well as Canadian provinces,

all to help you get more out of your getaway or vacation.

You can follow the **Best Low Cost Things to See and Do** exclusively, or you can intersperse low-cost attractions with more expensive commercial tourist attractions. You'll be surprised to learn how often the best attractions are also low cost. They are just less well advertised so you hear about them less frequently.

In many ways this is a vacation or getaway "wish book." You can check out the low-cost, but high rated attractions as you glance through this book to determine where you want to go next.

And amazingly enough, it's *not necessary* to spend thousands of dollars just to be entertained or informed on your next trip.

How to use this guide

Best Low Cost Things to See and Do is an adventure-filled, money-saving resource for budget minded travelers

•Organization

This Guide is organized **alphabetically** by state and then by major city. In Canada, the indexing is by province and then by major city. This means you can look ahead directly to the state you want and locate the city where you want to visit easily. To cover travel away from the major cities, there is a **"Statewide Attractions"** isting.

•Listings

State
Each listing has a quick reference guide to tell you about the area's **fame**. We add a **"you must"** suggestion to give you some ideas about those things that

are unique to the particular area.

City
Each major city has **"fame"** and we offer a quick few words of what this is. In addition, we also give you a **"you must"** suggestion.

Best choices
Here you have specific **attractions** to visit, along with a street address and, usually, a mailing address. We include directions to the attraction, a description of the attraction. as well as what to do there.

Prices are described at the end of the description, as well as the seasonal openings, if any.

Good Choices
This includes **other attractions** that were not selected as one of the top choices but that are still well worth a visit. For these choices, we give you a short description,

6

unless the topic is obvious from the name, and the city.

In other words, you have enough information so that referring to a local phone book or contacting a chamber of commerce can help you locate it. We list major chambers of commerce at the end of this book.

Uses for book
In all you can use this book in three ways:

1/ Plan your trip ahead of time and lay out a specific itinerary. You might even decide to write to specific attractions you want to visit, using this guide.

2/ Use this guide as you travel to find the best of the lowcost attractions. It is useful no matter what type of transportation you are using.

3/ After the trip is over, you can use the guide to refer back to your adventures. And you can read about another area--- and start dreaming about and

planning your next travel adventure.

About this Guide:
This *Guide* was compiled with the latest figures available at press time. But be aware that there may be somewhat of a fluctuation from season to season, even week to week, although common sense would suggest that these changes will be modest. Attractions have the right to change their rates at any time.

To our readers:
We'd like to hear about your experiences with this *Guide*. Drop us a line and share some of the things you've encountered---both the good and the bad. If you've found a special attraction you think others would be interested in, please nominate it for a future edition of **Best Low Cost Things to See and Do.**

Alabama

Fame: *Southern hospitality, Confederacy's first capital and the U.S.'s first "Space Capital."*
You must *visit a plantation mansion, see the Space and Rocket Center, Huntsville, or the Alabama Shakespeare Festival Complex, Montgomery.*

Statewide Attractions

•Best Choices:

Space and Rocket Center
Tranquility Base, Huntsville, 35807. (205) 837-3400, (800) 633-7280. 15 miles E of I-65 on AL 20.

There are three attractions: Space Camp, Space Flight Center and Spacedome. Hands-on astronaut-related exhibits at the Space Camp; escorted bus trips to the interiors of four NASA labs at the NASA-Marshall Space Flight Center and see Space Flight films at the Spacedome. **Museum: $5/adult; $3.25/sr citizen, military, child. Flight Center: $3.25/adult; $2.25/sr citizen, military, child. Dome: $3.50/adult; $2.25/sr citizen, military, child.** Jun-Aug, daily, 9-5. Rest of yr, daily, 8-6.

Constitution Hall Park
Mail to: 301 Madison St., Huntsville, 35801. (205)532-7551. Street address: 306 Franklin St.

Costumed guides lead visitors through the meeting place of Alabama's first Constitutional Convention and other reconstructed 1819 buildings, including cabinetmaker's shop, print shop, theatre, library, post office. Demonstrations. $3.50/adult; $1.50/child. Tues-Sat, tours begin at 10 am; Sun, 1 pm. Mar-Oct, tours end at 3:30 pm, Nov-Feb, tours end at 2:30 pm.

Jasmine Hill Gardens
1500 Jasmine Hill Road, Wetumpka 36092. (205)567-6463. Jasmine Hill Rd., off U.S. 231 north of Montgomery.

A full-scale reproduction of the ruins of the Olympic Temple of Hera is the centerpiece of 17 acres, ornamented by fountains and pools. **$3/adult; $1/child under 12. Tues-Sat, 9-5.**

Old N. Hull Historic District
310 N Hull St, Montgomery, 36104. (205)263-4355.

Tours of 24 restored 19th century buildings including the Ordeman-Shaw House, Lucas Tavern, the Pioneer Log Cabin, Doctor's Office, Grange Hall, Country Store and Church. Gives a view of 1850's city life. **$5/adult; $1.50/child. Mon-Sat, 9:30-3:30; Sun, 1:30-3:30.**

U.S.S. Alabama Battleship Memorial Park
Battleship Parkway, Box 65, Mobile 36601. (205)433-2703

The Battleship Alabama was home to a 2,500-man crew that saw extensive action in World War II. Explore this mighty battleship, the galley, wardroom, engine room and many compartments. **$5/adult; $2.50/child 6-11. Daily, 8 sunset. Closed 12/25.**

Sturdivant Hall
713 Mabry St, Box 1205, Selma 36702. (205)872-5626.

One of the south's most magnificent mansions, completed in 1853. The period furnishings and formal gardens featuring native plants contribute to the interest of this outstanding building. **$3/adult; $1.50/child over 11. Tues-Sat, 9-4; Sun, 2-4. Closed Mon. and holidays.**

Birmingham Museum of Art
2000 8th Av N, Birmingham 35203. (205)254-2565.

The Southeast's largest municipal art museum featuring the Kress collection of Renaissance art, excellent collections of Wedgewood and Remington bronzes as well as changing exhibitions of major historical, contemporary and regional art. **Free. Tues-Sat, 10-5; Thurs, 10-9; Sun, 2-6.**

•Good Choices:

Natural Scenery: Sequoyah Caverns, Valley Head.

Nature and Man: Birmingham Zoo, Birmingham/ Landmark Park, nature trails, wildlife exhibits, Dothan/ Noccalula Falls and Park, waterfall, botanical gardens, deer park, Gadsden/ Montgomery Zoo, Montgomery/ Bellingrath Gardens, beautiful flowers, waterfowl, azaleas/ Theodroe.

Science and Technology: Anniston Museum of Natural History, Anniston.

History and Culture: Ave Maria Grotto, miniature churches, shrines and buildings, Cullman/ Cullman County Museum, Cullman/ Fort Gaines, Civil War Fort, Dauphin Island/ Fort Morgan, Confederate Fort, Gulf Shores/ Tannehill Historical State Park, iron and steel museum, grist mill, pioneer farm, train ride, McCalla/ Fort Conde', 18th century French fort, Mobil/ Conde'-Charlotte Museum House, Mobile's history under 5 flags, Mobil/ Dexter Avenue King Memorial Baptist Church, Dr. Martin Luther King, Jr. memorial, Montgomery/ Mound State Monument, prehistoric temple mounds, reconstructed Indian village, Moundsville/ Pike Pioneer Museum, Troy/ Old Tavern Museum, Tuscaloosa/ Tuskegee Institute National Historic Site, Tuskegee.

Historic Houses: Arlington Antebellum Home and Gardens, Birmingham/ Gaineswood, large plantation mansion, Demopolis/ Shorter Mansion, Eufaula/ W.C. Handy Home and Museum, Florence/ Weeden House Museum, Huntsville/ Oakleigh Historic Com plex, antebellum home, Mobile/ First White House of the Confederacy, Montgomery/ Ivy Green, birthplace of Helen Keller, Tuscumbia.

Entertainment: Vulcan Park, world's largest cast iron statue, Birmingham/ Point Mallard Park, family golf, nature trails, ice/water amusement, Decatur.

Sports: Alabama International Motor Speedway & Motor Sports Hall of Fame, Talladega.

Alaska

Fame: One of the last frontiers; the land of the midnight sun. You must get out into the countryside to see the beauty of the area; visit a gold mine.

Anchorage

Fame: The home of mountains, glaciers and wilderness; the center of a historic gold rush.

You must *take a South Anchorage driving tour, encompassing Portage Glacier, Alyeska Resort and Ski Area, wildlife viewpoints and a historic gold mine; enjoy native culture and history.*

•Best Choices:

Portage Glacier/ Begich Boggs Visitor Center
Box 129, Girdwood 99587.

50 miles south of downtown along the Seward Highway. Five glaciers in the surrounding valley, stunning blue-white icebergs, naturalist hikes, displays of glacial ecology, wilderness and wildlife. Free. $1 to see movie, "Voices from the Ice."

Crow Creek Mine
Box 113, Girdwood 99587.

45 miles south of downtown along the Seward and Alyeska Highways. Historic, picturesque gold mine, older than the finds in Klondike, Nome and Fairbanks. Eight original buildings nestled in trees.

On National Register of Historic Sites. Gold panning, duck pond, barnyard animals, rushing, glacial Crow Creek, profuse flower beds, picnic pavilion and camping sites. **$2/sightseers, $4/gold panners. Open only during summer (June-early September).**

Potter Section House
Box 220587. Anchorage, 99522.
(907)345-2631.

12 miles south of downtown along the Seward Highway. Historic Alaska Railroad Section house depicts railroad history in the state and houses a ranger station for the southern section of Chugach State Park. **Museum: $1/person; $2/family.**

Alaska Zoo
4731 O'Malley, Anchorage 99517.
(907)346-2133

12 mi S of downtown. 2.2 mi from the intersection of O'Malley & Seward Hwy. Hundreds of animals; more than 50 species of Alaskan animals, including the only glacier bear in captivity; natural-land habitat for brown bears, aquarium for seals and otters. **$3.50/adult; $2.50/sr citizen, student, child; free/child under 2.**

Lake Hood Air Harbor
7 miles S of downtown, near Anchorage International Airport.

World's busiest float plane harbor, with more than 10,000 operations per year; starting point for flightseeing trips to Alaska wilderness. **Free. Contact visitors bureau for information about flightseeing trips.**

Oscar Anderson House
420 M Street, Anchorage 99501.
(907)274-2336.

Anchorage's first permanent frame residence. Guided tours offered through the summer, during Christmas season, and Fur Rendezvous celebration. **$2/adult; $1/child.**

Russian Orthodox Church/Native Spirit Houses
26.5 mi N of downtown, along the Glenn Hwy.

St Nicholas Russian Orthodox Church. Many Tanaina Indians converted to Russian Orthodoxy after contact with missionaries. Hand-hewn log prayer chapels on grounds. "Spirit" houses mark blend of native tradition and missionary influence. **Free.**

Anchorage Museum of History & Art
21 West 7th Av, Anchorage 99501.
(907)343-4326.

Downtown, entrance on 7th & A Street. Five-story atrium auditorium, gift shop and display rooms. Alaska Gallery shows history and people of Alaska, permanent and revolving art exhibits. **Free.**

•Good Choices:

Natural Scenery: Ship Creek Salmon Overlook/ Potter Point State Game Refuge/ Eagle River Visitors Center of Chugach State Park, wildlife displays, nature trails, hikes, beaver pond.

Nature and Man: Alaska Wildlife & Natural History Museum, dioramas, exhibits, films/ Imaginarium, hands-on discovery of Aurora Borealis and other scientific finds.

Historical and Cultural: Alaska Wilderness Museum/ Anchorage Museum of History and Art, prehistoric to contemporary art/ Ft Richardson Fish & Wildlife Center/ Elmendorf Wildlife Museum.

Commercial: David Green & Sons Fur Factory/ Anchorage Fur Factory.

Sports: Alaska Baseball League including Anchorage Bucs and Anchorage Glacier Pilots.

Statewide Attractions

•Best Choices:

Mendenhall Glacier
Box 2097, Juneau 99803. (907)789-0097.

One of the most accessible glaciers in Alaska. Overlook the foot of the glacier and see it drop 100 feet into Mendenhall Lake. Exhibits at the visitor center show how glaciers are made and how they advance and retreat with climatic changes. Well marked trails. Free. May-Sept, daily, 9-6; Oct-Apr, Sat-Sun, 9:30-5.

Alaska Chilkat Bald Eagle Preserve
Haines 99827.

18-22 miles N of Haines on the Haines Hwy, to council grounds. Thousands of eagles come to the Chilkat River to feast on chum salmon in a 3-mile stretch of warm water. During November the eagles are joined by visiting birds from hundreds of miles away. Turnouts at side of hwy allow watchers to park and scan trees for eagles. **Free.**

Klondike Highway
Downtown Skagway to the Canadian border at White Pass

Spectacular drive, of 15 miles, with amazing crevasses, beautiful waterfalls and an unusual cantilever bridge.

Danali National Park and Preserve
Box 9, Denali Park 99755. (907)683-2294.

240 miles N of Anchorage and 120 miles S of Fairbanks, on SR 3. The highest mountain in North America, Mount McKinley, is not

the only highlight of this park. Look for glaciers and wildlife, sheep, caribou, moose, grizzly bears, timber wolves and other animals. Free shuttlebus rides. Vehicle traffic is restricted during part of the year. **Free.** Shuttlebus runs late May mid Sept. Park open all yr.

•Good Choices:

Natural Scenery: Alaska Maritime National Wildlife Refuge, Aleutian Islands/ Yukon-Charley Rivers National Preserve, Eagle/ Wrangell-St. Elias National Park and Preserve, Glennallen/ Alaska Maritime National Wildlife Refuge, Homer/ Katmai National Park and Preserve, King Salmon/ Noatak National Preserve, Kotzebue/ Matanuska Glacier, east of Palmer, Mile 102 on Glenn Hwy/ Kenai Fjords National Park, Seward/ Sheridan Glacier, Cordova/ Kenai National Wildlife Refuge, Soldotna.

Nature and Man: Prince William Sound Aquaculture Corporation, largest pink salmon hatchery, Cordova/ Fairbanks Research Farm, farming and huge garden vegetables, Fairbanks/ Large Animal Research Station, herds of musk ox, reindeer, moose, caribou, Fairbanks/ University of Alaska Agricultural Experiment Station, dairy and crop testing, Palmer/ Musk Ox Development Corp, see and learn about the musk ox, Palmer/ Garnet Ledge, look for garnets, Wrangell.

Science and Technology: Palmer Tsunami Observatory, National Weather Service, Palmer.

History and Culture: Ft William H. Seward, arts center, businesses, Haines/ Independence Mine State Historic Park, former gold mining complex, Hatcher Pass/ Pratt Museum, Homer/ Alaska State Museum, Juneau/ Juneau Douglas City Museum, Juneau/ State Office Building, Juneau/ House of Wickersham, Juneau/ Saxman Totem Park, Ketchikan/ Tongass Historical Society Museum, Ketchikan/ Totem Heritage Center, Ketchikan/ NANA Museum of the Arctic, Eskimo history, Jade Mountain, Kotzebue/ Sitka National Historical Park, Sitka/ Russian Bishop's House, Sitka/ Klondike Gold Rush National Historic Park, Skagway/ Valdez Heritage Center, Valdez/ Frontier Village, restoration, Wasilla/ Knik Museum and Sled Dog Mushers Hall of Fame, Iditarod memorabilia, Wasilla/ Petroglyphs, Wrangell.

Entertainment: Alaskaland, theme park, Fairbanks/ Malemute Saloon, Robert Service poetry, ragtime music, Fairbanks/ Fire House Theater, music and R. Service poetry, Fairbanks/ Santa Claus House, gift shop, North Pole.

Commerce: Alaska Wild Berry Products, processing jellies and jams, Homer/ Reed's Jewelry Manufacturing Co, tour, Seward.

Sports: Hiking: "Juneau Trails," U.S. Forest Service, Juneau/

Dewey Lake Trail or Denver Glacier Trail, Skagway/ Funny River Trail, Soldotna/ Crater Lake Trail, Cordova.
 Seasonal Events and Festivals:

World Eskimo Indian Olympics, July, Fairbanks/ Southeast Alaska State Fair, Aug, Haines/ Iditarod Winter Carnival, Mar, Wasilla.

Arizona

Fame: *Grand Canyon, Sunshine.*
You must *See/buy some of the distinctive objects made by Indian craftspeople such as turquoise jewelry, weaving, Kachina dolls, rugs (be sure they are genuine), see the Grand Canyon.*

Mesa

Fame: *Gateway to Arizona.*
You must *visit the Superstition Mountains.*

•Best Choices:

Superstition Mountains
East of Mesa in beautiful Superstition Wilderness.

Hwy 360 to Power Rd; Power Rd N to Main (SR 60); SR 60 E to jct with SR 88; SR 80 N on Apache Trail. Three manmade lakes with boating, skiing, fishing, other water sports. **Free.**

Champlin Fighter Museum
4636 Fighter Aces Drive, Mesa, AZ 85205. (602)830-4540.

The world's largest private collection of flyable vintage fighter aircraft and home to the American Fighter Aces Association. **$4/adult; $2/child. Daily, 10-5.**

Mesa Southwest Museum
53 N. MacDonald, Mesa, AZ 85201. (602)834-2230.

Try panning for gold, see ancient Indian civilizations, experience the days of the frontier, look into the space age. Hands-on history of the Southwest. **$2.50/adult; $1/child. Mon-Sat, 10-5.**

Church of the Latter Day Saints Temple
525 E. Main, Mesa 85201. (602)964-7164.

Temple gardens have trees, shrubs, cacti from around the world. 10 ft reproduction of B. Thorvaldsen's Christus, and extensive collection of religious art and sculpture. Exhibits and audiovisual presentations of history, doctrines and programs of the Church. **Free. Daily, 9-9.**

Arizona Museum for Youth
36 N. Robson, Mesa 85201. (602)898-9046.

A child-oriented fine arts facility featuring changing exhibits of hands-on experiences and weekend workshops. $1.50. Tues-Fri, Sun, 1-5; Sat, 10-5.

•Good Choices:
Natural Scenery: Salt River,

tubing, popular summer recreation.
Nature and Man: Tortilla Flat, recreated stage coach stop/ Apache Canyon/ Roosevelt Lakes, man-made lakes, water sports.
History and Culture: Sirrine House, restored territorial Victorian home/ Galeria Mesa, contemporary art work.
Commerce: Fiesta Mall, enclosed shopping mall.
Sports: Chicago Cubs at Hohokam Park, spring training ground.

Phoenix

Fame: *Southwestern hospitality; Sonoran Desert.*

You must *spend time outside, soaking up the sunshine; sample the authentic Mexican cuisine*

•Best Choices:

Desert Botanical Garden
in Papago Park, 1201 N Galvin Pkwy, 85008. (602)941-1225.

Remarkable collection of desert plants, trees and flowers, from all the deserts of the world, growing naturally in a spectacular outdoor setting. $2.50/adult; $2/sr citizen; $.50/child 5-12. 9 to sunset.

Phoenix Zoo
in Papago Park, Box 5155, 5810 E Van Buren, 85010. (602)273-7771.

Nearly 1200 animals, many of them endangered species, are exhibited throughout 125 acres of jungle-like swamps and ponds, desert terrain, rocky buttes and other natural habitats. $5/adult; $2/child 4-12. Summer, daily,8-5; Rest of yr, daily, 9-5.

Heard Museum
22 East Monte Vista Road, 85004. (602)252-8848.

Large array of traditional Native American artifacts with an outstanding collection of contemporary paintings, graphics and sculptures. $3/adult; $2.50/sr citizen; $1/student; free/child under 6. Mon-Sat, 10-5; Sun, 1-5.10-5; Sun, 1-5.

Rawhide
23023 N Scottsdale Rd, Scottsdale 85261. (602)563-5111.

Theme park featuring stagecoach and burro rides, western animal exhibit, petting zoo, stunt show, shoot-outs. **Free. Charge of indiv attractions.** Daily, 5-10 pm.

Phoenix Art Museum
1625 N Central Av, 85004. (602)257-1222.

Permanent collection of over 18,000 objects featuring 18th, 19th and 20th century European, American, Western American and Asian art and costume design. $2/adult; $1/sr citizen, student; free/child.

•Good Choices:

Tucson

Fame: *Astronomy capital of the world, located in the Sonoran Desert, unique Mexican food prepared by local cooks.*

You must *eat some Mexican food, see Old Tucson, visit the Sonora Desert Museum.*

•Best Choices:

Flandrau Planetarium
Cherry Av and E University Blvd.

Astronomical and space science exhibits. **Free.** Open 1-5. 16 in telescope viewing, 7-10. Planetarium show. $3.50/adult; $2.75/sr citizen, student, child 3-16. Children under 3 not allowed in

Nature and Man: Karho Arabian Horse Farm.
History and Culture: Arizona Museum, Arizona history/ Hall of Flame, fire fighting equipment/ Pueblo Grande Museum, Hohokam Indian culture/ Tallesin West, Frank Lloyd Wright desert home/ Wrigley Mansion.
Commercial: Carefree Cactus Gardens, Scottsdale/ Cosanti, gallery with windbells, sculptures, art by artist Paolo Soleri, Scottsdale/ Old Town Shopping Area, Scottsdale.
Sports: Phoenix Firebirds, professional baseball/ Phoenix Greyhound Park/ Turf Paradise, horse racing.

theatre. Shows at 1:30, 2:30, and 3:30 pm.

Pima Air Museum
6000 E Valencia Rd.

Historical collection of over 120 civilian and military planes. **$4/adult; $3/sr citizen, military, $2/student 10-17; free/under 10.** Daily, 9-5.

Tucson Botanical Gardens
2150 N Alvernon Way. (602)326-9255.

Landscape plants, native wildflowers, tropical greenhouses, Mediterranean plants. Classes, special events. **$1.** Noon-4.

•Good Choices:

Natural Scenery: Saguaro National Monument, living museum, distinctive zoo/ Tohono Chul Park, trails, gardens, geology.

Nature and Man: Reid Park Zoo/ Sonoran Arthropod Studies, Inc/ Colossal Cave.

History and Culture: Arizona Historical Society Fremont House Museum, 1880s adobe home/ Tucson Museum of Art/ Titan Missile Museum, Green Valley.

Commercial: R W Webb Winery Tour.

Statewide Attractions

•Best Choices:

Grand Canyon National Park
Box 129, Grand Canyon 86023. (602)638-7778

The spectacular canyon of the Colorado River is more than a mile deep at its deepest point, more than 18 miles wide at its widest point. There are 3 separate areas: the South Rim, the North Rim and the Inner Canyon. Each has different facilities. Visitors can enjoy horseback trips, muleback trips, boat trips, hiking, museum. $5/car. Golden Eagle Passport. **South Rim open yr around; North Rim, mid-May to late Oct.**

1. Montezuma Castle and 2. Tuzigoot National Monuments
1. Box 219, Camp Verde 86322. (602)587-3322. 2. Clarksdale 86324. (602)634-5564.

These parks, 27 miles apart, preserve the remnants of two distinct cultures that once lived in the Verde Valley. The Hohokam, near Camp Verde, were cliff dwelling farmers who irrigated their land. The Sinagua, E of Clarksdale, were pithouse dwellers and dry farmers. Each site: $1/car. Golden Eagle Passport.

Tombstone
Box 917, Tombstone 85638. (602)457-3608.

A former boomtown that almost became a ghost town, it's now known as the "Town Too Tough to Die." There are many things to see and do in town, including Historama, O.K. Corral, Courthouse, Bird Cage Theatre, Crystal Palace Saloon, Tombstone Epitaph, Boothill Cemetery, Gabe's Doll Museum, Mine Tour and Stagecoach Ride. Free entry to Tombstone. **Some of the attractions have a charge but all are $3 or under.**

Sharlot Hall Museum
415 W Gurley St, Prescott 86302. (602)445-3122

Built around the original territorial governor's house, includes the first schoolhouse, Bashford House, old

Fort Misery and the Porter Locomotive. Donation requested. 4/1-10/31, Tues-Sat, 9-5; Sun, 1-5. Rest of yr, Tues-Sat, 10-4, Sun 1-5.

•Good Choices:

Natural Scenery: Mile Hi Ramsey Canyon Preserve, nature conservancy, Sierra Vista/ Catalina State Park, desert plants, wildlife, Tucson.

Science and Technology Lowell Observatory, Flagstaff/ Kitt Peak National Observatory Tours, Sells.

History and Culture: Casa Grande Ruins National Monument, ruins, museum, ranger talks, Coolidge/ Museum of Northern Arizona, archaeology, geology, Indian arts, Flagstaff/ Besh Ba Gowah, prehistoric ruins, Globe/ Oatman, ghost town, Hwy 66 near Kingman/ Arcosanti, prototype town, project by Paolo Soleri and the Cosanti Foundation, Prescott/ Yuma Territorial Prison State Historical Park, Yuma.

Commerce: Tlaquepaque, arts and crafts village, Sedona/ Old Town Tempe, Tempe.

Arkansas

Fame: *Beauty of nature; abundance of arts and crafts.*
You must *view some of the state's natural beauty by driving Scenic Hwy 7, Harrison to Hot Springs; or Talimena Scenic Drive from Mena, AR, toward Oklahoma; or canoe Buffalo National River; or explore a box canyon.*

Statewide Attractions

•Best Choices:

Crater of Diamonds State Park
Rte 1, Box 364, Murfreesboro 71958. (501)285-3113.

2 miles SE of Murfreesboro on SR 301. The only diamond hunting field in North America which is open to the public. Visitors' center, exhibits, naturalist interpretive programs. Amethyst, agate,jasper, quartz, calcite and barite are also found at the site. Visitors keep any gems that they find. $3/adult; $1/child 6-15. Mar-Nov, daily, 8-6.; Dec-Feb, daily, 8-5.

Ozark Folk Center
Box 500, Mountain View 72560. (501)269-3851.

On SR 9-5-14. State park for preservation of lore of the mountain people. During the day, craftspeople demonstrate activities such as candle making, weaving basketry, iron working, pottery and wild foods foraging. In the evening, except Sunday, traditional folk music is performed. **$4.50/adult; $2.50/child 6-15.** May-Oct, daily, 10-5, crafts forum; 8 pm, folk music.

Blanchard Springs Caverns
U.S. Forest Service, Box 1, Mountain View 72560. (501)757-2213.

Off SR 14 in the Sylamore District of the Ozark National Forest.Only cave operated by the U.S. Forest Service. Contains stalactites, stalagmites, soda straws, large flowstone and underground river. Cave tours, visitors' center with film and exhibits. **Per trail: $5/adult; $2.50/child 6-15.** Summer: Dripstone and Discovery Trails, 9-5. Rest of yr: Dripstone Trail, 9:30-4:30.

Mid-America Museum
400 Mid-America Blvd, Hot Springs 71901. (501)767-3461.

Off U.S. 270, in Mid-America Park, west of Hot Springs. A hands-on look at the principals of life, energy, matter and perception. Visitors interact with imaginativeexhibits. $3.50/adult; $2.50/child 6-17. **Summer, daily, 9:30-6. Rest of yr, Tues-Sun, 10-**

5. Closed Thanksgiving, Christmas and New Year's Day.

Arkansas Territorial Restoration
3rd & Scott Streets, Little Rock 72201. (501)371-2348

Located in the historic Quapaw Quarter. Interprets the 1820-1840 period of Arkansas's early statehood. Guided tour of 14 of the oldest buildings in Little Rock. Artists' gallery, gift shop and decorative arts exhibit. **$1/adult; $.25/child under 17.** Mon-Sat, 9-5, Sun, 1-5. Closed Christmas Eve, Christmas, New Year's Day, Easter, Thanksgiving.

•Good Choices:

Natural Scenery: Buffalo National River, bluffs, caves, farms, Harrison/ Mammoth Spring State Park, lake, restored depot, fish hatchery, Mammoth Spring/ Pinnacle Mountain State Park, exhibits, audio visual, nature walks, Roland.
Nature and Man: DeGray State Park, lake, mountains, recreation, Bismarck/ Hot Springs Mountain Tower, 1,040 ft above sea level, Hot Springs/
Queen Wilhelmina State Park, mountains, lodge, Mena; Little Rock Zoo, Little Rock; Arkansas Riverboat Co, paddlewheel riverboat excursions, North Little Rock.
Science and Technology: The University Museum, geological, historic, zoological, anthropologic

themes, Fayetteville/ Southeast Arkansas Arts & Science Center, Pine Bluff.

History and Culture: Onyx Cave Park/Gay 90's Museum, Eureka Springs/ Thorncrown Chapel, peaceful, inspiring, Eureka Springs/ Fort Smith National Historic Site, early forts, Fort Smith/ Arkansas Post National Memorial, historic exhibits, Gillett/ Louisiana Purchase Historic Marker & State Park, swamp, broadwalk, marker, Holly Grove/ Jacksonport State Park, Courthouse Museum & Mary Woods No. 2 Museum, period rooms, paddlewheel boat, Jacksonport/ Arkansas State Capitol, Little Rock/ Old State House, historic Arkansas exhibits, Little Rock/ Pea Ridge National Military Park, civil war battlefield covers 4,300 acres, Pea Ridge/ Potts Tavern, historic buildings, Pottsville/ Prairie Grove Battlefield Historic State Park, battlefield, historic buildings, Prairie Grove/ Toltec Mounds State Park, Indian mounds, Scott/ Shiloh Museum, history of Arkansas Ozarks, Springdale/ Old Washington Historic State Park, historic structures, Washington.

Historic Houses: The Castle & Museum at Inspiration Point, "point rock" building, early 1900 family furnishings, museum, Eureka Springs/ Rosalie House, period furnished home, Eureka Springs.

Special Interest Museums: Bible Museum, over 7,000 volumes, Eureka Springs/ Miles Musical Museum, musical instruments, wood carvings, seasonal exhibits, Eureka Springs/ Museum of Automobiles, antique autos, Morrilton/ Project 819, train restoration, Pine Bluff.

Art: Arkansas Arts Center, Little Rock/ Arkansas Arts Center Decorative Arts Museum, Little Rock.

Entertainment: Eureka Springs & North Arkansas Railway, train ride, Eureka Springs/ Arkansas Traveller Folk & Dinner Theatre, Hardy; Reader Railroad, train ride, Malvern/ Jimmy Driftwood Music Barn & Folk Hall of Fame, Mountain View; I.Q. Zoo (trained animals), Hot Springs; Josephine Tussand Wax Museum, Hot Springs.

Commerce: Post Family Winery Tours, Altus/ Wiederkein Wine Cellars & Weinkellar Restaurant, free tours, Altus/ Cowie Wine Cellars, Paris/ Daisy Manufacturing Company International Air Gun Museum, Plant Tours, Rogers.

Sports: Oaklawyn Race Track, thoroughbred racing, Hot Springs/ Southland Greyhound Park, greyhound racetrack, West Memphis.

California

Fame: *Golden state, innovation, flowers, giant redwoods.*
You must *see a California redwood, have a sip of California wine, pick a California poppy, dine California style.*

Los Angeles

Fame: Movie stars, beaches and Hollywood.
You must visit the beach areas of Venice, Santa Monica, Malibu or Marina Del Rey; see the walk of fame/Chinese Theater in Hollywood; take Universal Studios tour.

•Best Choices:

Paramount Television Audience Shows
780 N. Gower St., Los Angeles, 90038. (213)468-5575.

A major motion picture and television show production studio. Admission: Free to shows requiring audience viewing and participation. Schedule is seasonal and subject to change. Call for information.

NBC Studio Tour & Tickets
3000 W. Alameda Av., Burbank, 91523. (818)840-3537.

Watch your favorite TV shows. **Free.** M-F, 8-5; Sat-Sun, 9:30-4.

J. Paul Getty Museum
17985 Pacific Coast Hwy, LaCosta 90265. (213)458-2003.

Recreation of ancient Roman country house Villa dei Papiri. See Greek & Roman antiquities, European paintings and decorative arts, old master drawings. Parking reservations required. No walk-ins. Tues-Sun, 10-5.

Los Angeles Children's Museum
310 N Main St., Los Angeles 90012. (213)687-8800.

A "hands-on" museum where kids touch the world. In a play-like atmosphere, children make choices, invent, create, imagine, pretend and work together. $3. Wed-Thurs, 2-4; Sat-Sun, 10-5.

Los Angeles Dodgers
Dodger Stadium, 1000 Elysian Park Av, Los Angeles 90012. (213)224-1500.

Professional baseball in 56,000 seat stadium. **$4-7/adult; $2/child; sr citizen discount.** Apr.-Oct.

•Good Choices:

Nature and Man: Los Angeles State and County Arboretum, Arcadia/Descanso Gardens, La-Canada/Los Angeles Zoo, Los Angeles.

History and Culture: The Hollywood Studio Museum, Hollywood/Los Angeles: Los Angeles County Museum of Art, The Museum of Contemporary Art, Natural History Museum of Los Angeles County, The George C. Page Museum of La Brea Discoveries.

Entertainment: Hollywood Wax Museum, Hollywood/Mann's Chinese Theatre Complex, footprints of stars, Hollywood.

Commerce: Farmers Market and Shopping Village, Los Angeles/Fisherman's Village, shopping, dining, fishing, Marina del Rey/Ports O' Call Village, harbor tours, sailing, helicopter rides, Port of Los Angeles/Alpine Village, Bavarian Village with shopping and restaurant, Torrance.

Sports: Santa Anita Park, racetrack, Arcadia/Fairplex Park/L.A. County Fair Grounds, racetrack, Pomona.

Seasonal Events and Festivals: Tournament of Roses Parade, Jan 1, Pasadena.

Monterey Peninsula

Fame: *Mountains and sea; the most historic city in California.*
You must *follow Monterey's Path of History, walk through Carmel or drive the 17 Mile Drive.*

•Best Choices:

17-Mile Drive
Pebble Beach. (408)649-8500.

This legendary drive originated as a 17-mile carriage drive through the Del Monte Forest for guests of the old Hotel Del Monte. Includes ocean habitats, wildlife and seascapes, Lone Cypress. **$5/car.**

Path of History
Monterey. (408)649-7109.

This 2.7 mile walking tour may begin at any historic location in Monterey. It provides everyone, serious historians or casual strollers, with an array of stories and locations from the colorful past of Monterey. You'll see gardens, adobes, sidewalks made of whalebone, antique furnishings and many sites where history was made. **$1/adult.**

Carmel-by-the-Sea
(408)624-2522.

Cottage-style homes and quaint inns surrounded by gardens are a part of Carmel's unique atmosphere. Enjoy some of the regular activities of shopping, strolling, surfing, sun bathing, scenic painting and photography. You might get to see Mayor Clint Eastwood but more likely you'll enjoy the lovely city itself. **Free.**

Fisherman's Wharf
Monterey. (408)373-3720.

A wood-planked pier lined with restaurants, specialty and novelty shops as well as traditional open-air fish markets. A stroll down the wharf provides a variety of sights, sounds and smells, from feeding sea lions to seeing a musical at the Wharf Theatre. **Free.**

Cannery Row
Monterey. (408)375-3882.

Once the haunt of author, John Steinbeck, this area, which was in the past, filled with active sardine canneries and warehouses, has been renovated and now contains restaurants, antique stores, art galleries, hotels, novelty shops and the Monterey Bay Aquarium. The aquarium is one of the largest in the world and is well worth seeing even though it's too costly for our book. When your feet get tired, ride the Cannery Row Trolley to all points of interest. **Free. All-day unlimited use trolley tickets/$1.**

•Good Choices:
Natural Scenery: Point Lobos State Reserve, south of Carmel. **Nature and Man:** Lester Rowntree Arboretum, Carmel. **History and Culture:** Carmel: Carmel Art Association Gallery; Carmel Mission; Tor House/ Monterey: Colton Hall Museum, historic town hall, museum, jail; Allen Knight Maritime Museum, maritime history; Monterey Peninsula Museum of Art; Monterey State Historical Park/ Pacific Grove: Point Pinos Lighthouse; Pacific Grove Museum of Natural History/ Steinbeck House, Salinas.

Sacramento

Fame: *Center of the famed gold rush; California State Capitol.* **You must** *visit Old Sacramento Historic District.*

•Best Choices:

Old Sacramento Historic District
Historic area between I St Bridge and I-5.

Historic buildings have been restored to the period of the gold rush. Has shops, restaurants, historic buildings including California Railroad Museum , said to be the largest of its kind, with exhibits of lavishly restored locomotives and cars, as well as many other historic railroad artifacts. **Free.**

California State Capitol
State Capitol Museum, Room 124, Sacramento 95814. (916)324-0333.

The building itself has been restored to the grandeur of the 1900s. Seven historic museum rooms depicting the government at the turn of the century. Two public tours are offered during the day. 40 acres surrounding the capitol contain hundreds of trees and shrubs from around the world. **Free.**

Historic Governor's Mansion
16th and H Sts., Sacramento. (916)323-3047.

Regal 15-room Victorian mansion, home to 13 of California's governors until 1967. 14-ft. ceilings, oriental carpets, chandeliers, French mirrors and Italian marble fireplaces. **$1/adult; $.50/child.** Daily, 10-4. Tours on the hour.

Sutter's Fort State Indian Museum
27th and L Sts, Sacramento. (916)445-4209.

Depicts Sacramento's earliest settlement, founded by John Sutter, with highlights of his life. Demonstrations. Adjacent Indian Museum illustrates lifestyle of earliest California residents. **$1/adult; $.50/child.** Daily, 10-5.

•Good Choices:

Nature and Man: Folsum Zoo, Folsom Park/ Sacramento Garden and Arts Center.
Science and Technology Sacramento Science Center and Junior Museum.
History and Culture: B. F. Hastings Building/ Central Pacific Passenger Depot/ Crocker Art Museum/ Sacramento History Center/ Towe Ford Museum.
Entertainment: Fairyland Town, William Land Park.
Commerce: California Almond Growers Visitors Center, history and tour of plant.

San Diego

Fame: *Mediterranean climate, flowers, beaches.*
You must *visit a beach, enjoy the sunshine.*

•Best Choices:

Cabrillo National Monument
Box 6670, 92106. (619)293-5450.

Tip of Point Loma, San Diego. Commemorates the discovery of the coast of California by Juan Rodriguez Cabrillo. Exhibits, programs, Old Point Loma Lighthouse, glassed-in whale watching station with exhibits. Free. Daily, 9-5:15.

Scripps Aquarium Museum
8602 La Jolla Shores Drive, La Jolla 92093. (619)534-6933.

Colorful and interesting view of sea life from the Pacific. 22 marine life tanks. **Free.** Daily 9-5.

San Diego Hall of Champions
1649 El Prado/Balboa Park, 92101. (619)234-2544.

Dramatic exhibits with historic photos, uniforms, awards, memorabilia and videotapes of San Diego sports history. **$2/adult; $1/sr citizen, military, student; $.50/child 6-17.** Mon-Sat, 10-4:30; Sun, Noon-5.

Old Town
2645 San Diego Av., 92110. (619)237-6770.

The site of the first European settlement in California. Many historic buildings and gardens, plus souvenir and specialty shops, restaurants. **Free.** Walking tours led by park rangers at 2 pm daily across from the plaza.

•Good Choices:
Natural Scenery: Mission Bay Park, aquatic park, boating, swimming, San Diego.

Science and Technology Reuben H. Fleet Space Theatre & Science Center, San Diego.

Historic: Maritime Museum, 3 antique boats/ Aerospace Museum & International Aerospace Hall of Fame/ Villa Montezuma/ Jesse Shepard House.

Missions: Mission San Diego de Alcala/ Mission San Luis Rey, San Luis Rey/ Mission San Antonio de Pala, Pala/ Mission Santa Ysabel, Ysabel.

Art: Museum of Photographic Arts/ San Diego Museum of Art/ Timken Art Gallery, European Old Masters, Russian icons/ La Jolla Museum of Contemporary Art, La Jolla/ Mingel International Museum of World Folk Art, La Jolla.

Entertainment: Children's Museum of San Diego/ San Diego Model Railroad Museum.

Commerce: Bazaar del Mundo, in Old Town State Park/ Bernardo Winery tour/ Farmers Bazaar/ Seaport Village/ Deer Park Vintage Cars & Wines, Escondido/ Callaway Vineyard & Winery tour, Temecula.

Sports: Fishing from municipal pier/ San Diego Padres/ Windsurfing/ Del Mar Racetrack, Del Mar.

San Francisco and the Redwood Empire

Fame: *San Francisco's cuisine, cable cars and Golden Gate Bridge; Wine Country; Redwood Trees.*

You must *ride the cable cars, sample wine at a winery in Napa or Sonoma, walk under the redwoods.*

•Best Choices:

San Francisco walk
Kearny St bus to Broadway & Grant.

Walk N 3 blks on Grant (former "Beatnik" row), W 1 blk to Washington Square (Italian neighborhood -- St. Peter & Paul Church, N Beach Museum, Italian Delis, coffee houses, Lillie Coiti statue). Follow Columbus Av. to Taylor, 5 blks to Wharf (net menders, fishing boats, shops, cafes, Pier 39 complex, sailing ship museum Balclutha, submarine USS Pampanitor, tours of harbor, Alcatraz). W, board old ships at Hyde St. Pier, visit National Maritime Museum, the Cannery, Ghirardelli Sq. before boarding bus or Powell-Hyde Cable back to Union Sq.

Golden Gate Promenade
In San Francisco, along the N shore of San Francisco, from the Western end of Fisherman's Wharf to the old Civil War fort under the arch of Golden Gate Bridge, then up to the bridge for a leisurely stroll across and return to the Toll Plaza for a Golden Gate Transit bus to downtown San Francisco. Enjoy the brisk air, unparalleled view of San Francisco Bay, see boats coming under the bridge, people fishing off the sea wall near Ft Point.

Point Reyes National Seashore Walks
Point Reyes 94956. (415)663-1092.

Especially beautiful in spring. 65,000 acre sea shore area with high bluffs, meadows and marshlands, carpeted with wildflowers from mid-April to mid-summer. Get walking maps from Bear Valley Visitor Center. Visit lighthouse for ocean views and for whale-watching December-March. Lighthouse open Thurs-Mon, 10-4 except major holidays. Take a picnic lunch or have one made up at the General Store in Inverness.

Fort Ross State Historic Park
SR 1, Sonoma County. (707)865-2391.

---

12 miles N of the Russian River, coast town of Jenner. Reconstruction of fort established by Russian fur hunters from Sitka, Alaska, in 1841 after the seal population was killed and the remaining troops and hunters had been unsuccessful at agriculture. Rough-hewn fort with Russian Orthodox Church, granary storehouse, Commandant's House, barracks, guest house and corner blockhouses. Three times a year episodes in the history of the fort are acted out in costume. **$3/car.** Daily, 10-4:30. Closed major holidays.

Winery Tours
The visitors' guide to the Redwood Empire Wine Country lists 130 different wineries! Most offer free tours and wine tasting. Some have a small charge.

Jack London State Historic Ranch

N of Sonoma, 1 1/2 miles W of Glen Ellen. (707)938-5216.

A must for London fans! 795 acres including the famed "Wolf House," grave site, ranch winery, his widow's home and museum with mementos, the cottage where he lived, worked and died. Trails to Sonoma Mountain and around Lake, farm area. Horse trails, picnic areas. **$3/car. $.50/rider for bridle paths.** Museums 10-5.

Tall Trees Grove

Redwood Information Center south of Orick, in Humboldt County

In this grove is the world's tallest tree (367.8 feet). Shuttle buses transport visitors from the center to the head of the Tall Trees Trail. 1 1/3 mile walk to site of tallest trees. Trail down is gentle but the trip out is quite steep. **Fare for bus: $3/adult; $1.50/sr. citizen; $1/children 5-15.** Memorial Day to mid-Oct wknds.

•Good Choices

Natural Scenery: Arcata Marshland Restoration, Arcata/ Avenue of the Giants, Humboldt Redwood State Park/ Redwood National Park, Humboldt & Del Norte Counties/ Anderson Marsh Project, Lower Lake.

Nature and Man: Sequoia Park & Zoo, Eureka/ San Francisco: Steinhart Aquarium, CA Academy of Sciences Natural History Museum, Golden Gate Park/ Angel Island State Park, San Francisco Bay/ HSU Marine Lab Aquarium, Trinidad.

History and Culture: S.S. China Cabin, Belvedere/ Clarke Memorial Museum, Eureka/ Fort Humboldt State Historical Park, Eureka/ Maritime Museum, Eureka/ Ferndale Museum, Ferndale/ Fort DePot Museum, Fortuna/ Fort Ross State Historic Park, Jenner/ Kerbyville Museum, Kerby/ Petaluma Adobe State Historic Park, Petaluma/ Port Arena Lighthouse and Museum, Port Arena/ Alcatraz Island, San Francisco/ Luther Burbank Home & Gardens, Santa Rosa/ Mission San Francisco Solano, Sonoma/ Grace Hudson Museum & The Sun House, Ukiah.

Entertainment: Humboldt Bay-Boat Tours, Eureka.

Commerce: Coast Oyster Company, Eureka/ Victorian Village of Ferndale, Ferndale/ Loleta Cheese Factory, Loleta/ One Log House, Phillipsville/ The Chimney Tree-Hobbiton, U.S.A., Phillipsville/ Samoa Cookhouses, museum, mill, 1885 cookhouse serving meals, Samoa/ Chinatown, San Fancisco/ Fisherman's Wharf, San Francisco/ ride a cable car, San Francisco/ The Pacific Lumber Co, Scotia.

Statewide Attractions

•Best Choices:

Sequoia and Kings Canyon National Parks
Three Rivers 93271.

The giant sequoia is the largest living thing on earth. The diameter may exceed the width of many city streets. Also within the park boundaries, the highest mountain in the U.S. outside of Alaska, Mount Whitney, the Sierra crest, the Great Western Divide and at least two spectacular valleys. Extensive trails, campgrounds and lodging, food service, horseback riding, ski trails, snow play area, visitor centers, ranger walks. **$5/car.**

Death Valley National Monument
National Park Service, Death Valley 92328. (619)786-2331.

Noted for having the hottest, driest climate in North America with summer temperatures reach 120 to 200 degrees F. In more comfortable temps, you'll find uniquely adapted plants and wildlife and many historical structures such as Scotty's Castle, 19th and early 20th century mining structures. Desert landforms, including volcanic craters and evaporative lakebeds, date palm orchard, over 2,000 mine workings, charcoal kilns, sand dunes, historic buildings. Ranger guided tours and self-guided tours. **$5/car; $2/pedestrian/bicycle; $15/annual pass.** Open year around. Visitor Center: Nov-May, 8-8; Jun-Oct, 8-5.

Big Sur
Box 87, Big Sur 93920. (408)667-2100.

Along Highway One between Carmel and San Simeon, Big Sur refers to 90 miles of rugged, beautiful coastline, flanked on one side by the Santa Lucia Mountains and on the other by the Pacific Coast. Large areas set aside for public use include: Los Padres National Forest, Pfeiffer Big Sur State Park, J. P. Burns and Molera Parks, U.S. Forest Service campgrounds and picnic areas. There are no towns or villages. Activities include camping, hiking, fishing, swimming, nature walks and scenic driving. **Free.**

Yosemite National Park
Box 577, Yosemite National Park 95389. (209)372-4512.

Giant Sequoias, alpine meadows, waterfalls, lakes, trails, streams and rivers, high wilderness country. Indian culture demonstrators portray their ancestors' use of native materials. Naturalist conducted walks, evening programs. Explore the high country on horseback or on foot. **$5/car.**

•Good Choices:

Natural Scenery: Anza-Borrego Desert State Park, W of Borrego Springs/ Old Faithful Geyser of California, Calistoga/ Sierra National Forest, Fresno/ Point Reyes National Seashore, Inverness/ Lava Beds National Monument, SW of Tulelake/ Channel Islands National Park, Ventura.

Nature and Man: Mendocino Coast Botanical Gardens, Ft Bragg/ Crystal Cathedral, church resembling star set in 22 landscaped acres, Garden Grove/ Luther Burbank Memorial Gardens and Home, Santa Rosa.

History and Culture: Bodie State Historical Park (unrestored ghost town), Bridgeport; Museum of World Wars and Military Museum, Buena Park; Western Railway Museum, Fairfield; McConaghy Estate (Victorian farm house), Hayward; Mission San Juan Capistrano, San Juan Capistrano.

Commerce: Rellim Redwood Co. Demonstration Forest, Crescent City; Graber Olive House (industrial tour), Ontario; Marin French Cheese Company, Petaluma, Wineries, all over the state.

Colorado

Fame: *Fantastic mountain scenery and extraordinary mountain skiing.*

You must *take a walk in the Rocky Mountains in the summer or fall, ski or learn to ski in winter or spring.*

Colorado Springs

Fame: *at the foot of Pike's Peak, site of US Olympic Training Center, Air Force Academy.*
You must *drive Pike's Peak Highway.*

•Best Choices:

Pike's Peak Highway
Box 1575, Colorado Springs, 80901. (303)684-9383.

Exit Hwy 24 W at town of Cascade, follow the signs. This toll road takes you to the summit of Pike's Peak. The summit, at 14,110 ft., is about 20 miles. Although the drive is spectacular, don't take it if you're sensitive to high altitudes. Dress warmly even in the summer. $4/adult; $1/child 6-11. 6/10-Labor Day: 7-6:30. 5/1-6/9, Labor Day - 10/15: 9-3.

US Olympic Committee and Training Center
1750 E Boulder St, 80909. (303)578-4618.

Olympic athletes and future athletes train and live here throughout the year. Home to the US Olympic Committee and 19 national governing bodies. Tours are available throughout the day. **Free.** Mon-Sat, 9-4; Sun, Noon-4. Closed on Monday during the winter.

US Air Force Academy
Visitor Center, Bldg 2346, USAF, CO 80840. (303)472-2555.

This is where the cadets take their 4 yr college/military training. Films and displays on cadet life, planetarium, cadet parades, guided tours of area June-Aug. The 17-spire, six-story chapel is world-famous for its architecture. **Free.** Mon-Fri, 9-5. Closed Thanksgiving, 12/25, 1/1.

Garden of the Gods Park
Parks and Recreation Dept, 1401 Recreation Way, 80905. (303)578-6933.

Exit Hwy 24 W from I-25, turn right on 30th St, look for red sandstone formations on the left. Magnificent geological formations. Especially striking when seen at sunrise or sunset. **Free.** Apr-Oct, 5-11. After Oct inquire about times.

•Good Choices:

Natural Scenery: Seven Falls, waterfall, canyons/ Florissant Fossil Beds, petrified tree stumps, fossils dating back 38 million yrs.
Nature and Man: Cheyenne Mountain Zoo/ Royal Gorge Scenic Railway, ride, breathtaking views.
History and Culture: American Numismatic Association, world's largest coin collection/ Miramont Castle Museum and Conference Center, 9 different styles of architecture/ National Carvers Museum/ Cliff Dwellings Museum/ Pioneer Museum, regional and national history/ Cripple Creek and Victor, former mining boom towns/ May Natural History Museum, tropical giant insects, invertebrates/ White House Ranch Historic Site and Arboretum.
Entertainment: Buffalo Bill Wax Museum, figures of the old west/ Cameron's Doll & Carriage Museum/ Ghost Town/ Hall of the Presidents Living Wax Studio.
Commerce: Van Briggle Art Pottery, tours.
Sports: Pro Rodeo Hall of Champions and American Cowboy Museum/ World Figure Skating Hall of Fame and Museum/ Skate City, roller skating.

Denver

Fame: *The "Mile High City."*
You must *visit Cheesman Park to see the mountains and identify the peaks.*

•Best Choices:

United States Mint
322 W Colfax, Denver 80204. (303)844-3582.

Between cherokee and Delaware Sts. Established in 1862. 20 minute tours every half-hour. Learn how our money is made. **Free.** Mon-Fri, 8:30-3.

Molly Brown House Museum
1340 Pennsylvania, Denver 80203. (303)832-4092.

Restored home, built in 1890s, of the "Unsinkable Molly Brown" heroine of the *Titanic* sinking and famous Denver socialite. The house is furnished with period furniture and artifacts. Tours are conducted by costumed guides. **$3/adult or child over 6; $1.50/sr citizen.** Tues-Sat, 10-4:30.

Denver Botanic Gardens
1005 York St, Denver 80206. (303)575-3751.

Conservatory with tropical and sub-topical plants, orchid and bromeliad pavilion. Outdoor areas have demonstration gardens, rose, herb, Japanese and rock gardens.

$1.50/adult; $1/sr citizen, child 6-15. Mon-Sun, 9-4:45.

Museum of Western Art
1727 Tremont Place, Denver 80202. (303)296-1880.

One of the largest collections of Western art in the U.S. Contains the works of over 50 artists including Moran, Russell, Remington, O'Keefe. Permanent and changing exhibits housed in historic landmark building with a colorful history. **$3/adult or child over 7; $1.50/sr citizen.** Tues-Sat, 10-4:30.

Cheesman Park
Franklin and E 8th Av.

Park affords a spectacular view of the mountains and a dial and pointers help to identify the mountain peaks. **Free.**

•Good Choices:

Nature and Man: Denver Zoo. **Science and Technology** Charles C. Gates Planetarium/ Chamberlain Observatory, Observatory Park. **History and Culture:** Denver Museum of Natural History, City Park/ State Capitol/ Colorado State Museum - Colorado Historical Society/ Denver Art Museum/ Denver Center for the Performing Arts, tours/ Grant-Humphreys Mansion, living history/ Pearce-McAllister

Cottage, lifestyle of the 20s/ Forney Transportation Museum/ Comanche Crossing Museum.

Entertainment: Children's Museum/ IMAX Theatre, Museum of Natural History.

Statewide Attractions

•Best Choices:

Rocky Mountain National Park
Estes Park, 80517-8397. (303)586-2371.

3 mi W of Estes Park on US 36. The park varies from lowland meadows to alpine tundra, from forests to snowy peaks to steep canyons. Temperatures vary from the 70s to the 40s as you travel from lowland to mountain peaks. Forests and meadows are filled with plants and wildlife. There are four visitor centers. Moraine Park Museum, on Bear Lake Road, and the Alpine Visitor Center, on Trail Ridge Road, are open only during the summer, while the headquarters, at the east entrance, and the Kawuneeche center, at the west end, are open year around. Guided tours, campfire talks, conservation talks and other daily events. Facilities for bicycling, fishing, hiking, horseback riding, rock climbing and cross-country skiing. **$5/car; $2/cyclist, hiker or bus passenger.** Open year around.

Dinosaur National Monument
Box 210, Dinosaur, 81610. (303)372-2216.

From Rangely take Hwy 64, 18 miles NW. The Yampa and Green Rivers have cut magnificent, steep canyons through the mountains. A quarry contains the fossils of dinosaurs and other early animals. **Free.** Summer, daily; Winter, Mon-Fri; 8-4:30.

Mesa Verde National Park
Box 8, Mesa Verde National Park, 81330. (303)529-4461.

US 160 from Cortez. Contains notable and best preserved pre-Columbian cliff dwellings in the United States in caves of the canyons. Stop first at the Far View Visitor Center, 16 miles S of park entrance. The dwellings are only open on ranger guided tours. In the summer there are five dwellings to visit, with hundreds of rooms, while in the winter only one of the dwellings may be visited. Self-guided driving tours may be taken to see up to 30 dwellings from viewing points. **$5/car; $2/cyclist, hiker, bus passenger.** Open all year long. Museum and visitors center open 8-5.

Black Canyon of the Gunnison National Monument

Box 1648, Montrose, 81402-1648. (303)374-2216.

From Montrose take Hwy 50 E to Hwy 347 to S Rim. This is the breathtakingly beautiful canyon of the Gunnison River. The narrow, shadowed space between the two walls, the steep depth of the sides, the darkness of the aged rock give the canyon its name. Visitor center, interpretive programs. **$3/car; $1/cyclist, hiker, bus passenger.** Open year around, visitor center open irregularly in winter.

Colorado National Monument

Fruita, 81521. (303)858-3617.

I-70 from Grand Junction or Fruita. Millions of years of wind and rain have eroded the sandstone to create sheer canyons, rounded domes, massive monoliths and other strange formations. In addition to the spectacular scenery the area is home to many forms of wildlife. **$1/car.** Open 24 hours a day, visitors center may be closed on holidays.

Great Sand Dunes National Monument

Mosca, 81146. (303)378-2312.

From Alamosa take US 160 E to SR 150 N. These dunes were formed, in thousands of years, from winds blowing through the Sangre de Cristo Mountains. Considered the largest in the United States, the dunes trapped in this place by the mountains, continually change color, size and shape. Nature walks and campfire programs. **$3/car; $1/cyclist, hiker, bus passenger.** Open year around, 24 hrs. Visitors center: summer, 8-8; winter, 8-5.

•Good Choices:

Natural Scenery: Royal Gorge, Canon City/ Mount Pisgah Scenic Drive, Cripple Creek/ Temple Canon Park, Canon City/ Big Thompson Canyon drive, Estes Park/ Scenic Drives, Fort Collins/ Scenic Drives, Glenwood Springs/ White River National Forest, Glenwood Springs/ Grand Mesa National Forest, Grand Junction/ Curecanti National Recreation Area, Gunnison/ Scenic Drives, Steamboat Springs.

Nature and Man: Glenwood Hot Springs Pool, Glenwood Springs.

Science and Technology Fiske Planetarium and Science Center, U of CO, Boulder/ Sommers-Bausch Observatory, U of CO, Boulder/ National Bureau of Standards, National Oceanic and Atmospheric Administration, Boulder/ National Center for Atmospheric Research, Boulder/ Colorado-Big Thompson Project, Estes Power Plant, Estes Park.

History and Culture: Ashcroft Mining Camp, preserved ghost town, Aspen/ Ghost Towns, near Breckenridge/ Cripple Creek-Victor Narrow Gauge Railroad, Cripple Creek/ Southpark City Museum, restored mining town, Fairplay/ Dinosaur Valley, animated scientifically exact dinosaurs, Grand Junction/ Bent's Old Fort Historic Site, restored fort, La Junta/ Colorado Car Museum, Manitou Springs.

Gold Mines: Central Gold Mine & Museum, Central City/ Lost Gold Mine, Central City/ Mollie Kathleen Gold Mine, Cripple Creek.

Historic Buildings: Old Homestead, restored gold rush brothel, Cripple Creek/ Healy House-Dexter Cabin, Leadville/ Tabor Opera House, Leadville/ Rosemount Vic

torian House Museum, Pueblo/.

Indian Settlement Ruins: Lowry Pueblo Ruins, Cortez/ Ute Mountain Tribal Park, Cortez.

Entertainment: Royal Gorge Scenic Railway, ride, Canon City/ Aerial Tramway, ride, Estes Park/ Argo Town, USA, reproduction of mining town, Idaho Springs.

Commerce: Buckskin Joe, restored boom town, attractions, Canon City/ Estes Hi-Flyer, industrial tour - model rockets, kites, Canon City/ Coors Brewery, tours, Golden.

Sports: Colorado Ski Museum and Hall of Fame, Vail.

Connecticut

Fame: *Maritime Heritage, Colonial History, New England.* **You must** *visit the shoreline, Litchfield Hills.*

Statewide Attractions

•Best Choices:

Gillette Castle State Park
67 River Rd, Hadlyme 06439. (203)526-2336.

Off Rte. 82, Rte. 9, Exit 6 or 7. Built in 1919 as private home of actor William Gillette, this fieldstone mansion resembles medieval castle. On hilltop overlooking Connecticut River. **$1/adult; $.50/child.** Memorial Day-Columbus Day, daily 10-5; Columbus Day-12/18, weekends only 10-4.

USS Nautilus Memorial
US Naval Submarine Base, Rte 12, Groton 06340. (203)449-3174 or 449-3558. I-95, Exit 86.

The world's first nuclear-powered submarine. Submarine Force Library, Museum with history of Submarine Force from Revolutionary War to present. Submarine control room, working periscopes.

Free. 4/15-10/14, Wed-Mon, 9-5; 10/15-4/14, Wed-Mon, 9-3:30. Closed Tues, 3rd week of Mar, Jun, Sep, 2nd week of Dec, Thanksgiving, 12/25, 1/1.

Stamford Museum & Nature Center
39 Scofieldtown Rd, Stamford 06903. (203)322-1646.

Rte 15, Exit 35. 19th Century working farm with farm animals, farm tools exhibit, nature trails, wildlife, picnic area, art, country store. **$3/adult; $2/sr citizen, child.** Mon-Sat, 9-5, Sun, holidays, 1-5. Closed Thanksgiving, 12/25, 1/1. Planetarium shows Sun, 3:30 pm; Observatory Fri night, 8-10 pm.

Old State House
800 Main St, Hartford 06103. (203)522-6766.

I-91, Exit 31, I=84, Exit 52. Designed by Charles Bullfinch, this is the oldest state house in the nation. Gilbert Stuart's portrait of George Washington in restored interior, chamber concerts, changing exhibits, outdoor concerts in summer. **Free.** Mon-Sat, 10-5; Sun, 12-5.

Yale University
344 College St, New Haven 06511. (203)432-2300.

I-95, Exit 47. Guided one-hour walking tours of historic campus. Start at Phelps Gateway, across from New Haven Green. **Free.** Mon-Fri, 10:30, 2; Sat-Sun, 1:30.

•Good Choices:

Natural Scenery: Kent Falls, Kent/ White Memorial Foundation, large nature center, Litchfield.

Nature and Man: Hungerford Outdoor Center, farm animals, wildlife, trail system, Kensington/ White Flower Farm, gardens, fields, greenhouse, Litchfield.

Science and Technology Copernican Space Science Center, planetarium & observatory, New Britain.

History and Culture: Old Newgate Prison & Coppermine, copper mine, prison, East Grandby/ Fort Griswold State Park, Revolutionary War site, Groton/ Yale University Art Gallery, medieval to 20th century, New Haven/ Wadsworth Atheneum, art museum covering every major period, Hartford/ State Capitol, Hartford.

Entertainment: Shoreline Trolley Museum, East Haven/ Connecticut River Ferries, Glastonbury-Rocky Hill or Chester-Hadlyme/ New England Air Museum, Windsor Locks/ Connecticut Trolley Museum, Warehouse Point.

Commerce: Haight Vineyard & Winery, Litchfield/ Hopkins Vineyard, New Preston.

Sports: Shallowbrook Equestrian Center, equestrian sports, Somers/ Plainfield Greyhound Park, greyhound racing, Beehive Field/ New Britain Red Sox-baseball, New Britain/ Bridgeport Jai-Alai, Bridgeport/ Hartford Jai-Alai, Hartford/ Milford Jai-Alai, Milford.

District of Columbia

Washington

Fame: *Our Nation's Capital.*
You must *at least drive by the White House, the Capitol Building and the Supreme Court, to view the seats of the three divisions of our nation's power, the judicial, the executive and the legislative branches.*

•Best Choices:

All Washington attractions are free to the public. The attractions that we have chosen for "best choices" are the attractions that annually attract the most visitors.

National Air & Space Museum
6th St & Independence Av, SW, 20560. (202)357-2700.

Contains 23 galleries detailing the evolution of aviation and space technology. Films in the Langley Theatre on a 50 ft. high screen. Planetarium, original Wright Flyer, Lindbergh's Spirit of St. Louis, space capsule, space station, Apollo II command module. **Free.** Daily, 9-5. Closed 12/25.

National Gallery of Art
4th & Constitution Av, NW, 20565. (202)737-4215.

Extensive collections of Western European and American works. The West Building contains works by Old Masters from 13th century to 19th century. The East Building contains contemporary works. One of the world's great art museums. **Free.** Mon-Sat, 10-5; Sun, Noon-9. Closed 12/25, 1/1.

National Museum of Natural History
10th St. & Constitution Av, NW, 20560. (202)357-2700.

More than 81 million items, including dinosaur skeletons, a living coral reef, insect zoo, displays of early man and the 45.5 carat Hope Diamond. Discovery Room has objects that may be handled. **Free.** Daily, 9-5. Closed 12/25.

Vietnam Veteran's Memorial
Constitution Av between Henry Bacon Dr. & 21st St, NW. (202)426-6841.

Memorial inscribed with the names of 58,022 people who died or remain missing in the Vietnam War. Built with the contributions of American citizens. **Free.** Daily, 24 hrs.

Lincoln Memorial
West Potomac Park at 23rd St, NW.
(202)426-6841.

The famous memorial to Abraham
Lincoln, shaped like a Grecian
temple, overlooking the massive
Reflecting Pool on the National
Mall. A 19-ft. statue of Lincoln is
inside and some of his most
famous speeches are on the walls
of the memorial. **Free.** Daily, 24
hrs. Closed 12/25.

National Museum of American History
14th St and Constitution Av, NW,
20560. (202)357-2700.

The history of the U.S. and its
people in exhibitions that highlight
scientific, cultural, political and
technological developments. Includes original Star Spangled Banner, gowns of the First Ladies,
Ford's original Model T,
memorabilia of our national pas-
times. **Free.** Daily, 9-5. Closed
12/25.

John F. Kennedy Center for the Performing Arts
New Hampshire Av at Rock Creek
Pkwy, 20566. (202)254-3600.

Drama, dance, music and film in
five theatres. Home of the National
Symphony, the American National
Theater, the Washington Opera and
the American Film Institute
Programs. **Free tours.** Daily, 10-1.

Jefferson Memorial
Tidal Basin (South Bank), West
Potomac Park.

Memorial to the third U.S. president. A 19-ft. statue is inside and
the walls are filled with quotes
from the Declaration of Independence and other writings. **Free.**
Daily, 24 hrs. Closed 12/25.

National Zoo
3000 block of Connecticut Av, NW,
20008. (202)673-4717.

More than 3,000 animals including
Smokey the Bear, the giant pandas,
Ling-Ling and Hsing-Hsing. **Free.**
Daily, 4/1-10/15, Buildings 9-6;
10/16-3/31, Buildings 10-4:30.

Library of Congress
10 First St, SE, 20540. (202)287-5458.

One of the world's largest libraries,
containing over 80 million items in
470 languages, in three buildings.
Also offers rotating exhibits, concerts, poetry readings and lectures
to the public. **Free tours.** Mon-Fri,
9-4. Exhibit halls open Mon-Fri,
8:30-9:30; Sat, 8:30-6.

•Good Choices:
Nature and Man: US National Ar-
boretum/ US Botanic Garden/
Cherry Trees, late March or early
April.
Science and Technology National
Geographic Society, Explorers
Hall.

History and Culture: Hirschhorn Museum and Sculpture Garden, 19th and 20th century painting and sculpture/ US Capitol/ Washington Monument/ White House/ National Archives, original American documents/ US Supreme Court/ Ford's Theatre & Lincoln Museum/ FBI Headquarters/ Bureau of Engrav

ing, printing of U.S. dollars and stamps/ Pentagon, headquarters for Army, Navy, Air Force and Coast Guard/ Frederick Douglass Memorial Home/ The Washington Post, hourly tours/ The Washington Times, tours/ Arlington National Cemetery/ Capital Children's Museum/ National Portrait Gallery.

Delaware

Fame: *Brandywine Valley, Atlantic coastline.*
You must *visit Brandywine Valley museums and/or the historic town of New Castle.*

Statewide Attractions

•Best Choices:

Hagley Museum and Eleutherian Mills
Box 3630, Greenville 19807. (302)658-2400.

In Wilmington, on Route 141. 3 miles northwest of Wilmington via SRs 52 and 141. Indoor and outdoor exhibits depict evolution of American industry and 19th century millworkers' lifestyles. Located on Brandywine River amid over 200 acres of trees and flowering shrubs, Eleutherian Mills was the home of five generations of du Ponts. **$5/person.** 4/1-12/31: Daily, 9:30-4:30; 1/2-3/31: Sat-Sun, 9:30-4:30. Weekdays tour: 1:30 pm.

Delaware Art Museum
2301 Kentmere Parkway, Wilmington 19806. (302)571-9590.

Works of Howard Pyle, Winslow Homer, Robert Indiana, N. C. Wyeth, Andrew Wyeth, Frank Schoonover, John Sloan and others. Largest public collection of pre-Raphaelite art in the U.S. Children's White Whale Gallery. **Free.** Mon-Sat, 10-5; Sun, 1-5. Closed Thanksgiving, 12/25, 1/1.

Rockwood Museum
610 Shipley Rd., Wilmington 19809. (302)571-7776.

A 19th-century country estate, includes a manorhouse, conservatory, porter's lodge, gardener's cottage, carriage house and out-buildings. Furnishings include 17th, 18th and 19th century decorative arts. The only surviving example of Rural Gothic architecture and of Gardenesque landscape design. **$3/person.** Tues-Sat, 11-3. Closed major holidays.

Wilmington & Western Railroad

Box 5787, Wilmington, 19808. (302)998-1930.

Six miles NW of Wilmington, Greenback Station at SRs 2 & 44. Ride a steam-powered train through woods, past historic sites and rolling farm lands. Special events scheduled regularly. **$5/adult; $3/child 3-12.** 5/17-10/25, Sun, Noon, 1:15, 2:30, 3:45 pm.

George Read II House and Garden

42 The Strand, New Castle, 19720. (302)322-8411.

A prominent lawyer and son of a signer of the Declaration of Independence undertook constructing the grandest residence in Delaware. Designed in the Federal fashion, surrounded by a landscaped garden in the style of Andrew Jackson Downing. **$3/person.** 4/1-12/31, Tues-Sat, 10-4: Sun, Noon-4. Closed major holidays.

Historic Houses of Odessa

Main Street, Odessa, 19730. (302)378-2681.

A trio of houses dating back to 18th and 19th centuries, the Corbit-Sharp House, the Wilson-Warner House and the Brick Hotel Gallery. See fine examples of historic architecture and furnishing in a village setting. **$3/house; $5/2 houses.** Mar-Dec, Tues-Sat, 10-4:30, Sun, 1-4:30. Closed Easter, 7/4, Thanksgiving, 12/24, 12/25, Jan-Feb, Mondays.

•Good Choices:

Natural Scenery: Delaware Seashore State Park, Bethany Beach/ Fort Delaware State Park, Pea Patch Island, Delaware City/ Fenwich Island State Park, Fenwick Island/ Trap Pond State Park, Laurel/ Cape Henlopen State Park, Lewes/ Trussum Pond, near Lowe/ Prime Hook National Wildlife Refuge, Coastal Sussex County/ Bombay Hook National Wildlife Refuge, Smyrna.

Nature and Man: Delaware Agriculture Museum, Dover/ Delaware Museum of Natural History, Greenville/ Delaware Nature Education Society, forest, fields, marshes, trails, Hockessin/ Abbott's Mill Nature Center, mill, nature walks, Milford/ Brandywine Zoo, Wilmington.

History and Culture: Brandywine River Museum, restored mill, American paintings, Chadds Fort/ John Dickinson Plantation, Dover/ Old State House, 2nd oldest state house in U.S., Dover/ Lewes Historical Complex, restored buildings, Lewes/ Zwaanendael Museum, maritime and Dutch artifacts, Lewes/ Amstel House Museum, 18th century house, New Castle/ New Castle on the Delaware, residential area with houses from Colonial era, New Castle.

Commerce: Container Port of Wilmington, Wilmington/ General Motors Assembly Div tour, Wilmington.

Sports: Harrington Raceway, Harrington/ Delaware Park, racetrack, Stanton/ Brandywine Raceway, Wilmington.

Florida

Fame: *Tropical land surrounded by water.*
You must *put a foot, hand or body in the ocean.*

Fort Myers/Lee Island Coast

Fame: *Shelling.*
You must *go shelling, explore some of the abundant natural scenery.*

•Best Choices:

Edison Winter Home
2350 McGregor Boulevard, Fort Meyers 33901. (813)334-3614.

Thomas Edison's 14-acre, riverfront estate, authentically maintained. Included in the estate, are his home, tropical gardens, laboratory, experimental gardens and a museum that contains his collection of rare antique automobiles and over 200 Edison phonographs. Tours are conducted continuously throughout the day. **$4/adult;** **$1/child, grades K-12.** Mon-Sat, 9-4; Sun, 12:30-4, Closed Thanksgiving, 12/25.

Turner Beach
between Sanibel and Captiva Islands.

There is no one to entertain you here, but this beautiful beach is the perfect place to visit if you want to try your hand at shelling. It's also an excellent vantage point for sunsets. **Free.**

J.N. "Ding" Darling National Wildlife Refuge
on the N side of Sanibel Island. (813)472-1100.

This 4,900 acre tract is named after the pioneer conservationist and political cartoonist Jay Norwood Darling. You'll find delightful walkways, winding canoe trails and a five-mile scenic drive lush with vegetation. One is also likely to encounter a wealth of native birds and mammals, reptiles and marine life. **Free.** Open from sunup to sundown unless otherwise posted.

Nature Center of Lee County & Planetarium
3840 Ortiz Av, Fort Myers 33905. (813)275-3435.

Rustic boardwalks lead visitors on a tour of an Everglades-style swamp environment. Inside many permanent and changing exhibits are on display. The planetarium features shows and laser effects. **Nature Center: Free. Planetarium: $3.50/adult; $3/sr citizen; $2.50/child under 12.** Mon-Sat, 9-4; Sun: 11-4:30.

•Good Choices:
Natural Scenery: Sanibel-Captiva Conservation Foundation, wet lands, trails, observation tower, nursery, Sanibel-Captiva Islands/ Bowman's Beach, Gulfside, Sanibel-Captiva Islands/ Carl E. Johnson Park - Lover's Key, park, Ft. Myers Beach/ Ft Myers Beach Park, Ft Myers Beach/ Imperial River, canoeing, Bonita Springs/ Cayo Costa Island & State Preserve, island accessible by boat, Pine Island - Boca Grande/ Cabbage Key, island accessible by boat, Pine Island.

Nature and Man: Nature's Wonderland Children's Museum, toys, sea shells, fossils, N Ft Myers/ Everglades Wonder Gardens, native wildlife, Bonita Springs.

History and Culture: Ft Myers Historical Museum, depicts ancient civilizations, historic businesses, Ft Myers/ Koreshan State Historical Society, site of 1890s religious sect, Estero, Bonita Springs/ Sanibel Lighthouse, Sanibel Island.

Commerce: The Shell Factory, shop for shells, N Ft Myers.

Sports: Naples-Fort Myers Dog Track, Bonita Springs.

Miami

Fame: *Sunshine, Surf, Sand.* **You must** *eat a Cuban meal and swim in the ocean.*

•Best Choices:

Art Deco District
13th St and Ocean Drive, Miami Beach. (305)672-2014.

The only National Historic District built in the 20th century. Tours provided by the Miami Design Preservation League. **Tours: $5/person.** Sat, starting at 10:30.

Fairchild Tropical Garden
10901 Old Cutler Rd, Miami 33156. (305)667-1651.

The largest tropical botanical garden in the country. Winding paths take you among many diverse and colorful plants and trees from around the world. Tram rides are available. **$4/adult; free/child under 13.** Daily, 9:30-4:30. Closed 12/25.

Orchid Jungle
26715 SW 157th Av, Homestead 33031. (305)247-4824.

A natural Florida jungle provides a tropical setting for orchids from every part of the world displayed among huge oak trees. **$5/adult; $4/student 13-17; $1.50/child 6-12.** Daily, 8:30-5:30.

Vizcaya Museum and Gardens
3251 S Miami Av, Miami 33129. (305)579-2708.

An magnificent Italian Renaissance palace furnished with 15th to 19th century European antiques,

surrounded by 10 acres of beautiful formal gardens. This was the winter home of the late James Deering. Daytime guided tours, Sunday evening sound and light shows. **$5/adult; $3.50/sr citizen, student.** Daily, 9:30-5.

•Good Choices:

Nature and Man: Fruit and Spice Park, botanical garden, Homestead. **Science and Technology:** Miami Museum of Science and Space Transit, Miami. **History and Culture:** Metro-Dade Cultural Center, art, museum, library, Miami/ Miccosukee Indian Village, family campsite, culture, alligator wrestling, airboat, Rte 41, 25 mi W of Miami/ Barnacle State Historical Site, restored home and grounds, Coconut Grove/ Ancient Spanish Monastery, North Miami. **Entertainment:** Gold Coast Railroad Museum, rides, Miami. **Commerce:** Bayside Market Place, $93 million retail & restaurant complex, Biscayne Bay/ Calle Ocho, "Little Havana," cuban culture, Miami/ Coconut Grove, Miami's Greenwich Village, Biscayne Bay. **Sports:** Miami Jai Alai, Miami/ Hialeah Race Track, Miami.

Orlando/Kissimmee Area

Fame: *Disneyworld.*
You must *visit Disneyworld and Sea World, both too high priced for our*

book, but take time to enjoy the terrific lowcost attractions, too.

•

•Best Choices:

Gatorland Zoo
14501 S Orange Blossom Trail, Orlando 32801. (305)855-5496.

5 miles N of Hwy 192 on US 441. Largest alligator attraction in Florida. Scenes from Indiana Jones and the Temple of Doom were filmed here. Actual alligator farm with zoo and products for sale. **$5/adult; $3.75/child 3-11.** Mon-Sun, 8-7.

Xanadu, Home of the Future
4800 W Hwy 192, Kissimmee 32741. (305)396-1992.

Jct of SR 535 and US 192 in Kissimmee. Home designed for the year 2001, with 15 rooms of sculptured walls, talking computers and computer-controlled gadgets. **$4.75/adult; $3.50/child 4-17.** Daily, 10-10.

Morse Museum of Art
113 Wellbourne Avenue, Winter Park 32789. (305)644-3686.

In Winter Park, just off Park Av. Largest collection of Tiffany art nouveau directly from the estate of Louis Tiffany. Many works were rescued from the charred ruins of Tiffany's mansion on Long Island. Exhibits often include other acclaimed artists of the art nouveau style. **$2.50/adult; $1/child over 6.** Tues-Sat, 9:30-4; Sun, 1-4.

Leu Gardens and House
1730 N Forest Av, Orlando 32803. (305)849-2620.

55-acre botanical garden. Magnificent gardens showcase spectacular flowers, sculptures, fountains, archways of oaks, camphor trees and memorial garden. Inside the gardens is Leu House, a turn-of-the-century Florida farmhouse which has been carefully restored to reflect the way people lived during the period from 1910-1930. **Gardens: $3/adult; $1/child 6-16. House: $1 in addition to garden admission.** Daily, 9-5.

Orlando Museum of Art
Loch Haven Park, 2416 N Mills Av, Orlando 32803. (305)896-4231.

Noted for its quality and variety of art exhibits. The pre-Columbian gallery houses more than 250 pieces representing a variety of styles dating from 1200 BC to 1500 AD. Permanent collections include rotating exhibits of American and African art. Changing exhibits include a broad range of styles, periods and mediums. **Free.** Tues-Fri, 10-5; Sat-Sun, Noon-5.

Orlando Science Center
Loch Haven Park, 812 E Rollins St, Orlando 32803. (305)896-7151.

A museum and a planetarium, the Science Center features a variety of exhibits on health, astronomy, physical science and natural history. Many of the exhibits are designed to encourage viewer participation. **$4/adult; $3/sr citizen, child; $10/family.** Mon-Thurs, 9-5; Fri, 9-9; Sat, Noon-9; Sun, Noon-5.

Reptile World Serpentarium
US 192, 4 miles E of St Cloud. (305)892-6905.

60 different species of reptiles from Florida and other parts of the world. The snake venum produced here is used in biomedical research in the US, Europe and Asia. **$3.25/adult; $2.25/student 6-17; $1.25/child 3-5.** Daily, 9-5:30. Closed Mon. Venom extractions at 11, 2, 5.

•Good Choices:

Natural Scenery: Big Tree Park, 3,500 year old bald cypress, Longwood.

Nature and Man: Bok Singing Tower Gardens, flowers, pools and carillons, Lake Wales/ Audubon House, art gallery, gift shop, raptor aviary, Maitland/ Beal Maltbie Shell Museum, thousands of different shells, Winter Park/ Genius Drive, wild peacocks, Winter Park.

Science and Technology John Young Planetarium, Orlando.

History and Culture: Central Florida Railroad Museum, historic railroad memorabilia, Winter Garden/ Cornell Fine Arts Center, Old Masters, 19th century American, Rollins College, Winter Park/ Fire Station No. 3, fire memorabilia, Loch Haven Park, Orlando/ Fort Christmas Museum, 1837 fort of Seminole Wars, Christmas/ Maitland Art Center, contemporary art, Maitland/ Orange County Historical Museum, Orlando/ Polasek Foundation, former estate, galleries of sculptor-painter Albin Polasek, Winter Park.

Entertainment: Cartoon Museum, cartoon art and collections, Orlando/ US Navy Recruit Graduation Exercises, Fri am, Naval Training Center, Orlando/ Places of Learning, 1-acre map, lifesize chess set, parent's store, Orlando.

Commerce: Flea World, 104 acre Flea Market, Orlando/ Tupperware World Headquarters, factory tour, container museum, Kissimmee/ Old Town, Kissimmee.

St. Petersburg/Clearwater

Fame: *Sunshine, beaches, ambience, Greek sponge divers.*
You must *buy a native sponge.*

•Best Choices:

Suncoast Seabird Sanctuary

18328 Gulf Blvd, Indian Shores 33535. (813)391-6211.

Brown pelicans, cormorants, white herons, birds of prey, song birds and other species are on exhibit in this refuge and rehabilitation center for injured and permanently crip-

44

pled birds. **Free.** Daily, daylight
hours.

Boyd Hill Nature Trail
1101 Country Club Way S, St
Petersburg 33705. (813)893-7326.

Contains 216 acres of land, filled
with wildlife and vegetation. Six
trails lead you through Florida's
various ecosystems. Special
programs include educational
shows, day camps, nature photography classes and bird walks.
$.75/adult; $.35/child. Daily, 9-5.

Salvador Dali Museum
1000 Third Street S, St Petersburg
33701. (813)823-3767.

The world's most extensive collection of work by the famous
Spanish surrealist, valued at more
than $125 million. **$3/adult; $2/sr
citizen, student.** Tues-Sat, 10-5,
Sun, 12-5.

Captain Anderson II
Box 3332, Clearwater, 33515.
(813)462-2628.

Docked at the Clearwater Beach
Marina. Sightseeing cruises.
$4.50/adult; $2.50/child. Oct-
May, Tues-Sat, 2 pm.

Tarpon Springs
Community with unique Greek
heritage that gives the visitor the
impression of strolling through a
seaside Mediterranean village.
Originally settled by Greek sponge
divers, the community still shows
many reminders of the formerly
thriving sponge center and of the
Greek settlers. Waterfront sponge
docks, Greek foods and hand-
icrafts, and an outstanding Greek
Cathedral.

•Good Choices:

Natural Scenery: Moccasin Lake
Nature Park, environmental center,
Clearwater/ Caladesi Island, undis-
turbed barrier island, boat access
only, Dunedin/ Honeymoon Island,
undisturbed barrier island, Dunedin
Causeway/ Sawgrass Lake Park,
park and environmental center, St
Petersburg.
Nature and Man: Tiki Gardens,
tropical gardens, Indian Rocks
Beach/ Suncoast Botanical Gar-
dens, 60-acre garden, Largo.
Science and Technology Marine
Science Center, area marine life,
Clearwater.
History and Culture: Yesterday's
Air Force, aircraft museum, St
Petersburg-Clearwater Internation-
al Airport/ Railroad Historical Is-
land, Dunedin/ Heritage Park and
Museum, restored homes and build-
ings, Largo/ Haas Museum, res-
tored homes and buildings, St
Petersburg/ Museum of Fine Arts,
French impressionists, American,
pre-Columbian, Far Eastern art, St
Petersburg.
Entertainment: London Wax
Museum, St Petersburg Beach.
Commerce: Boatyard Village,
shop in 1890s recreated fishing vil-
lage, Clearwater/ John's Pass Vil-

lage & Boardwalk, shopping district, Madeira Beach.

Sports: Derby Lane, greyhound racing, St Petersburg.

Statewide Attractions

•Best Choices:

Spaceport USA
Visitors Center, TWA 810, Kennedy Space Center 32889. (305)452-2121.

A selection of short movies throughout the day at Spaceport Central; hands-on activities for children at Exploration Station; walk among exhibits from each stage of the space program at Rocket Garden; multimedia presentation on space exploration in Galaxy Theater; IMAX film "The Dream is Alive;" air conditioned bus tours of Kennedy Space Center or Cape Canaveral Air Force Station; guided walking tours of some exhibits; free kennel facilities; free use of camera; take a picture with the center's "spaceman." **Free admission to all but IMAX and bus tour. Tour: $4/adult; $1.75/child 3-12. IMAX movie: $2.75/adult; $1.75/child 3-12.** Daily, 9-7:30.

Everglades National Park
Box 279, Homestead 33030. (305)247-6211.

The largest remaining tropical wilderness in the United States. Fresh and salt water, mangrove forests, open prairies, wildlife. The area teems with wildlife, mostly visible during the winter months.

Trails have been set up by the National Park Service to make a safe trip into the glades possible for visitors. **$5/car.**

Naval Aviation Museum
Naval Air Station, Pensacola 32508. (904)452-3604.

The nation's finest collection of historic Navy, Marine and Coast Guard aircraft. Early wood and fabric prototypes to the modern era of jets and space exploration. **Free.** Daily, 9-5. Closed Thanksgiving, 12/25, 1/1.

Overseas Highway
This is an extension of US 1 from Miami to the Keys. It covers 113 miles of roadway and 42 bridges moving from key to key. The well-known 7-mile bridge is a part of this thoroughfare. The visitor driving the highway can see the sea, swaying palms, water-rooted mangroves and rustling pine. Sunrises and sunsets are spectacular. Look for mile markers (small green signs with white numbers) on the right shoulder of the road that begin on US 1, with number 126, just S of Florida City and end with zero in Key West. Key's residents use them when giving directions. Although the drive can be made in less than 3 hours, you'll

want to allow more time to enjoy this beautiful drive.

•Good Choices:

Natural Scenery: National Key Derr Refuge, smallest of all white-tailed deer, Big Pine Key/ Lignum-viae Key State Botanical Site, hardwood forest, trails, historic house, Islamorada/ Corkscrew Swamp Sanctuary, Naples/ Gulf Islands National Seashore, barrier islands and keys, Gulfport, MS, to Destin, FL.

Nature and Man: Jacksonville Zoological Park, Jacksonville/ Key Wet Aquarium, Key West/ Brevard Zoological Park, Melbourne/ Ocala Stud Inc, Bonnie Heath Farm, horse farms, Ocala/ Ravine State Gardens, 85 acre garden, ravines, Palatka/ Marie Selby Botanical Gardens, tropical plants, Sarasota.

Science and Technology Discovery Center Museum, science, art and history, Fort Lauderdale/ Jacksonville Museum of Arts and Sciences, planetarium, changing exhibits, Jacksonville.

History and Culture: Museum of Arts and Sciences, art of Cuba & Florida, European, American, Daytona Beach/ Florida State Museum, natural and social history, U of FL, Gainsville/ Ernest Hemingway Home and Museum, Key West/ Audubon House and Gardens, house, garden, engravings, Key West/ Henry Morrison Flagler Mansion, Palm Beach/ Fort Pickens, pre-Civil War fortress, Pensacola/ Fort Barrancas, pre-Civil War fortress, Pensacola Naval Air Station/ Lightner Museum, eclectic collection of oriental art, Art Nouveau, mechanical musical instruments, etc, St. Augustine/ St Augustin Antiguo, restoration area, St Augustine.

Entertainment: Ringling Museum, complex of residence, gardens, art museum, theater and circus museum, Sarasota.

Commerce: Annheuser-Busch Brewery, Jacksonville/ Seville Historic District, shopping, Pensacola/ Pabst Brewing Company, Tampa/ Villazon & Co, cigar factory, Tampa/ Ybor City, Cuban, Spanish, Italian area, Tampa.

Sports: Daytona International Speedway, auto racing, Daytona Beach/ Spring Garden Ranch, harness racing track, De Land/ Gulfstream Park racetrack, Hallandale/ International High-goal Polo, Palm Beach Polo and Country Club, W Palm Beach.

Seasonal Events and Festivals Circus Winter Quarters, Jan-Feb, Venice.

Georgia

Fame: *Southern Hospitality, Antebellum Homes, Atlanta.*
You must *visit Atlanta, an antebellum home.*

Atlanta

Fame: *The home of Coca Cola and "Gone with the Wind."*
You must *see "Gone with the Wind" at the CNN Cinema 6.*

•Best Choices:

Cyclorama
Georgia and Cherokee Av, SE, Atlanta 30315. (404)658-7625.

Immense circular painting of 1864 Civil War Battle of Atlanta. Completed in 1885, the action revolves around the reviewer. Over the years three dimensional figures, sound and light effects, narration and a rotating seating platform have been added. There are also other exhibits and a film. Listed on the National Register of Historic Places. **$3/adult; discount for sr citizen, child.** Daily, 9:30-5.

Atlanta Historical Society
3101 Andrews Drive, NW, Atlanta 30305. (404)261-1837. 26 acres of formal gardens, wildflower trails. Includes two historical houses, the Swan house and Tullie Smith House. Rotating exhibits, archives, library. Tours every half hour.

$4.50/adult; $4/sr citizen; $2/child 6-12. Mon-Sat, 9-5:30; Sun, Noon-5.

Carter Presidential Center
1 Copen Hill, Atlanta 30307. (404)331-3942.

The 30-acre center includes a museum with a full-scale replica of the oval office, films, videos and displays portraying President Jimmy Carter's life and administration. **$2.50/adult; $1.50/sr citizen; free/under 16.** Mon-Sat, 9-5; Sun, Noon-5.

CNN Studio Tour
1 CNN Center, Marietta St at Techwood Dr, Atlanta 30335. (404)581-2161.

The headquarters of the two 24-hour news networks, CNN and Headline News. Visitors may tour the studios and watch writers, editors, producers, technicians and journalists on-the-air at work producing live news coverage. **$4/adult; $2/sr citizen, student, child.** Mon-Fri, 10-6, Sat-Sun, 10-4.

Zoo Atlanta
Grant Park, 800 Cherokee Av, SE, Atlanta 30315. (404)624-ROAR.

Big cats, elephants, llamas, monkeys, exotic birds and a large reptile collection. Look for Willie B, the lowland gorilla, and Starlet O'Hara, the African elephant. **$3/adult; $2/child 4-11.** Daily, 10-5.

Martin Luther King Jr Historic Site
Auburn Av between Jackson and Randolph Sts, Atlanta 30312.

Two blocks associated with the civil rights leader have been designated as a historic site. The historic buildings and store fronts have been restored or are currently being restored to turn-of-the-century condition. Included in this are **Dr King's birth home** , 501 Auburn Av. Restored circa 1929. **Free.** Oct-Apr, 10-3; May-Sept, 9-5. **Ebenezer Baptist Church** , 407 Auburn Av. Sunday worship services open to the public. **No charge. Donations accepted.** Mon-Fri, 9-5, Sat, 9-2. **Dr King's Gravesite** , within the grounds of the M. L. King Jr Center for Non-violent Social Change, 449 Auburn Av. Also in the center are a movie, exhibits and a gift shop. **Movie: $1.** Daily, 9-5:30.

High Museum of Art
1280 Peachtree St, NE, Atlanta 30309. (404)892-3600.

The building was designed by Richard Meier in 1983. Collections of European and American paintings, sculpture, decorative arts, photography, bold prints and graphics. International traveling exhibits. The kids will enjoy the multi-sensory exhibit. **$3/adult; $1/sr citizen, student over 11. All are free on Thurs, 1-5.** Tue-Sat, 10-5; Wed, 10-9; Sun, Noon-5.

•Good Choices:

Nature and Man: Atlanta Botanical Garden, Atlanta/ Yellow River Wildlife Game Farm, native GA animals, Lilburn.
Science and Technology Fernbank Science Center, planetarium, exhibits, garden, nearby trails, Atlanta.
History and Culture: Governor's Mansion, Atlanta/ Herndon Home, house museum, Atlanta/ High Museum of Georgia-Pacific, rotating exhibits from High Museum, Atlanta/ Federal Reserve Bank, Monetary Museum, history of money, Atlanta/ Georgia State Capitol, Atlanta/ Oakland Cemetery, look for famous and Civil War inhabitants, Victorian funeral statuary, Atlanta/ Emory Museum of Art and Archaeology, prints & drawings 13th century to present, Middle & Far East artifacts, Atlanta/ Wren's Nest, historic home of Uncle Remus author J. C. Harris, Atlanta.
Entertainment: Stone Mountain Park, mountain carved with images

of Civil War heros plus nearby attractions, Stone Mountain/ Piedmont Park, free concerts, Atlanta.
Commerce: DeKalb Farmers Market, Decatur.
 Sports: Atlanta Braves Baseball games, Fulton County Stadium, Atlanta.

Statewide Attractions

•Best Choices:

Rome
Rome Tourist & Convention Comm., Box 5823, Rome 30161. (404)295-5576.

This city is filled with attractions and the admission is often free. Among the interesting viewing that you'll find is Oak Hill, Martha Berry's antebellum plantation, Old Clock Tower, giant water wheel, Chieftains Museum with the art and history of the Cherokee Indians and a walking tour of downtown. You'll even find a forest with virgin trees and wildflowers.

Babyland General Hospital
19 Underwood St, Cleveland 30528. (404)865-5505.

This is for Cabbage Patch Kids fans. Once a real medical clinic, the hospital is the home of the original Kids and is now filled to the brim with the creatures. If you're lucky, you may even see an actual delivery with doctors and nurses scurrying around. If you want to, you can adopt your own baby here and buy all the accessories it'll ever need, but you can also just come to see the collections, including the world's largest gathering of limited edition CPKs. **Free.** Mon-Sat, 9-5; Sun, 1-5. Closed Easter. Thanksgiving, 1/1, 7/4, 12/24, 12/25.

Providence Canyon State Park
Rte 1, Box 158, Lumpkin 31815. (912)838-6202.

7 miles W of Lumpkin on SR 39C. Sometimes called the "Little Grand Canyon" because of its unusual colored sand formations and magnificent erosion gullies. Spend a day hiking, picnicking and enjoying nature's exhibition. Interpretive Center. **Free.** Daily, 9/15-4/14, 7-6; 4/15-9/14, 7-9.

Madison
Madison-Morgan Chamber of Commerce, Box 826, Madison 30650. (404)342-4454.

On US 441 and 278, 2 mi N of I-20, Exit 51. If you're traveling through this part of the state, you'll want to drive through Madison. General Sherman spared this town in his march to the sea, leaving an abundance of Victorian and antebellum homes and buildings. A large part of the town has been designated as a National Historic District. **Free.**

•Good Choices:

Natural Scenery: Chehaw Wild Animal Park, African animals, Albany/ Lake Lanier Islands, recreation, scenery, Buford/ Okefenokee National Wildlife Refuge, freshwater swampland, Folkston/ Richard B Russell Scenic Highway, Helen/ Beaches of the Golden Isles, St Simons Island, Sea Island, Jekyll Island.

Nature and Man: State Botanical Gardens, Athens/ William Weinman Mineral Center & Museum, rocks, minerals, gemstones, Cartersville/ gold panning, Dahlonega/ Helen, town looks like an Alpine village/ American Camellia Society Gardens and Headquarters, Perry/ The Andersonville Trail, Perry/ Rose Test Garden, Thomasville/ Georgia Agrirama-Agricultural Heritage Center, living history, forestry, farmsteads, Tifton/ Southern Forest World, active involvement in history of forestry, Waycross.

Science and Technology Savannah Science Museum, aquarium, planetarium, science exhibits, Savannah.

History and Culture: New Echota Historic Site, last capital of the Cherokee Nation, Calhoun/ Etowah Indian Mounds & Archaeological Area, museum, Cartersville/ Heritage Tour, historic buildings, Columbus/ Uncle Remus Museum, cabin, woodcarvings, paintings, museum, Eatonton/ Westville, living history village, Lumpkin/ Trolley Tour, Milledgeville/ Ft McAllister Historical Park, Confederate earthworks, museum, Richmond Hill/ Ft Frederica National Monument, museum, field exhibits, movie, St Simons Island/ Ft Pulaski National Monument, demonstrations of military arts, Savannah/ Great Savannah Exposition, multimedia exposition, history of city, Savannah/ Chickamauga & Chattanooga National Military Park, Civil War memorabilia and sites, 9 mi S of Chattanooga, TN.

Historic Houses & Plantations: Historic Homes Tour, Athens/ Hofwyl-Broadfield Plantation Historic Site, Darien/ Taylor-Grady Home, Athens/ Hay House, Macon/ Old Cannonball House & Macon-Confederate Museum, Macon/ Old Governor's Mansion, Milledgeville/ Telfair Mansion and Art Museum, Savannah/ Plantation Tours, Thomasville/ The Crescent, Colonial house, Valdosta/ Little White House, Warm Springs/ Callaway Plantation, Washington.

Special Interest Museums: Mary Miller Doll Museum, 4,000 dolls, Brunswick/ Museum of Antique Dolls, Savannah/ Ships of the Sea Museum, maritime museum, Savannah.

Entertainment: Riverboat Jubilee excursion, Columbus.

Commerce: Chateau Elan Winery, Braselton/ seafood plants, shrimp boat docks and plants, Brunswick/ Claxton Bakery, world's most popular fruitcake, Claxton/ Tom's Foods, Inc, peanut processing, Columbus/ Habersham Winery, Habersham County/ Cranshaw's One Horse Farm and

Gardens, Perry/ Heileman Brewing Company, Perry.

Seasonal Events and Festivals
Georgia Mountain Fair, early Aug, Hiawassee/ Oktoberfest, 6 wknds, Sept-Oct, Helen/ Christmas in Savannah, mth in Dec, Savannah.

Hawaii

Fame: *Exotic island paradise, melting pot of races and cultures.*

You must *enjoy the tropics, spend time at the beach, learn the hula and look at the flowers.*

Hawaii

Fame: *largest of the islands, two active volcanos and scene of many of the state's historic events.*
You must *see a volcano and visit one of many spectacular gardens.*

•Best Choices:

Hawaii Volcanos National Park
Hwy 11, about 30 miles from Hilo. (808)967-7311.

Two active volcanos, steaming craters, unique volcanic formations, sulphur pits, fern grottos, lunar landscapes and a volcanological museum make this one of the top scenic attractions on the state. Possible visitor activities include auto tours, walking, hiking, camping, backcountry, picnicking, fish-

ing and interpretive programs. $2 Daily, 24 hrs.

Hilo Tropical Gardens
1477 Kalanianaole Av, Hilo 96720. (808)935-4957.

Native Hawaiian plants, water lily pools, waterfalls, spectacular tropical orchids and a Japanese garden with pond and footbridge are viewed from paved walkways. This is one of the most beautiful of the many gardens in Hilo. **Free.** Daily.

Kaimu Black Sand Beach
Hwy 137, near Kalapana on the SE coast.

The island of Hawaii is famed for its black sand beaches, made of pulverized lava. This beach is one of the most photographed of those beaches with coconut palms lining the shore and a savage surf pounding the shore. Bring your camera but not your swim suit. **Free.**

Rainbow Falls
Rainbow Dr, off Walanuenue Av, Hilo.

One of the island's most captivating waterfalls. Views are best from 9 to 10 am when rainbows rise in the mist. Two miles farther down Walanuenue you'll find the Boiling Pots, pools that appear to be boiling as water flows over the lava beds. **Free.**

Panaewa Rain Forest Zoo
Just outside Hilo on Stainback Hwy, off of Hwy 11. (808)959-7224.

40 acres with a tropical rain forest and the animals of the forest, as well as local vegetation and animals. There are exotic birds and a children's zoo. **Free.** Daily, 9-4:30.

•Good Choices:

Natural Scenery: Akaka Falls, spectacular falls, vegetation, Honomu village/ Anaehoomalu Beach, white sand, fishponds, petroglyphs, Kohala Coast/ Chain of Craters Road, marvelous views, Volcano House to SE coast/ Kaumana Cave, lava tube, Kaumana Dr/ Papakolea Green Sand Beach, South Point.

Nature and Man: Akatsuka Orchid Gardens, between Hilo and Volcano/ Barry's Nut Farm, botanical gardens, Kona/ Hawaii Tropical Botanical Garden, streams, flowers, Onamea Bay/ Kona Gardens, home sites, lava formations, petroglyphs, Keauhou-Kona/ Kualoa Farms, anthuriums, other tropical flowers, Hilo/ Kulani Flowers Anthurium Farm, Hilo/ Liliuokalani Gardens, Japanese gardens, Waiakea Peninsula/ Nani Mau Gardens, trees, flowers, Hilo.

Science and Technology Richardson Ocean center, aquatic information, displays, Hilo.

History and Culture: Lyman House and Museum, missionary home, Hilo/ Nihon Japanese Culture Center, art gallery, restaurant, Hilo/ Wailoa Center, Hawaiian history, Hilo/ Pu'uhonoua o Honaunau National Historical Park, prehistoric house sites, scenery, Honaunau/ Hulihee Palace, restored royal vacation home, Kailua-Kona/ Mokuaikaua Church, 1838 lava rock & coral, Kailua-Kona/ Lapakahi State Historical Park, 600 yr old fishing village, Kawaihae Harbor/ Kaloko-Honokohau National Historical Park, Hawaiian culture, Kona coast/ Kamuela Museum, Hawaiian royal artifacts, Waimea town/ Puukohola Helau National Historic Site, temple ruins, Waimea-Kohala.

Commerce: Orchids of Hawaii, orchid farm, Hilo/ Mauna Loa Macademia Nut Mill and Orchard, Hilo/ Suisan Fish Market, Hilo/ Royal Kona Coffee Mill and Museum, Kealakekua Bay.

Sports Hiking: Waipio Valley, 50 miles N of Hilo/ Kilauea Visitor Center, Volcano National Park/

Kailua-Kona walking tour, Kona Activities Center/ Swimming at beaches.

Kauai

Fame: *Scenery so beautiful that it has served as a backdrop for many Hollywood movies.*
You must *visit Waimea Canyon or Kalakau Lookout to see the spectacular beauty of this island.*

•Best Choices:

Waimea Canyon
Hwy 50 to Waimea Canyon Dr.

The best view is from Puu Ka Pele lookout. You'll stand at the top of a 3,657 ft gorge looking into a chasm that is a mile wide and 10 mi long. The gorge has been compared to the Grand Canyon. It's smaller but, at times, its colors are brighter.
Free.

Kalakau Lookout
4 miles from Kokee State Park.

Said to be one of the most beautiful views on earth. And, on the same island as Waimea Canyon, too! It's a 4,000 ft drop from the forest above to the sea below.
Free.

Grove Farm Homestead
Box 1631, Lihue, Kauai, 96766. (808)245-3203.

In Nawiliwill. A look at a Hawaiian sugar plantation of the 1800s. Founded in 1864 by George Wilcox, the homestead is now a museum complex that includes the family plantation home, wash house, tea house, guest cottage and other buildings. The structures are furnished with antiques in a warm, casual manner which imparts a "lived in" look. Tours are usually booked far in advance so you'll need reservations. **$3/adult; $1/child 5-12.** Tours, Mon, Wed, Thur, 10 am, 1:15 pm.

•Good Choices:

Natural Scenery: Hanalei Valley Overlook, Hwy 580, Princeville/ Kokee State Park, wilderness, wildlife, trails, Waimea Canyon Rd/ Opaekaa Falls, Wailua/ Spouting Horn, geyser-like breakers, Poipu/ Waikapalae and Waikanaloa Dry Caves, Haena.
Nature and Man: Kiahuna Gardens, landscaped gardens, pools, S of Lihue/ Kukuiolono Park, Japanese gardens, above Kalaheo/ Smith's Tropical Paradise, gardens, cultural villages, Kapaa/ Salt Pond Beach Park, salt beds, Hanapepe.
History and Culture: Kamokila, restored settlement, Hwy 580 in-

land from Wailua/ Kauai Regional Library, batik mural, programs, films and art shows, Hardy St/ Kilauea Lighthouse, great view, Kilauea/ Waioli Mission House, 1834 station, Hanalei. **Entertainment:** Kilohana, rides, exhibits, arts, crafts, Lihue. **Commerce:** Koloa Town, 1st sugar plantation, S of Lihue.
Sports: Go to the beaches for swimming, snorkeling, windsurfing, scuba diving and sunbathing/ try hiking on State Park and Forest Reserve trails.

Maui

Fame: *Haleakala, the 10,023 ft high dormant volcano.*
You must *stand at the rim of the crater to look into the volcano.*

•Best Choices:

Haleakala National Park
Box 369, Makawao 96768. (808)572-9177.

From Kahului take Hwy 37 to Hwy 377 to Hwy 378. The site of the world's largest volcano. It's been over 200 years since its last eruption. You'll need to walk or ride horseback to make the 2 mile ascent to the top of the crater but, if you're physically up to the climb, it's worth it. A public observatory is on the rim of the crater. $3. Daily, park open 24 hrs; observatory 8:30-3.

Maui Tropical Plantation
Honoapiilani Hwy, Waikapu. (808)244-7643.

A showplace of tropical agriculture. In a scenic tour aboard a tram you will explore the Waikapu Valley through acres planted to sugar cane, macadamia nuts, bananas, pineapples, papayas, orchids, anthuriums and proteas. **Plantation: free. Tour: $5.** Daily, 8-4.

Brig Carthaginian
Lahaina Harbor. (808)661-3262.

This 19th century square-rigged ship from Germany has been restored. It's now a floating museum with artifacts and films relating to the days when Maui was a center for whalers. $2. Daily, 8:30-4:30.

•Good Choices:

Natural Scenery: Seven Sacred Pools, beautiful but difficult to reach, Haleakala National Park/ Wailua Gulch, twin waterfalls, beyond Hana/ Kanaha Bird Sanctuary, Kahului.
Nature and Man: Kepaniwai Heritage Gardens, gardens, pagodas, pools, Iao Valley Park/ Kula Botanical Gardens, tropical plants, flowers, Haleakala/ Maui Zoological and Botanical Garden,

native plants, animals, Wailuku/
Seven Sacred Pools, beautiful but
difficult to reach, Haleakala National Park.

History and Culture: Hale
Hoikeike, historical museum,
Wailuku/ Baldwin Home, home of
missionary doctor, Lahaina/ Hale
Pai Museum, missionary printing
house, Lahaina/ Olowalu

Petroglyphs, Lahaina/ Pioneer Inn,
whaling memorabilia, Lahaina/
Whaler's Village Museum,
Kaanapali Beach Resort.

Commerce: Flora Hawaii, jewelry factory tours, Kahului/ Tedeschi
Vineyards, Ulupalakua Ranch.

Sports: Beaches offer surfing and
swimming for viewing or participating/ hiking.

Oahu

Fame: *Waikiki Beach, Arizona
Memorial.*

You must , *after you've been to the
beach, visit the Arizona and get away
from Waikiki Beach to see downtown
Honolulu, other parts of the island.*

•Best Choices:

Arizona Memorial at Pearl Harbor
Kamehameha Hwy (Rt 99) at Pearl
Harbor.

The site of the devastating opening
attack of World War II, in the
Pacific. Over half the fatalities
were aboard the battleship, USS
Arizona. Start by getting a tour
number for a boat trip to the
memorial at the information desk.
In the busy season, you'll probably
have to wait unless you get there
very early. The visit to the
memorial is a moving and impressive experience. **Free. No children
under 6.** Tues-Sun, 8-3. Closed
Mon.

Kodak Hula Show
Kapiolani Park next to Waikiki Shell.
(808)833-1661.

This is an impressive show of
authentic dance and music, by
skilled dancers. Of course, there
are many photo opportunities, but
it's well worth your time even if
you don't have a camera. **Free.**
Tues-Thurs, 10 am.

Falls of Clyde
Pier 7, Honolulu Harbor. (808)536-6373.

The world's only surviving fullrigged, four-masted schooner. Tour
through the Hawaiian Maritime
Center to learn about the boat's history as well as the Hokule'a, ancient Polynesian canoe. **$3/person.**
Daily.

Iolani Palace
downtown, corner of Richards and S.
King Sts. (808)538-1471.

1882 palace of King Kalakaua and Queen Kapiolani. Restoration of this beautiful palace cost $6 million. Tours cover the private chambers, dining room, music room and throne room. **$4/adult; $1/child 5-12.** Tours Wed-Sat, every 15 min. until 2:15 pm.

National Cemetery of the Pacific
Punchbowl, Puowaina Drive. (808)541-1430.

27,000 servicemen, who died in the Pacific during World War II, the Korean War and the Vietnam conflict, are buried here in the crater of an extinct volcano. From the rim of the crater one can see a spectacular view of Honolulu below. **Free.** Daily, 3/1-9/30, 8-6:30; 10/1-3/1, 8-5:30.

Foster Botanic Garden
180 N Vineyard Blvd. (808)533-3214.

15 acres of rare and unusual tropical vegetation including orchids, gingerbread palms, sunshine tree and the cannonball tree. A marvelous place to escape from the heat. **$1/adult.** Daily, 9-4.

Mission Houses
553 S King St. (808)531-0481.

The missionaries and their influence on the history of Hawaii become animate as you visit these three buildings: the Frame House, home of the missionary families, the printing house and the warehouse. Restored to the period of 1821-1860, the buildings are furnished with original furniture and other missionary artifacts. **$3.50/adult; $1/child 6-16.** Daily, 9-4.

•Good Choices:

Natural Scenery: Ala Moana Beach Park, swimming, tennis, Honolulu/ Blow Hole, geyser, Kalanianaole Hwy/ Diamond Head, extinct volcano crater/ Hanauma Bay, great snorkeling, Kalanianaole Hwy/ Kuhio Beach Park, Waikiki/ Nuuanu Pali Lookout, Pali Hwy/ Round Top Tantalus Drive, mountain drive, Makiki St/ Waikiki Beach.
Nature and Man: Haiku Gardens, ponds, trees, flowers, restaurant, Kaneohe/ Honolulu Zoo, animal collection, Wed evening shows Jun-Aug, Honolulu/ Kapiolani Rose Garden, Honolulu/ Porpoise Feeding, Kahala Hilton Hotel/ Waikiki Aquarium, Waikiki. **History and Culture:** Fort Randolph, army museum, Fort DeRussy/ Tropic Lightning Historical Center, army museum, Schofield Barracks/ Contemporary Arts Center, Hawaiian artists, Honolulu/ Honolulu Academy of Arts, Hawaiian, Asian, Pacific art, Honolulu/ Bishop Museum, Hawaiian artifacts, Kalihi.
Entertainment: Royal Hawaiian Band Concerts, Iolani Palace/ Young People's Hula Show, Ala Moana Shopping Center/ Hula

Show, Royal Hawaiian Shopping Center.

Commerce: Dole Pineapple Factory, movie or tour, Honolulu/ Hilo Hattie's Factory Tour, muumuus, aloha shirts, Honolulu.

Sports: Surfing clinics, Kapiolani Beach Park/ rent a surf board from concessions at or near the large beaches/ Joggers Clinic, Kapiolani Park/ Ice Palace Chalet, ice skating, Honolulu.

Statewide Attractions

•Good Choices:

Natural Scenery: Molokai: Kalaupapa Lookout, 1,600 ft above the sea, Palaau Park/ Kalokoeli Fishpond, ancient ponds, between Kaunakakai and Kawela/ Phallic Stone, ancient sacred site, Palaau Park. Lanai: Garden of the Gods, eroded canyon, multi-colored rocks/ Hulopoe Bay, beautiful beach, Kaunolu Village/ Lanaihale, view from highest spot on island.

History and Culture: Kalaupapa, village for banished victims of Hansen's Disease, hike down a steep trail, Molokai/ Luahiwa Petroglyphs, Hwy 441 S of Lanai City, Lanai.

Commerce: Kaunakakai, the largest town on the island, Molokai/ Big Wind Kite Factory, Maunaloa, Molokai.

Sports: Swimming at the beaches/ Hiking.

Idaho

Fame: *Rugged scenery with forests, rock, meadows, mountains, lakes, streams.*
You must get out and enjoy the outdoors.

Statewide Attractions

•Best Choices:

Craters of the Moon National Monument
Box 29, Arco 83213. (208)527-3257.

18 miles W of Arco on US 20, 26, 93. Lava outbursts through the earth's crust over thousands of years have produced a strange landscape with craters, caves, cones, tubes and bridges. There is a 7 mile circular drive for autos. Interpretive programs, nature walks, campfire talks. **$5/car.** Visitor Center open year around, but road is closed from late Nov to mid-Apr. Daily, Jun-Sept, 8-8; Sept-Jun, 8-5.

•Good Choices:

Natural Scenery: Crystal Ice Cave, American Falls/ Grand Canyon in Miniature, Challis/ Scenic Drives, Coeur D'Alene/ Nezperce National Forest, rivers, forest, Grangeville/ The Lavas, fissures, caves, flows, Idaho Falls/ Auto Tours, scenic and historic, Lewiston/ Bruneau Canyon, Gruneau Dunes State Park, Mountain Home/ Idaho Panhandle National Forests - Kanikau, Priest River/ Shoshone Falls, Twin Falls.
Nature and Man: Julia Davis Park, zoo, rose garden etc, Boise/ Howard Platt Gardens and Union Pacific Depot, Boise/ World Center for Birds of Prey, tour of endangered species program, Boise.
Science and Technology Experimental Breeder Reactor Number 1, nuclear reactor tour, Arco.
Historical and Cultural: Idaho State Historical Society Museum, Pacific Northwest, Boise/ Boise Gallery of Art, American, Oriental, European, Boise/ Old Idaho Penitentiary, Boise/ Ghost Mining Town, Challis/ Old Mission State Park, restored Indian mission, Kellogg/ Stanrod House, restored Victorian mansion, Pocatello/ Ghost Mining Towns, Stanley.
Entertainment: Boise Tour Train, Boise/ Sierra Silver-Lead Mine, Wallace.
Sports: Appaloosa Horse Museum, Moscow/ hiking, biking, skiing, fishing, swimming, boating throughout the state.

Illinois

Fame: *Frank Lloyd Wright Architecture, Chicago, Abraham Lincoln's home state.*
You must *visit Chicago or visit the historic towns of Galena, Nauvoo or Springfield.*

Chicago

Fame: *Architecture, lakefront, museums, music theater, professional sports.*

You must *walk around the loop to see the architecture; walk down Michigan Avenue from the river to Oak Street; take a bus tour of Chicago.*

•Best Choices:

Museum of Science and Industry
57th St and Lake Shore Dr, Chicago, 60637. (312)684-1414.

Over 2,000 exhibits, designed for visitor participation, in 75 exhibition halls. Among the displays are a full-scale replica of an underground coal mine, a ride on the Augernaut to the center of the earth, a World War II German submarine, an Appollo 8 capsule, a walk through a pulsating 16-ft. high heart, the Circus with 22,000 hand-carved figurines. **Free.** Daily, Memorial Day-Labor Day, 9:30-5:30. Rest of yr, Mon-Fri, 9:30-4; Sat, Sun, holidays, 9:30-5:30.

Lincoln Park Zoo and Conservatory
Fullerton and Cannon, 2200 N Cannon Dr, Chicago 60614. (312)294-4660.

The zoo has more than 2,000 animals, birds and reptiles from all over the world. Naturalistic habitats make the zoo a last refuge for many endangered species and encourage breeding of the animals. New areas, just opened, are children's zoo, farm-in-the-zoo and lion house. The conservatory has 4 glassed buildings with changing floral exhibits and permanent collections of exotic trees and plants. **Free.** Daily, 8-5:15; Buildings, 9-5.

Art Institute of Chicago
Michigan Av at Adams St, Chicago, 60603. (312)443-3600.

Internationally acclaimed Impressionist and Post-Impressionist pictures, Japanese prints, ancient Chinese bronzes, African wood carvings. Some of the finest art ever produced, in a world renowned institution. **$5/adult; $2.50/sr citizen, student, child. Free on Tues.** Wed-Fri, Mon, 10:30-4:30; Tues, 10:30-8; Sat, 10-5; Sun and holidays, Noon-5. Closed Christmas Day.

Field Museum of Natural History

Roosevelt Road at Lake Shore Drive, Chicago, 62521. (312)922-9410.

A preeminent natural history museum. Internationally famous collections of American Indian, Africa, Egypt, Chinese, Tibetan cultures and primitive art. Other exhibits include minerals and meteorites, botanical displays, dioramas. **$2/adult; $1/student, child 6-17; $.50/sr citizen; Free/teacher, child under 6, military.** Daily, 9-5.

Adler Planetarium

1300 S Lake Shore Dr, Chicago, 62521. (312)322-0300.

Exhibits of solar telescope, an amateur telescope maker's shop, modern astronomy, early scientific instruments. Highlighted are "Race to the Moon," "The New Universe," "The Discovery of Uranus." A multimedia sky show is presented throughout the day. **Sky Show: $2.50/adult; $1.50/child 6-17; Free/sr citizen.** Daily, 9:30-4:30, Fri until 9.

Shedd Aquarium

1200 S Lake Shore Dr, Chicago, 62521. (312)939-2438.

The aquarium displays more than 8,000 fish, reptiles, amphibians, invertebrates and mammals. Among the popular exhibits is "Coral Reef Exhibit," a 90,000 gallon tank filled with sharks, sea turtles, moray eels and other colorful fish. At 11, 2 and 3 a diver hand feeds the animals in the Coral Reef while talking to visitors through an underwater microphone. **$2/adult; $1/child 6-17; $.50/sr citizen. Free on Thurs.** Daily, 9-5.

Sears Tower

233 S Wacker Dr, Chicago, 60606. (312)875-9696.

Currently the world's tallest building, the 103rd floor skydeck is 1,353 ft. above the ground. You can ride an express elevator to this floor in just over one minute. On a clear day, portions of 4 states can be viewed from the skydeck. **$3.25/adult; $1.75/child 5-15.** Daily, 9-11:30.

Chicago Public Library Cultural Center

78 E Washington St, Chicago 60602. (312)744-6630.

5 galleries, a museum, a theater and a concert hall with a library collection of over 500,000 books, recordings, film and other materials are housed in a Chicago landmark with Tiffany glass domes, marble walls and mosaics. Over 500 different free programs

and exhibits are presented annually. **Free.** Mon-Thur, 9-7, Fri, 9-6, Sat, 9-5. Closed Sun and holidays.

Here's Chicago
163 E Pearson St at Michigan Av, Chicago 60611.

Located in the Water Tower Pumping Station. A 45-minute "sound and sight" show about the city. Includes a 63-projector slide show, a giant screen 70mm film that takes you flying down the Chicago River and soaring over the Sears Tower, a narrated walk through Chicago's operating historic water system and, finally, Chicago's gift shop filled with fascinating souvenirs. **$3.75/adult; $2/child under 13.** Daily starting at 9:30 am.

•Good Choices:
Natural Scenery: Lakeshore, you can walk for miles/ parks.
Nature and Man: Navy Pier, picnics, biking, fishing, exhibits, programs/ Buckingham Fountain, Grant Park/ Garfield Park Conservatory.
Historical and Cultural: Museum of Contemporary Art/ Chicago HIstorical Society, American & Chgo history, participatory exhibits/ Prairie Av, between 18th & Cullerton Sts, restored area, house tours/ Chicago Fire Academy, firefighter training facilities/ Chicago Academy of Sciences, natural history.
Entertainment: Double decker bus rides, narrated 1 hr tour from Sears Tower/ narrated boat tour, memorial day-labor day from planetarium, aquarium or Field museum/ Ripley's Believe It or Not Museum/ walk along Rush Street at night, Illinois to Division St/ Concerts in Grant Park, June-Aug.
Commercial: State of Illinois Center, shopping, art, architecture/ Chicago Board of Trade visitors gallery/ State Street mall, shopping/ Water Tower Place, shopping/ N Michigan Av, shopping on the "Magnificent Mile"/ Chinatown, Wentworth S of Cermak Rd/ James W Jardine Water Purification Plant, industrial tour/ Chicago Tribune, tour/ Chicago Sun-Times, tour/ US Post Office, 2 hr guided tour.
Sports: Chicago White Sox, baseball from bleachers, Comiskey Park/ Chicago Cubs, baseball from bleachers or upper deck reserved, Wrigley Field/ biking or walking malls, lakeshore, shopping areas, parks/ beaches/ fishing/ ice skating/ tennis/ horseracing.

Statewide Attractions

•Best Choices:

Brookfield Zoo

31st St and 1st Av, Brookfield 60513. (312)485-0263. Rt 5 S to 1st Av and 1st to 31st.

204 acres with more than 2,000 animals in areas similar to their natural habitats. Among the 24 exhibits are Tropic World, Children's Zoo, Seven Seas and Pachyderm House. **$3.25/adult; $1.50/sr citizen, child 6-11. Free Tues. Additional charge for some exhibits.** 5/1-9/30, daily, 9:30-6. Rest of yr, 10-5.

Frank Lloyd Wright Walking Tour
951 CHicago Av, Oak Park 60302. (312)848-1978.

Tour Wright's home and studio, Unity Temple, or the National Historic District. There are examples of early Wright as well as much later products of his prairie style of architecture. **$4/adult; $2/sr citizen, child 10-18.** Daily, inquire for schedule.

Chicago Botanic Gardens
Lake Cook Road, Glencoe 60022. (312)835-5440.

From Rt 41, take Lake Cook Rd exit E for 1/2 mile. 300 spectacular acres of lakes, waterfalls, islands, brooks, trails sprinkled with gardens. When you want to leave the outdoors, you may visit the educational center, greenhouses, exhibition hall, library, floral arts museum, gift shop or restaurant to visit. **Free. Tours: $2/adult; $1/sr citizen, child under 17.** Daily, 8-Sunset.

Bishop Hill State Historic Site
Box D, Bishop Hill 61419. (309)927-3345.

I-80 to Atkinson Exit, turn S for 15 miles following Bishop Hill signs. Bishop Hill was settled by a group of Swedish religious dissidents. The communal colony was started in 1846 and was finally abandoned in 1861. Today the site contains a living history village with many restored buildings including the Colony Church, Blacksmith Shop, school, store and Bjorklund Hotel. **Free. Some buildings charge a small fee.** Daily, 9-5.

Nauvoo
Nauvoo Restoration, Inc, Visitors' Center, Box 215, Nauvoo 62354. (217)453-2237.

Said to be one of the nation's finest restorations. It is famous for its association with Joseph Smith, founder of the Mormon Church. The restored town includes a visitors center, Seventies Hall, Noble-Smith House, Brigham Young Site and Residence, Heber C. Kimball Home, Jonathan Browning Houses and Workshops, Printing Office Complex, Webb Wagon and Blacksmith Shop, Old Smith Homestead and Smith Mansion. **Free.** May-Oct, daily, 8-8. Nov-Apr, daily, 8-7.

Shawnee National Forest
Greater Harrisburg Chamber of Commerce, Harrisburg National Bank

Annex, Harrisburg 62946. (618)252-4192.

I-57 runs S directly into the forest. It stretched across 240,000 acres of southern Illinois with hills, valleys, parks, wilderness and recreation areas. There are unusual and magnificent rock formations and scenic vistas. Public roads and trails traverse the forest. **Free.**

•Good Choices:

Natural Scenery: Wildlife Prairie Park, natural prairie and wildlife, Hanna City/ Ferne Clyffe State Park, canyons, caves, nature preserve, Marion/ Bird Haven-Robert Ridgway Memorial, arboretum and bird sanctuary, Olney.

Nature and Man: National Shrine of Our Lady of the Snows, shrine and gardens, Belleville/ Miller Park Zoo, Bloomington/ Lord's Park, zoo and recreation, Elgin/ Ladd Arboretum, Evanston/ Grosse Point Lighthouse, nature center and maritime museum, Evanston/ Morton Arboretum, Lisle/ Glen Oak Botanical Garden, Peoria/ Abraham Lincoln Memorial Garden and Nature Center call in advance for tour, Springfield/ Cantigny Gardens, country estate, Wheaton.

Science and Technology Fermilab National Accelerator Laboratory, subnuclear Particle research - call for reservation, Batavia/ Lakeview Museum of Arts and Sciences, planetarium, natural science, Peoria/ John Deere Planetarium, Augusta College, Rock Island.

Historic: Macon County Museum Complex, restored prairie village, Decatur/ Galena-Jo Daviess Historical Museum, Galena/ General Store Museum, Galena/ Old Market House State Historical Site, Galena/ Old Stockade and Underground Refuge, Galena/ Vinegar Hill Lead Mine and Museum, Galena/ Naper Settlement, outdoor history museum village, Naperville/ Old Graue Mill and Museum, operating gristmill, Oak Brook/ Lincoln's New Salem State Park, Petersburg/ Rockford Museum Center - Midway Village, historic artifacts, restored village, Rockford/ Cahokia Mounds State Historic Site, remains of prehistoric Indian city, St Louis/ Illinois State Museum, anthropology, natural history, geology, Springfield/ Illinois State Capitol, Springfield/ Lincoln and Herndon Building Museum, Springfield/ Lincoln Tomb State Historic Site, Springfield/ Teutopolis Monastery Museum, Teutopolis.

Historic Houses: David Davis Mansion, restored mansion, Bloomington/ Vermillion County Museum, restored 1850 home, Danville/ Ronald Regan Boyhood Home, Dixon/ Dawes House, restored home, Evanston/ The Belvedere, Dowling House, Turney House, restored houses, Galena/ U.S. Grant Home State Historic Site, Galena/ Carl Sandburg State Historical Site, Galesburg/ Grove

National Historic Landmark, nature preserve, restored homes, Glenview/ Lincoln Home National Historic Site, Springfield. **Special Interest Museums:** Fox River Trolley Museum, historic trolleys and ride, Elgin/ Grant Hills Antique Auto Museum, Galena/ Lolly's Doll and Toy Museum, Galena/ Hartung's Automotive Museum, Glenview/ The Time Museum, Rockford/ Garfield Farm Museum, St Charles.
Art: Terra Museum of American Art, Evanston.
Entertainment: Blackberry Historical Farm Village, replica 19th century village, crafts, children's rides, Aurora/ Bolingbrook Aquatic Center, indoor wave-generating pool, Bolingbrook/ The Lambs, shops, children's farmyard, rides, Libertyville/ Bradford Museum of

Collector's Plates, exhibit of 1,200 limited edition plates, Morton Grove/ Rockford Trolley, Rockford.
Commercial: Kolb-Lena Cheese Factory, factory viewing, Freeport/ Haeger Potteries, factory tour, Macomb/ Deer & Company, industrial tour equipment manufacturer, Moline/ Sara Lee Visitors Center, factory tour, Northbrook/ Antique Markets I, II, III, St. Charles.
Sports: Hawthorne Race Track, horse racing, Cicero/ Fairmout Park Race Track, horse racing, Collinsville/ Balmoral Park Race Track, horse racing, Crete/ Quad City Downs, horse racing, East Moline/ Maywood Park Race Track Harness Racing, Maywood.

Indiana

Fame: *Hoosier Hospitality.*
You must *see some of the countryside: go for a drive in the country, see a small town, a farm, the Amish areas or frolic in the sand dunes at Indiana Dunes National Lakeshore.*

Statewide Attractions

•Best Choices:

Indiana Dunes National Lakeshore
1100 N Mineral Springs Road, Porter 46304. (219)926-7561.

This is an unusual and changing environment, with many plants and animals not normally found in this area. See stabilized dunes with permanent vegetation, shifting dunes. Also visit Bailley Homestead and Chellberg Farm. Interpretive

programs and field trips. **$2/car.**
Daily, 8-5. Closed holidays.

Auburn-Cord-Duesenberg Museum

1600 S Wayne St, Auburn 46706.
(219)925-1444.

Displayed in original Art Deco factory showroom of the Auburn Automobile Co are 140 classic, antique and special interest cars. See historic fashions, art, toys, radio and TV equipment. **$4/adult; $2.50/sr citizen, child 6-18; $10/family.** Apr-Oct, daily, 10-5; May-Sep, 9-9. Closed Thanksgiving, 12/25, 1/1. Annual Festival.

Children's Museum

30th and N Meridian Sts, Indianapolis 46208. (317)924-5431.

One of the largest museums for children in the world. Signs read "please touch." Children barter for goods in a trading post, sit in the cockpit of a race car, explore a cave, ring bells, operate pulleys, light lights and handle feathers, skins, shells and rocks. Preschoolers enjoy Playscape. **Free. Carousel is $.50/adult; $.35/child under 12.** Tues-Sat, school holidays, Mon between Memorial Day and Labor Day, 10-5; Sun, noon-5. Closed Thanksgiving, 12/25, 1/1.

Marengo Cave Park

SR 64, Marengo 47140. (812)365-2705.

10 miles N of I-64. Two tours are available. Crystal Palace has formation filled rooms, huge flowstone deposits and a special underground pageant. Dripstone Trail features totem pole stalagmites and delicate sodastraw structrures. Marengo Cave has been open since 1883 and is a U.S. National Natural Landmark. **Crystal Palace Tour: $4.50/adult; $2.25/child 6-12; Dripstone Trail Tour: $5/adult; $2.75/child 6-12.** Daily 9-5, Memorial Day-Labor Day, 9-6.

Lincoln Boyhood National Memorial

Lincoln City 47552. (812)937-4757.

SR 162, just N of Lincoln City. The farm where Lincoln lived from 1816 to 1830. Includes the restored homestead, the grave of his mother, Nancy Hanks, and a visitor center. The farm still harvests the kinds of crops his family grew. **$1/adult; Free/sr citizen, child under 12.** Daily, 8-5

•Good Choices:

Natural Scenery: Bluespring Caverns, Bedford/ Indiana Dunes State Park, Chesterton/ Eagle Creek Park, one of largest city parks, Indianapolis/ Wyandotte Caves, Leavenworth/ Brown County State Park, fall foliage, wildlife, spectacular scenery, Nashville.
Nature and Man: Mesker Zoo, Evansville/ Children's Zoo, Ft. Wayne/ Foellinger-Freimann

Botanical Conservatory, Ft Wayne/ Indianapolis Zoo, Indianapolis/ Wolf Park, wolf packs, Lafayette/ International Friendship Gardens, 200 floral specimens, Michigan City/ Hayes Regional Arboretum, forest, greenhouse, bird sanctuary, rose garden, Richmond/ Round Barns of Fulton Co, drive, Rochester.

Science and Technology Evansville Museum of Arts and Science, Evansville/ Wilbur H. Cummings Museum of Electronics, growth of electronics, Valparaiso Technical Institute, Valparaiso.

Historic: Columbus Visitors Center, driving/walking tour to see modern architectural design, Columbus/ Angle Mounds State Historic Site, restored Indian mounds and dwellings, Evansville/ Historic River Cruises, Historic Ft Wayne, Ft Wayne/ Howard Steamboat Museum, restored mansion, steamboat models, shipyard artifacts, Jeffersonville/ John A Hook Drug Store restored pharmacy, Nashville/ Wayne County Historical Museum, tools of early settlers, log cabin, store, loom house, cobbler, blacksmith, print shop, Richmond/ Covered Bridges, Park County Tourist Information Center, biking/driving tour, Rockville/ Historical Museum of the Wabash Valley, victorian house, recreated shops/buildings, Terre Haute/ Early Wheels Museum, antique vehicles, Terre Haute/ George Rogers Clark National Historic Park, Revolutionary campaign, Vincennes/ Fort

Quientenon, 18th Century Trading Post, West Lafayette.

Historic Houses: Madison County Historic Home, Anderson/ Governor Hendrick's Home, living history, Corydon/ Ruthmere Museum, restored Beau Arts Mansion, Elkhart/ Limberlost State Historic Site, 14 rm log cabin home of author - naturalist - photographer Gene Stratton Porter, Geneva/ James Whitcomb Riley Home, one of finest Victorian restorations, Indianapolis/ President Benajamin Harrison Memorial Home, restored home and artifacts, Indianapolis/ Barker Mansion, Michigan City/ T C Steele Historic Site, home, studio, trails, forest, Nashville/ Culbertson Mansion, Empire-style residence, New Albany/ William Henry Harrison Mansion, Vincennes.

Historic Restored Villages: Historic Fort Wayne, reconstruction, Ft Wayne/ Spring Mill State Park, gristmill, restored pioneer village, space exhibits, caves, Mitchell/ Historic New Harmony, history and historic homes, New Harmony/ Conner Prairie, 30 building living history museum, Noblesville/ Billie Creek Village, Civil War Village, Rockville.

Art: Midwest Museum of American Art, Elkhart/ Indianapolis Museum of Art, Oriental, Old Masters, Post Impressionists, park, Indianapolis/ Greater Lafayette Museum of Art, Lafayette/ Century Center, art gallery, Studebaker Museum, South Bend.

Entertainment: Muncie Children's Museum, Muncie/ University of Notre Dame, South Bend.

Commercial: Kimball Piano & Organ Co, industrial tour, French Lick/ Art Chemical Products, factory tour - modeling clay, Huntington/ Amish Acres, restored farm, bakery, cheese shop, Nappance/ Hillerich & Bradsby Co, factory tour - baseball bats, golf clubs, Jeffersonville/ Possom Trot Vineyards, winery tour, Nashville.

Sports: Indianapolis Motor Speedway & Hall of Fame Museum, Indianapolis/ National Track & Field Hall of Fame, Indianapolis/ International Palace Sports Hall of Fame, wax figures, portraits, trophies, tape recordings, Warsaw.

Seasonal Events and Festivals: 500 Festival, May, Indianapolis/ East Race Waterway, artificial whitewater rapids races, South Bend/ Auburn-Cord-Duesenberg Festival, Sept, Auburn/ Johnny Appleseed Festival, Sept, Ft Wayne/ Chautauqua of the Arts, Sept, Madison/ Festival of the Hunters Moon, Ft Quiatenon, Oct, Lafayette/ Parke County Covered Bridge Festival, Oct, Rockville.

Iowa

Fame: *A prosperous farm state.*
You must *visit the Amana Colonies, eat locally produced foods.*

•Best Choices:

Amana Colonies
Box 8, Amana 52203. (319)622-3828.

The colonies were originally settled in the 1850s by German immigrants belonging to a religious sect. Now the heirs of the original settlers are stockholders in the corporation. The Amana brand name is a respected name on manufactured goods, but the main occupation of most stockholders is still farming. There are six villages in the colonies: East, West, South, Middle, High Amana, Amana and Homestead. Among the places to visit are **Amana Home and Blacksmith Shop Museum Complex,** in Homestead, a restored early house and museum containing blacksmith tools and other community artifacts. **$1/adult.** 4/1-11/30, Mon-Sat, 10-5; Sun, noon-5.

Kitchen, Hearth Oven Bakery and Coopershop, in Middle Amana. Shows these work areas as they originally looked in the early colony. **$1/adult; $.75/child under 12.** 4/25-11/1, daily, 10-5.

Barn Farm Museum, in South Amana. Miniature buildings show the typical Amana settlement and farm in the late 1800s.

$1.50/adult; $.50/child 6-11. 4/1-10/15, Mon-Sat, 9-5; Sun, noon-5. **Krauss Furniture Shop,** near South Amana. Workshop tours. **Free.** 5/1-12/31, Mon-Sat, 8-5, Sun, 1-4. **Woolen Mill,** in Amana. Factory tours. **Free.** Summer, Mon-Fri, 9-10:30 and 11:30-4; Winter, Mon-Fri, 9-3:30. **Museum of Amana History,** in Amana. Museum. **$2/adult; $.75/child under 12.** 4/15-11/15, Mon-Sat, 10-5, Sun, noon-5. Also available are winery tours, restored house tours, other manufacturers.

Humboldt County Historical Museum

Box 247, Dakota City, 50529. (515)332-3392.

1/2 mi S of SR 3 on CRP 56. A group of 6 buildings that demonstrates early rural life in the county. Included are house, barn, school, log cabin, jail and chicken house. The restored buildings have displays of artifacts and tools appropriate to the buildings and other reconstructed shops. **$1/adult; $.25/child 7-11.** 6/1-Labor Day: Sun, 1:30-4:30; Mon-Tues, Thurs-Sat, 1-4:30; Labor Day-9/30: Sun, 1:30-4:30.

Herbert Hoover National Historic Site

Box 607, West Branch, 52358. (319)643-2541.

This park contains the cottage in which President Hoover was born, the Quaker Meetinghouse he at-tended, a reconstruction of his father's blacksmith shop, the school he attended, the presidential library and museum, the graves of President and Mrs. Hoover and a restored native prairie. **Library/museum: $1/adult; free/child under 16. Other exhibits are free.** Daily, 8-5. Closed Thanksgiving, 12/25, 1/1.

•Good Choices:

Natural Scenery: Crystal Lake Cave, Dubuque/ E B Lyons Prairie Woodlands Preserve, plants, wildlife, Dubuque/ Lacey-Keosauqua State Park, wildlife, plants, cliffs, ravines, lake, Keosauqua/ Spook Cave, McGregor/ DeSoto National Wildlife Refuge, wildlife, trails, recreation, Missouri Valley.
Nature and Man: Iowa Arboretum, Ames/ Des Moines Botanical Center, more than 1,000 species of plants, Des Moines/ Dallas County Forest Park and Museum, arboretum and museum, Perry/ Schield International Museum, artifacts from travels and canoe expedition, Waverly.
Science and Technology: The Bettendorf Museum, hands-on exhibits for pres-schoolers - adults, Bettendorf/ Des Moines Center of Science and Industry, planetarium, biological, physical sciences, Des Moines/ Keokuk Dam, hydroelectric plant tours, Keokuk/ Grout Museum of History and Science, restored shops, earth science, planetarium, Waterloo.

Historical and Cultural: Boone and Scenic Valley Railroad, 15 min rides, Boone/ Historic Pottawattamie County Jail, unusual jail, tours, Council Bluffs/ State Capitol, Des Moines/ Sidewheeler William M Black and Fred W Woodward Riverboat Museum, Dubuque/ Effigy Mounds National Monument, burial mounds, walking tour, Marquette/ Fort Dodge Historical Museum Fort and Stockade, exact replica of original fort, Fort Dodge/ Buffalo Bill Museum, Le Claire/ Lidtke Mill, Lime Springs/ Van Horn's Antique Truck Collection, Mason City/ Pella Historical Village Museum, recreated Dutch village, Pella/ Bily Clock Exhibit, hand carved clock collection, Spillville.

Historic Houses: Mamie Doud Eisenhower Birthplace, restored home of first lady, Boone/ Historic General Dodge House, restored residence, Council Bluffs/ Hoyt Sherman Place, restored mansion, art gallery, auditorium, Des Moines/ Salisbury House, replica of the King's House in Salisbury, England, Des Moines/ Terrace Hill, governor's mansion, restored Victorian, Des Moines/ Mathias Ham Historic House, Dubuque/ Plum Grove, restored governor's residence, Iowa City/ Liberty Hall Historic Center, restored home of Joseph Smith III, Lamoni/ Buffalo Bill Homestead, McCausland/ Nelson Homestead Pioneer Farm and Craft Museum, Oskaloosa/ Cedar Rock - The Walter Residence, Frank Lloyd Wright designed home, Quasqueton.

Art: Davenport Art Gallery, American, European, Haitian art, Davenport/ Des Moines Art Center, mid-18th century to present, modern sculpture, Des Moines/ Fisher Foundation Collection of Paintings, impressionists, Marshalltown/ Muscatine Art Center, 19th century American paintings, sculpture, oriental rugs, decorative arts. Muscatine.

Entertainment: Trainland USA, toy trains demonstrate railroad history, Colfax/ Fenelon Place Elevator, incline railway ride, Dubuque.

Commercial: John Deere Des Moines works, farm machinery factory tour, Des Moines/ Winnebago Industries Visitor Center, factory tour, Forest City/ Shaeffer Eaton, pen factory tour, Fort Madison/ Maytag Dairy Farm, maker of blue cheese, seasonal, Newton/ John Deere Ottumwa Works, farm machinery factory tour, Ottumwa/ John Deere Tractor Works, farm machinery factory tour, Waterloo.

Kansas

Fame: *Frontier history, natural beauty of prairie and flint hills.*

You must *visit a recreated cowtown, take a driving tour of the flint hills and prairie.*

Statewide Attractions

•Best Choices:

Eisenhower Center

SE Fourth St, Abilene 67410. (913)263-4751. Dwight D. Eisenhower's boyhood home, a museum featuring his career in the military and presidency, a library housing the archives of his administration's papers and the Place of Meditation -- burial place of Dwight and Mamie Eisenhower. Covers 22 acres of landscaped grounds. **$1/adult; free/child under 16.** Daily, 9-5. Closed Thanksgiving, 12/25, 1/1.

Kansas Cosmosphere and Discovery Center

1100 North Plum, Hutchinson 67501. (316)662-2305.

An Omnimax movie projector and a six-channel sound system give the viewer a feeling of actually participating in the screened experience. The Hall of Space contains a complete set of original spacecraft, a collection of space suits, a comprehensive camera exhibit and other space artifacts. In the Discover Center is a planetarium with sky lectures and laser shows. **Planetarium: $1.50 Laser Shows: $4.** Movies: Mon-Fri, 11, 1, 2, 3; Sat, 11, 1, 2, 3, 4; Sun, 1, 2, 3, 4; Tues, Thurs-Sat evenings, 7, 8.

Historic Wichita Cowtown

1871 Sims Park Dr, Wichita 67203. (316)264-0671.

A historic site museum displaying the first residence in Wichita, a general store, drug store, saloon, schoolhouse and artifacts. Craftspeople and musicians entertain on summer weekends. The Variety Theatre makes 19th Century stage and literture presentations as well as plays. There are 44 buildings on 73 acres of grounds. **$2.50/adult; $1.50/child.**

Boot Hill Historic Front Street

500 W Wyatt Earp, Dodge City 67801. (316)227-8188.

An authentic reproduction of historic Front Street with the Long Branch Saloon, Rath and Wright General Store, Boot Hill Memorial

Cemetery and Museum. During the summer the Long Branch Variety Show is performed every night and gunfights are staged daily. **$2.75/adult; $2/child.** Daily, Memorial day-3rd wknd in Aug, 8:30-10; rest of yr, 9-5. Closed Thanksgiving, 12/25, 1/1.

Topeka Zoological Park
635 Gage Blvd, Topeka 66606. (913)272-5821.

In Gage Park. This zoo has over 400 animals and is considered one of the finest in the nation. The tropical rain forest has the largest waterfall in Kansas, lush tropical vegetation, birds in free flight. A replica of a 19th century Santa Fe train moves across the park. **$2/adult; $.50/sr citizen, child 5-15.** Daily, 9-5.

Fort Larned National Historic Site
Rte 3, Larned 67550. (316)285-3571.

Fort Larned was one of the crucial military posts on the Indian Frontier and the Santa Fe Trail from 1859-1878. Four of the nine military buildings are open and restored: the barracks, hospital, commissary storehouse and officer's quarters. Living history programs operate on summer weekends. Films on Sundays. **Free.** Daily, 8-7; Sept-May, 8-5.

•Good Choices:
Natural Scenery: El Dorado State Park, 3,890 acres, prairie, recreation, game preserve, El Dorado/ Flint Hills National Wildlife Refuge, Emporia/ Kanopolis State Park, lake, canyon, petroglyphs, Lindsborg/ Wilson State Park, lake, deep canyons, hills, chimney rocks, Russell/ Cedar Bluff State Park, lake, stream, chalk beds, Castle Rock, Wakeeney.

Nature and Man: Finnup Park and Lee Richardson Zoo, Garden City/ Cheyenne Bottoms Wildlife Management Area, wildlife refuge and hunting area, Great Bend/ Ralph Mitchell Zoo, Independence/ Sunset Park and Zoo, Manhattan/ Children's Farmstead, barnyard animals to pet and feed, Overland Park/ Kansas State Fish Hatchery, aquariums, exhibits, ponds, Pratt/ Bartlett Arboretum, Wellington/ Sedgwick County Zoo, Wichita.

Science and Technology Agriculture Hall of Fame and National Center, Bonner Springs/ Lake Afton Public Observatory, Wichita.

Historical and Cultural: Fort Scott Historic Site, 1842 military post, Ft Scott/ Old Fort Hays, historic site, Hays/ Frontier Army Museum, Ft Leavenworth, Leavenworth/ Lawrence Museum of Natural History, Lawrence/ Spencer Museum of Art, University of Kansas, Lawrence/ Old Mill Museum, restored buildings, Indian, pioneer, Swedish artifacts, Lindsborg/ Birger Sandzen Memorial Gallery, works of Sandzen and other artists, Lindsborg/ Dalton Gang Hideout,

Meade/ State Capitol, murals, paintings, Topeka/ Wichita Art Association, galleries, Wichita.

Commercial: General Motors Assembly Plant, industrial tour - reservations, Kansas City.

Kentucky

Fame: *Where North meets the South, blending of scenic beauty with southern hospitality.*
You must *drive past a horse farm to see the fine thoroughbred race horses in the pasture, view one or several historic restorations to see the Kentucky of the past, get into the country to enjoy the natural scenery of Kentucky.*

Lexington

Fame: *Thoroughbred horses and bluegrass horse farms.*
You must *drive through the countryside past the famous horse farms, visit the Kentucky Horse Park (only slightly too high for our choices).*

•Best Choices:

Mary Todd Lincoln Home
578 W Main St, 40507. (606)233-9999.

A reconstruction of the house in which Mary Todd spent her girlhood and student years. In 1839 she left to visit her sister in Springfield, IL, and met Abraham Lincoln. This is the first shrine to a first lady in America. **$3/adult; $1/child 7-12.** 4/1-12/15, Tue-Sat, 10-4. Closed Thanksgiving.

Kneeland Race Course
US 60 W, Versailles Rd. (606)254-3412. (800)624-3477.

A model racetrack, with regular races including the final major prep race for the Kentucky Derby. Visitors are also welcome to watch the morning workouts during the season (6-10 am). The Keeneland Library is open year around, Mon-Fri. **$2/person.** Apr-Oct, Tues-Sat, 1:30 pm, post time.

Festival Market
325 W Main St, 40507.

Shopping area filled with pastry shops, food stalls, old-fashioned push carts, restaurants and boutiques. A classic musical carousel represents the horse industry and dancers musicians and clowns provide year around festival atmosphere. **Free.** Mon-Thurs, 10-9; Fri-Sat, 10-10; Sun, 12-6.

•Good Choices:

Natural Scenery: Jacobson Park/ Raven Run Nature Sanctuary, streams, meadows, woodlands, trails.

Nature and Man: Masterson Station Park, equestrian programs.

Historical and Cultural: Ashland - Henry Clay Estate/ Gratz Park, public park with historic background/ Headley-Whitney

Museum, jeweled bibelots, oriental porcelains, changing exhibits/ Hopemont, The Hunt-Morgan Home/ Lexington Cemetery/ Loudon House, art exhibits in castellated Gothic villa/ University of Kentucky Museum of Anthropology and Art Museum/ Waveland State Historic Site, antebellum house and grounds.

Commercial: Dudley Square, shopping center/ Old Kentucky Candy Co, factory tour.

Sports: American Saddle Horse Museum, heritage and story of American Saddlebred/ Red Mile Harness Track.

Louisville

Fame: *Kentucky Derby, Bluegrass Festival.*

You must *visit the Kentucky Derby Museum, hear some Bluegrass music.*

•Best Choices:

Kentucky Derby Museum
Churchill Downs, 704 Central Av, 40201. (502)582-2547.

I-65 to Eastern Parkway exit to Eastern Parkway, left on 3rd St, right on Central. The world's largest equine museum, featuring a 360-degree audio visual presentation about the Kentucky Derby, hands-on computerized simulated racing, miniature model of Churchill Downs, memorabilia. **$3/adult; $2.50/sr citizen; $1.50/child 5-12.** Daily, 9-5.

Kentucky Show
651 Fourth Av, 40202. (502)585-4008.

I-65 to Broadway exit, W on Broadway to 4th Av. An audiovisual presentation that uses 40 projectors, 3700 slides and a 5-channel soundtrack to provide a 52 minute tour of the people, places and lifestyles of Kentucky. **$3/adult; $2.50/sr citizen; $2/child under 15.** Shows every hour, Mon-Sat, 10-5 P; Sun, noon-3.

J. B. Speed Art Museum
2035 S Third St, 40208. (502)636-2893.

I-65 to Eastern Parkway exit W, right on 3rd St. Kentucky's largest and oldest museum. Among the ex-

74

hibits are traditional and contemporary art, including Old Masters, sculpture, tapestries, furniture, American Indian and African exhibits. **$2/adult; $1/sr citizen, free/student.** Tues-Sat, 10-4; Sun, 1–5.

•Good Choices:

Nature and Man: Cave Hill Cemetery, cemetery and botanical garden/ Kentucky Botanical Gardens/ Louisville Zoological Gardens, animals in natural environments.
Science and Technology Rausch Memorial Planetarium/ Museum of History & Science, hands on learning.
Historical and Cultural: Farmington, historic home designed by Thomas Jefferson/ Brennan House, Victorian townhouse/ Genealogical Research Library, for research on family tree/ Kentucky Railroad Museum, railroad memorabilia, ride/ Locust Grove Historic Home, plantation mansion home of Louisville's founder/ Howard Steamboat Museum, riverboat history, Jeffersonville, IN/ Culbertson Mansion, restored mansion, New Albany.
Commercial: Louisville Stoneware Co, factory tour/ Hillerich & Bradsby Co, factory tour - Louisville Slugger bats, Jeffersonville, IN/ American Printing House for the Blind, factory tour/ Hadley Pottery, factory tour.
Sports: Louisville Downs, harness racing/ hiking/ biking/ fishing.
Seasonal Events and Festivals: Kentucky State Fair and Horse Show, Aug.

Statewide Attractions

•Best Choices:

My Old Kentucky Home State Park
Box 323, Bardstown 40004-0323. (502)348-3502.

US-150, 1 mile E of Bardstown. The famous mansion that inspired Stephen Foster to compose "My Old Kentucky Home" in 1852. The house has been restored to its former splendor and tour guides in period costumes host tours daily.

$3.50/adult; $1/child. Daily, Jun-Aug, 9-6; Sept-May, 9-5.

Abraham Lincoln Birthplace National Historic Site
US 31 E, Hodgeville 42748. (502)358-3874.

Enclosed in a granite and marble memorial shrine is the cabin where Abraham Lincoln, our 16th president, was born on February 12, 1809. The grounds include 100 acres of the original farm. The memorial is reached by 56 steps, one for each year of his life. Also exhibits, movie, picnic areas, trails. **Free.** Jun-Labor Day, daily, 8-6:45. Apr-May, Sept-Oct, 9-5:45. Nov-Mar, 8-4:45. Closed Thanksgiving, 12/25, 1/1.

Old Fort Harrod State Park
Box 156, Harrodsburg 40330. (606)734-3314.

The site of the first permanent pioneer settlement west of the Alleghenies, built in 1774. This is an accurate reconstruction of the fort; also on the property is the cabin in which Abraham Lincoln's parents were married and the George Rogers Clark Memorial. **Fort: $1.50/adults; $1/children 6-11. Fort and museum: $2/adults; $.75/children 6-11.** 3/16-11/30, daily, 8:30-5; 12/1-3/15, Tues-Sun, 8:30-5.

Mammoth Cave National Park
Mammoth Cave 42259. (502)758-2251.

I-65, Exit 53. The longest known cave system in the world with over 300 miles of mapped passageways. In the park are 52,370 acres with over 30 miles of hiking trails, campfire programs, handicraft exhibits and scenic boat trips, all above the ground. Cave tours range from 1 1/4 to 6 hrs in length. **Free parking. Cave tours: $3.50-5.50/adult; $1.75-2.75/child under 16.** Summer, daily, 6:30 am - 6:30 pm. Rest of yr, 8-5:20.

Cumberland Falls State Resort Park
Rte 6, Box 411, Corbin 40701-8814. (606)528-4121.

In Daniel Boone National Forest, I-75, Exit 25, to US 25 W to KY 90. The largest, most impressive waterfall east of the Rocky Mountains except for Niagara. During a full moon, the mist of the falls creates a Moonbow, seen nowhere else in the western hemisphere. **Free.**

Land Between the Lakes
between Kentucky Lake and Lake Berley in western Kentucky and Tennessee. Managed by Tennesse Valley Authority.

A 170,000 acre, 40 mile long peninsula, used as a national demonstration area for outdoor education and recreation. In the area are a small buffalo herd, Golden Pond Visitor Center with orientation and astronomy programs, Environmental Education Area with wildlife in natural settings, Woodland Nature Center with slide shows, outdoor activities and wildlife exhibits, Empire Farm which demonstrates a self-sufficient lifestyle with organic gardening, sheep shearing, solar energy and bee keeping. The Homeplace is a living history exhibit of the lifestyle of a rural family in the 1850s. **Woodlands Nature Center: $1/adult; $.75/sr citizen and child; Empire Farm: $1/adult; $.75/sr citizen, child; Homeplace:**

$2.50/adult; $1/sr citizen, child. Daily, 9-5.

•Good Choices:

Natural Scenery: Crystal Onyx Cave and Campground, Cave City/ Breaks Interstate Park, "Grand Canyon of the South," Elkhorn City/ John James Audubon State Park, bird sanctuary, nature center, Henderson/ Cumberland Gap National Historical Park, Alleghenies pass, Middlesboro/ Carter Caves State Resort Park, caves, cliffs, lake, trails, Olive Hill/ Natural Bridge State Resort Park, spectacular view from 65 ft natural bridge, Slade.

Nature and Man: Bernheim Forest Arboretum and Nature Center, Clermont.

Science and Technology Owensboro Area Museum, science museum with planetarium, live reptiles etc, Owensboro.

Historical and Cultural: St. Joseph's Cathedral, 17th century paintings, 1st Catholic church W of Allegheny Mtns, Bardstown/ Blue Licks Battlefield State Park, Revolutionary War Battlefield, Blue Lick Springs/ Columbus-Belmont Battlefield State Park, Civil War battlefield, Columbus/ Jefferson Davis Monument, 351 ft obelisk, log house, Fairview/ Patton Museum of Cavalry and Armor, memorabilia related to WWII and Gen Patton, Ft Knox/ Frankfort Cemetery, burial site of Daniel Boone - many old graves, Frankfort/ Kentucky History Museum, Frankfort/ State Capitol, Frankfort/ Owensboro Museum of Fine Art, 18th & 19th century paintings, Owensboro/ Perryville Battlefield, Civil War Battlefield, Perryville.

Historic Houses: Hobson House, restored mansion, Bowling Green/ General Butler State Resort Park, restored home, Carrollton/ William Whitley House, restored home, Crab Orchard/ Mc Dowell House, home and office of pioneer surgeon, Danville/ Historic Frankfort Houses, Frankfort/ Old Governors Mansion, Frankfort/ White Hall, restored estate house of emancipationist, Cassius Marcellus Clay, Richmond.

Entertainment: B & B Riverboats, cruises, Covington.

Commercial: Churchill Weavers, factory tour, Berea/ General Motors Corvette Assembly Plant, factory tour, Bowling Green/ Schmidt's Museum of Coca-Cola Memorabilia, Elizabethtown/ Old Grand-Dad Distillery, factory tour, Frankfort/ Ancient Age Distillery, factory tour, Frankfort.

Louisiana

Fame: *Bayous hung with Spanish moss; Cajun cooking and music; plantations; New Orleans jazz.*
You must *see a plantation; sample Cajun or other Louisiana style cooking and music; enjoy the uniqueness of the area you visit.*

Baton Rouge

Fame: *Plantation homes, historic attractions, Mississippi River seaport.*

You must *visit some plantation homes on the banks of the Mississippi, take a swamp cruise through the Afchafalaya Basin.*

•Best Choices:

Louisiana Governor's Mansion
1001 Capital Access Rd, 70802. (504)342-5855.

A replica of one of the state's plantation mansions, built in 1963. Reservations necessary. **Free.** Mon-Fri, 9-11 am, 2-4 pm.

Louisiana State Capitol
State Capitol Drive, 70804. (504)342-7317.

A 34 story building overlooking the Mississippi River with extraordinary marble, stone and bronze work. From the 27th floor observation deck the visitor gets a sweeping view of the countryside. A lovely sunken garden surrounds former governor, Huey Long's grave. Steps commemorating the 50 states lead to the entrance of the building. **Free.** Daily, 8-4:30.

Magnolia Mound Plantation
2161 Nicholson Dr, 70802. (504)343-4955.

This restored building emphasizes the way of life in Colonial Louisiana. Furnished with a striking collection of Louisiana-made furniture. Includes restored overseer's house, detached kitchen and garden. Accredited by the American Association of Museums. **$3.50/adult.** Tues-Sat, 10-4; Sun, 1-4.

Louisiana Arts & Science Center - Riverside
North Blvd at River Rd. (504)344-9463.

A former railway station converted to house permanent and changing exhibits in art, history and science. Includes Discovery Depot for children. **$1.50/adult; $.75/child**

6-12; **Free/sr citizen, student, child under 6.** Tues-Fri, 10-3, Sat, 10-4, Sun, 1-4.

Samuel Clemens Riverboat
Florida St at River Rd. (504)381-9606.

Riverboat offering sightseeing harbor cruises. **$5/adult; $3/child.** Mar-Sept, daily, 10, noon, 2; Oct-Feb, Wed-Sun, 10, noon, 2.

•Good Choices:

Nature and Man: Greater Baton Rouge Zoo, more than 500 animals in natural settings/ Cohn Memorial Arboretum/ LSU Hilltop Arboretum.

Lafayette

Fame: *Cajun food and Cajun music.*

You must *dine on Cajun food while listening to a Cajun band.*

•Best Choices:

Acadian Village
Rte 3, Box 1976, 70505. (318)981-2364

H. Mouton Rd, off Hwy 342. A replica of an early bayou settlement with Acadian houses, church, blacksmith shop and gardens. Distinctive Acadian architecture. Crafts are displayed and sold. **$3/adult; $2/sr citizen; $1.50/child 6-14.** Daily, 10-5. Closed major holidays.

Science and Technology
Louisiana Arts & Science Center - Planetarium.

Historical and Cultural: Former Governor's Mansion, each rm dedicated to a former governor/ LSU Rural Life Museum, 19th century bldgs of rural South/ USS Kidd, WWII Fletcher Class Destroyer/ Old Bogan Fire Station, art exhibits, fire equip/ Old State Capitol, Gothic Revival Castle.

Plantation Homes Mount Hope Plantation/ Rosewood Manor/ Glynwood Plantation Home, Glynn/ McHugh House Museum, Zachary/ Nottoway Plantation, White Castle.

Sports: Evangeline Downs, race track.

Lafayette Museum
1122 Lafayette St, 70501. (318)234-2208.

Listed in the National Register of Historic Places, this is the home of former Louisiana Governor Alexandre Mouton. The museum now has displays of Mardi Gras costumes, antiques and Civil War artifacts. **$2/adult; $1/child.** Tues-Sat, 9-5; Sun, 3-5.

Live Oak Gardens
284 Rip Van Winkle Rd, New Iberia 70560. (318)367-3485.

Located on Jefferson Island. The 1870s home of stage actor Joseph Jefferson has been restored and furnished with period furniture. The grounds are covered with camellias, azaleas, crepe myrtles and live oaks. Restaurant and gift shop. **$5/adult; $3.50/sr citizen; $2.50/child 5-16.** Daily, 9-5.

Jungle Gardens and Bird Sanctuary
Avery Island, 70513. (318)365-8173.

Tropical plants, camellias, azaleas and iris provide a magnificent show in the tropical gardens. An ancient Buddha is found among the flowers in the Chinese garden. Egrets, herons, cranes, ducks and other fowl are protected here and may be seen in huge flocks seasonally. **$3.75/adult; $2.75/child 6-12.** Daily, 9-5.

•Good Choices:

New Orleans

Fame: *The French Quarter, the Mardi Gras, New Orleans jazz, Creole culture.*

You must *visit the French Quarter, listen to New Orleans jazz, eat a beignet.*

•Best Choices:

French Quarter Walking Tour
available from Visitor Information Center, 529 St Ann St, 70116. (504)566-5031.

Natural Scenery: Acadiana Park Nature Station and Trail/ Cypress Lake, natural swamp environment, Univ. of SW LA.

Nature and Man: Lafayette Natural History Museum, Planetarium and Nature Station.

Historical and Cultural: University Art Museum, permanent and special exhibits, U of SW LA/ Chretien Point Plantation, historic plantation, Sunset/ Shadows-on-the-Teche, restored plantation, New Iberia/ Mintmere Plantation and Armand Broussard House, restored, New Iberia/ Longfellow Evangeline State Commemorative Area, craft shop, museum, picnic area, St. Martinville.

Commercial: Tabasco Pepper Sauce Factory, factory tours, Avery Island/ Konriko Company Store and Rice Mill, New Iberia.

Sports: Evangeline Downs, race track.

Probably the very best way to see the highlights of the French Quarter. This tour is highly recommended if your time and legs will allow you to take it. **Free.**

Preservation Hall
726 St Peter St, 70116. (504)522-8939.

Arrive early if you want to get one of the very few seats, otherwise you'll stand. You'll hear traditional New Orleans jazz concerts by the top talents that happen to be in town and other great players that have never left. No drinks are served so bring the kids. They'll love this too. **$2/person.** Nightly, 8 pm - 12:30 am.

Superdome
1500 Poydras St, 70112. (504)587-3810.

The site of the Sugar Bowl game and of many other sports, concerts, theatre and conventions. This is the largest enclosed stadium in the world. It seats up to 80,000 people with no posts to obstruct your view. Guided tours **$4/adult; $3/child 5-12.** Daily, 9-4, except during certain special events.

St Charles Streetcar
board on St Charles St.

This trolley has been operating since 1835 and has been designated a National Historic Landmark. In addition to the fun of riding this old streetcar, this is the least expensive tour you'll be able to find. Among the highlights are riding through the Garden District, with antebellum houses surrounded by gardens, but you'll see historic and interesting sights all the way from downtown to uptown and back. **$.60/person each way.** Daily, 24 hrs, at frequent intervals.

Old French Market
700-1000 Decatur St.

This area has been a market since the 1700s. You'll wander past stalls piled high with fresh fruit and vegetables guaranteed to make you hungry. And if you don't mind a few calories you can buy a cafe' au lait (coffee with milk) and beignets (a fried bread) or pralines. Guaranteed to take more time than you expect. Daily, 24 hrs.

Pitot House
1440 Most St, 70119. (504)482-0312.

Home of Mayor James Pitot, first elected mayor of the incorporated city of New Orleans. This is one of the few remaining West Indian plantation house with wide galleries on 3 sides. **$3/adult; $1.50/child.** Wed-Sat, 10-3.

•Good Choices:

Nature and Man: Audubon Park and Zoological Center.
Historical and Cultural: Jean Lafitte National Historic Park, Barataria, Chalmette, French Quarter and Islenos units, interpretive exhibits, walking and auto tours/ The Cabildo, state museum/ St Louis Cathedral, built in 1794/ New Orleans Museum of Art, Faberge objects, 19th century French, 13-18th century Italian/ U.S. Customs House, renovated bldg, historic displays/ Musee' Conti Historical Wax Museum, figures from historic New Orleans/ St Louis Cemeteries Nos. 1, 2 and 3, cities of the dead/ Historic New Orleans Collection, museum, historic homes, research center.

Historic Mansions: Longue Vue House and Gardens/ Gallier House/ Bosque Home/ Madame John's Legacy/ Destrehan Plantation, Destrehan/ San Francisco Plantation, Garyville.
Entertainment: Sky Line Gondola Rides/ Ferry ride across the Mississippi from Canal St.
Sports: Fair Grounds, horse racing/ City Park and Audubon

Park for tennis and golf
. **Festivals:** Mardi Gras, starting 13 days before the beginning of Lent and ending on Shrove Tuesday, the last day before Lent/ New Orleans Jazz and Heritage Festival, late April or early May/ Spring Fiesta, tours of historic homes, art show, parade, pageant, first Friday after Easter/ The Food Festival, early July.

Statewide Attractions

•Best Choices:

Creole Nature Trail
Lake Charles. I-10 to SR 27, 15 miles SW.

Follow SR 27 in a circle going back to Lake Charles. Following the route one can view bayous, oil platforms, beaches, wildlife refuges and intracoastal waterway. It is the winter habitat of flocks of ducks and geese. Also visible are a large alligator population, shrimp, crab, animals, oaks and wildflowers. For a map of the route contact the Tourist Bureau, Box 1912, Lake Charles 70601.

Laurel Valley Village
Box 1847, Thibodaux 70302. (504)446-7456.

On Bayou Lafourche (SR 308) 2 miles S of Thibodaux. The largest intact authentic 19th century plantation complex in the US. 70 original buildings in their original state plus

a restored general store with a rural life museum, local arts and crafts. Has provided the background in several movies. **Free.** Daily, 10-4.

Wedell-Williams State Aviation Museum
Box 655, Patterson 70392. (504)395-7067.

The official state aviation museum has distinctive planes, many with historical significance. Among the exhibits are a Beech D 17-S Staggerwing, a 1931 Curtiss Jr. pusher, President Dwight Eisenhower's Aero-Commander 680, and a full-scale flying replica of the "44" racer that was the first land plane to travel faster than 300 mph. **Free.** Check with museum for tour times.

Louisiana State Arboretum
in Chicot State Park near Ville Platte. (318)363-6287.

82

Within nearly 6,000 wooded acres of the park, the arboretum covers 301 acres. It has more than 150 species of plants native to Louisiana which can be viewed from nature trails. **Free.**

Center for Traditional LA Boat Building

Box 2783, Nicholls State University, Thibodaux 70310. (504)448-4626.

In the lobby and behind the Nicholls State Library. This center is dedicated to the collection and preservation of the traditional Louisiana art of building wooden boats by hand. Visitors may view boats and descriptions and may talk with builders as they construct wooden boats. **Free.** Mon-Fri, 8-4:30. Closed University holidays.

•Good Choices:

Natural Scenery: Kisatchie National Forest, trees, flowers, lakes, bayous, wildlife, Alexandria/ Cypremont Point State Park, marsh, beach, access to Gulf of Mexico, Franklin.

Nature and Man: Vacherie - Lucher ferry across the Mississippi, SR 641 between Baton Rouge and New Orleans/ Wildlife Gardens, Gibson/ Swamp Gardens and Wildlife Zoo, Morgan City/ The Great Wall, view river traffic from walkway, Atchafalaya River, Morgan City/ Barnyard Zoo, Morgan City/ Louisiana Purchase Gardens

and Zoo, Monroe/ National Fish Hatchery Aquarium, Natchitoches/ R. S. Barnwell Memorial Garden and Art Center, Shreveport/ American Rose Center, Shreveport.

Historical and Cultural: R. W. Norton Art Gallery, European and American paintings, including Remington, Russell, Shreveport/ Edward Douglas White Museum, 1790 raised cottage, Thibodaux.

Plantation Mansions: Kent House, Alexandria/ Blythewood Plantation, Amite/ Houmas House Plantation, Convent/ Destrehan Plantation, Destrehan/ Oakland Plantation at Gurley, Ethel/ Arlington Plantation, Franklin/ Southdown Plantation House, Houma/ Asphodel Village and Plantation House, Jackson/ Milbank, Jackson/ Madewood Plantation Home, Napoleonville/ Beau Fort Plantation, Natchitoches/ Melrose Plantation, Natchitoches/ Oaklawn Plantation, Natchitoches/ Parlange Plantation, New Roads/ San Francisco Plantation, Rserve/ Cottage Plantation, St Francisville/ Greenwood Plantation, St Francisville/ The Myrtles Plantation, St Francisville/ Rosewood Plantation, St Francisville/ Longfellow-Evangeline State Commemorative Area, St Martinville/ Oak Alley Plantation Home, Vacherie/ Oak Alley Plantation, Vacherie/ Glencoe Plantation, Wilson.

Entertainment: "Louisiana Hayride" Country Music Show, Bossier City.

Maine

Fame: *Wilderness, coastal scenery, lobsters.*
You must *see Acadia National Park, eat fresh Maine seafood.*

Statewide Attractions

•Best Choices:

Acadia National Park
RFD 1, Box 1, Bar Harbor, 04069.
(207)288-3338.

2 mi N of Bar Harbor, off of Rte 3 in Hull's Cove. A park filled with all of the marvelous scenery we associate with Maine. There's rugged seacoast with surf pounding on the shore, foggy ports, towering mountains, high cliffs, tree lined valleys, lakes, ponds, birds, wildflowers and wildlife. First stop after you enter the park should be the visitors' center. Among the highlights are the 27 mile Park Loop Road, the nature center at Sieur de Monts Spring, the Robert Abbe Museum or Acadia Wild Gardens. Popular activities are bicycling, bird watching, boating, clamming, hiking, horseback riding, skiing, snowmobiling, swimming. **$5/car.** Park open year around. Visitors' center and park programs 5/15-10/30.

Maine State House and State Museum
State and Capitol (Route 201), Augusta 04333. (207)289-2301.

In the museum, exhibits depict Maine's natural resources, special history and manufacturing heritage. Among the exhibits are shipbuilding, ice harvesting, lumbering and fishing. Nearby guided tours are available in Blaine House, the state executive mansion. **Free.** Mon-Fri, 9-5. State Museum is also open Sat, 10-4; Sun, 1-4.

L.L. Bean
Main St (Rte 1), Freeport 04032.
(207)865-4761.

The famous catalog firm, noted for its outdoor gear, has its headquarters in Freeport. It is open 24 hrs a day, 365 days a year, and it's said that you'll find the store full of customers even at 2 a.m. More than 3 million shoppers a year visit the store, described as Maine's number one man-made attraction. It's worth setting a few hours aside for a stop if you're in the neighbor-hood. **Free.**

•Good Choices:

Natural Scenery: Allagash Wilder-ness Waterway, a national wild river/ Mast Landing Sanctuary, self-guided tours, Freeport/ Moosehead Lake, ME's largest lake, wilder-ness, Greenville/ Baxter State Park, wilderness, Mount Katahdin, Mil-linocket.

Nature and Man: Maine State Ferry Service, Camden/ Mount Desert Oceanarium, Maine marine life, Southwest Harbor.

Science and Technology Jackson Laboratory, medical research, lec-tures, audio visual, Bar Harbor.

Historical and Cultural: Nor-lands Living History Center, 19th century working farm, Auburn/ Boothbay Railway Village, railway memorabilia, rides etc, Boothbay Harbor/ Old Conway House Com-plex, restored 18th century farm, Camden/ Brick Store Museum, Kennebunk/ Shaker Museum, Poland Spring/ Portland Museum of Art, Portland/ Portland Head-light, oldest operating lighthouse, Portland/ Owls Head Transporta-tion Museum, Rockland/ Pownal Borough Court House and Museum, Wicassset/ York Village, self-guided tour, church, jail, school, etc, York.

Historic Houses: Moses Mason House, Bethel/ Chapman-Hall House, Damariscotta/ John Black Mansion, Ellsworth/ The Nott House, Kennebunkport/ Sarah Orne Jewett House, Kittery/ Sayward-Wheeler House, Kittery/ Hamilton House, Georgian House, garden, Kittery/ Campobello Inter-national Park, F. D. Roosevelt sum-mer home, Lubec/ Ruggles House, Machias/ Portland Historic Trail, self-tour, see Chamber of Com-merce, Portland/ Marrett House and Garden, Sebago Lake/ Montpelier, 1795 house, Thomas-ton/ Castle Tucker, mansion, Wis-casset.

Marine Museums: Maine Maritime Museum, restored man-sion, boatyard, boat ride, Bath/ Moosehead Marine Museum, Greenville/ Kittery Historical and Naval Museum, Kittery/ Penobscot Marine Museum, Searsport.

Entertainment: Maranbo II, boat trip, Boothbay Harbor/ Betselma, Penobscot Bay cruise, Camden.

Commercial: Georgia-Pacific Corp, paper mill tour, Calais/ Old Town Canoe Company, industrial tour, Old Town.

Seasonal Events and Festivals: Windjammer Days, Jul, Boothbay Harbor/ Maine Lobster Festival, Aug, Rockland/ Common Ground Country Fair, demonstrations, foods, entertainment, Sept, Windsor/ Fryeburg Fair, old-time country fair, Oct, Fryeburg.

Maryland

Fame: *Scene of many historic events, diverse terrain, major cities of Baltimore and Annapolis.*
You must *visit a famed historic site such as Fort McHenry, Star Spangled Banner Flag House, the Naval Academy.*

Baltimore

Fame: *Inner Harbor waterfront, seafood, ethnic neighborhoods.*
You must *visit the Inner Harbor, eat steamed crabs and crabcakes.*

•Best Choices:

Fort McHenry
Foot of E Fort Av. (301)962-4299.

During the War of 1812, Fort McHenry survived 25 hrs of continuous bombardment and kept British troops from occupying Baltimore. The sight of the United States flag still flying over the fort inspired Francis Scott Key to write the Star Spangled Banner. In the summer, soldiers recreate the 1814 battle in the restored fort, guided tours and special programs are given. Visitor center and fort buildings are open year around. **$1/adult; free/sr citizen, child under 12.** Memorial Day-Labor Day, 9-8; rest of year, 9-5. Closed 12/25, 1/1.

Baltimore Museum of Art

Charles and 32nd St, 21218. (301)396-7101.

This museum is noted for its outstanding collections. It has a permanent collection of over 120,000 objects, including Old Masters, 18th and 19th century American, African, European, sculptures, furniture, silver. Changing exhibitions are in a new wing. **$2/adult over 21; free/member, student under 22. Thurs free.** Tues-Fri, 10-4; Sat-Sun, 11-6.

Druid Hill Park
Druid Park Lake Dr, 21217. (301)396-6106.

The most beautiful of Baltimore's parks, covering 760 acres. Within the park are two zoos, a conservatory, athletic fields, tennis courts, picnic areas. The **Baltimore Zoo** covers 150 acres and houses more than 1200 animals. Highlights include a colony of black-footed penguins, African Plains area, elephant park, hippopotamus and flamingo pool. **$2.50/adult; $1/sr citizen, child.** The **Conservatory** contains a large, magnificent collection of tropical plants, desert plants, and flowers. **Free.** Daily, 10-4.

B & O Railroad Museum
Pratt & Poppleton Sts, 21201. (301)237-2387.

This museum houses the Baltimore and Ohio Railroad's large collection of locomotives, the most extensive assortment of railroad memorabilia in the United States and the second largest train exhibit in the world. **$2.50/adult; $1.50/sr citizen, child.** Wed-Sun, 10-4. Closed holidays.

Top of the World
27th floor, World Trade Center, Inner Harbor. (301)837-4515. This is the prime place to view the Inner Harbor activity. It has five glass sides which provide a magnificent view of the world below. The area contains a multimedia presentation and exhibits about Baltimore, the port and the neighborhoods. **$1.50/adult; $1.25/sr citizen, children.** Mon-Fri, 10-5. Summer: Sat, 10-8; Sun, noon-7. Winter: Sun: noon-5.

Lexington Market
Lexington and Eutaw Sts. (301)685-6169.

Baltimore is famous for its municipal markets and this 204 year old market is the oldest of those markets. The indoor market has kept its original feeling, continuing to specialize in fresh produce and traditional local foods. **Free.** Mon-Sat, 8:30-6.

•Good Choices:
Nature and Man: Cylburn Arboretum, gardens, trails, children's nature museum/ Sherwood Gardens, tulip gardens.

History: Baltimore Maritime Museum, submarine USS Torsk, Lightship Chesapeake/ Federal Hill, historic landmark, harbor view/ Baltimore Center for Urban Archaeology, 12,000 yrs of artifacts, archeologists at work/ Baltimore Museum of Industry, early industries, working people/ Baltimore Streetcar Museum, historic streetcars, ride/ Public Works Museum/ Eubie Blake Cultural Center/ U.S. Frigate Constellation/ Shot Tower, 234 ft historic tower/ Washington Monument.

Historic Houses: Carroll Mansion, 19th century winter home of Charles Carroll/ Edgar Allan Poe House/ 1840 House, 19th century row house/ H.L. Mencken House/ Star-Spangled Banner Flag House and War of 1812 Museum.

Art: Peale Museum, art displayed in oldest museum in nation/ Walters Art Gallery, 6,000 yrs of art, Mesopotamia and Egypt to 19th century Europe.

Entertainment: Baltimore City Hall, tour/ Baltimore Fire Department, tour at any firehouse/ Baltimore Police Department, tour of municipal headquarters/ The Baltimore Sun papers, tour/ WBAL TV, tour/ Baltimore Patriots II & III, harbor cruises/ Defender and Guardian, cruises.

Commercial: Mount Vernon Place, residential & shopping center/ Eagle Coffee Company, factory tour/ General Motors, factory tour/ Joseph E Seagram & Sons, tour/ McCormick & Company, tour of spice factory/ Moore's Candy Company, tour.

Sports: Baby Ruth Birthplace and Maryland Baseball Hall of Fame/ Pimlico Race Course.

Statewide Attractions

•Best Choices:

U.S. Naval Academmy
King George and Randall Sts, Annapolis. (301)263-6933.

Among the interesting places to visit on the campus are the chapel, museum, Bancroft Hall Dormitory, statue of Tecumseh. John Paul Jones' crypt is beneath the chapel. Dress parades are held in the fall and spring. **Free.** Mon-Sat, 9-5; Sun, noon-5. @ATTRACTION = State House
State Circle, Annapolis. (301)269-3400.

The first capitol of the United States (11/26/1783 - 8/13/1784), this is also the oldest state house in continuous use. Exhibits show Annapolis in colonial times, there is an audio-visual program and guided tours. **Free.** Daily, 9-5. Closed Thanksgiving, 12/25, 1/1.

Chesapeake and Ohio Canal National Historical Park
Box 4, Sharpsburg 21782. 11710 MacArthur Blvd, Potomac. (301)299-3613.

This canal, which was an operating canal from 1850 to 1924, follows the shore of the Potomac River from Georgetown to Cumberland, Maryland. 1 1/2 hr mule drawn canal boat trip, costumed guides describe canal boat life, music of the era. The Great Falls Tavern and Museum, in Potomac, shows a film and has exhibits on the history of the canal. **Boat Trips: $4.50/adult; $3/sr citizen, child under 13. Museum, visitor center and rest of canal is free.** Museum: Daily, 9-5, except holidays. Boat trip: June-Sept: Wed-Sun, 10:30, 1, 3; Sun also at 5. Apr-Jun & Sept-Oct: Fri-Sun.

Paul E. Garber Facility
Rte 414 to Silver Hill Rd, Silver Hill. (202)357-1400.

This is the facility for restoration and storage of aircraft and spacecraft for the Smithsonian Air & Space Museum. Tours take 3 hours and reservations must be made 2 weeks in advance. Write to Tour Scheduler, National Air & Space Museum, Smithsonian Institute, Washington, D.C. 20560. **Free.** Mon-Fri, 10; Sat-Sun, 10, 1.

Calvert Marine Museum
Rte 2, Solomons. (301)326-2042.

Exhibits on local maritime history, fossil collection, locally built boats and fishing boats. Also on the grounds is the Drum Point Lighthouse. Oyster Packing House is nearby. Cruises are available on the Wm B Tennison, a converted 1899 bugeye, the oldest oyster buy boat on the bay. **Museum: Free. Harbor tours: $3.50/adult; $2.50/child 5-12; $12/family. Lighthouse and Oyster Plant: $1/adult; $.50/child 5-12.** May-Oct: Mon-Sat, 10-5; Sun, noon-5. Nov-Apr: Mon-Fri, 10-4:30; Sat-Sun, noon-4:30

•Good Choices:

Natural Scenery: Assateague State & National Seashore Parks, barrier island, wild ponies, wildlife, Belin/ Battle Creek Cypress Swamp Sanctuary, Calvert County/ Blackwater National Wildlife Refuge, Church Creek.
Nature and Man: Helen Avalynne Tawes Garden, botanical garden, Annapolis/ William Paca Garden, terraced 18th century garden, Annapolis/ Ladew Topiary Gardens & Manor House, seasonal blooming gardens, topiary hedges, Jacksonville/ Oxon Hill Children's Farm, Oxon Hill/ Salisbury Zoological Park, natural habitats, Salisbury/ Brookside Gardens, conservatory, formal and specialty gardens, Wheaton.
Historical and Cultural: Hammond-Harwood House, Georgian residence, Annapolis/ Liriodendron, restored mansion, Bel Air/ Fort Frederick, British stone fort, Big Pool/ Historic St Mary's City, restored city buildings, St Mary's City/ Chesapeake Bay Maritime Museum, floating craft, aquarium, St Michaels/ Antietam National Battlefield, Civil War battlefield, Sharpsburg/ National Capital Trolley Museum, antique streetcars, ride, Wheaton.
Commercial: Ziem Vineyards, tour, Fairplay/ Boordy Vineyards, tour, Hydes/ Linganore Wine Cellers, Berrywine Plantations, tour, Mt Airy/ Elk Run Vineyard, tour, Mt Airy/ Byrd Winery, tour, Myersville/ Calvert Cliffs Nuclear Power Plant, Prince Frederick/ Montbray Wine Cellars, tour, Westminster.
Sports: Rosecroft at Ocean City, horse racing, Berlin/ Freestate Parkway, horse racing, Laurel/ Laurel Race Course, horse racing, Laurel/ Rosecroft Raceway, horse racing, Oxon Hill/ Steeple Chases.

Massachusetts

Fame: *The site of Plymouth Rock, the Massachusetts Bay and Plymouth Colonies, the home of many key people in the history of the United States.*
You must *visit several of the sites that relate to the early history of the U.S. and visualize history coming to life.*

Boston

Fame: *Seafood, Freedom Trail.*
You must *walk the Freedom Trail, sample the seafood.*

•Best Choices:

Freedom Trail
Boston Common Visitor Information Booth, Park Street.

A tour that allows a visitor to see 16 different historic sites in Boston in a short period of time (about 3 hours). The trail guides the visitor to Boston Common, the State House, Park Street Church, Granary Burying Gournd, King's Chapel, the First Public School and Ben Franklin Statue, the Old Corner Book Store, Old South Meeting House, Old State House, Boston Massacre Site, Faneuil Hall, Paul Revere House, Old North Church, Copp's Hill Burial Ground, U.S.S. Constitution, and Bunker Hill Monument. Although there are fees at some of the sites, most are free and a tourist taking the entire tour can spend only $5 per person. If you go any day between 10 am and 3:30 pm you'll be able to see everything. Most are open 9 am to 5 pm.

John Fitzgerald Kennedy Library Museum
Columbia Point, Corchester. (617)929-4523.

The building, designed by I.M. Pei, is a magnificent example of modern architecture. Inside visitors may view a 30 min film, see exhibits that center around the administration, the "Cuban Missile Crisis," the childhood, the presidential campaign and various other highlights in J.F.K's life as well as a film on Robert Kennedy. **$2.50/adult; $1.50/sr citizen; free/child under 16.** Daily, 9-5. Closed Thanksgiving, 12/25, 1/1.

Museum of Science
Science Park, Charles River Dam Bridge. (617)742-6088.

An excellent science museum with many hands-on exhibits. Displays are on natural history, physical science, astronomy, medicine, technology, transportation. The museum also has a Children's Discovery Room and Omnimax Theatre. **$5/adult; $3/sr citizen, child 4-16.** Tues-Sun, 9-5. Closed Thanksgiving, 12/25.

Museum of Fine Arts
465 Huntington Av. (617)267-9377.

This museum has a spectacular modern design. Permanent exhibits include Japanese, Chinese, Indian, Greek, Roman, Egyptian, European and American paintings and sculpture. The west wing holds major traveling exhibits. Varied programs for many varied interests are continuously scheduled. **$4/adult; $3/sr citizen; Free/child under 16.** Tues-Sun, 10-5.

Boston Tea Party Ship and Museum
Congress St Bridge, on Harbor Walk. (617)338-1773.

A re-creation of the Boston Tea Party, on a replica of the original ship. Visitors get to participate in dumping the tea. Costumed guides, films, artifacts, complimentary tea. **$3.25/adult; $2.60/sr citizen; $2.25/child 5-12.** Daily, 9-dusk.

Black Heritage Trail
Museum of Afro-American History, Smith Court, 46 Joy St. (617)742-1854.

A walking tour that explores the history of Boston's 19th century black community. The tour visits African Meeting House, Smith Court Residences, Abiel Smith School, George Middleton House, Robert Gould Shaw and 54th Regiment Memorial, The Phillips School, John J. Smith House, Charles Street Meeting House, Lewis and Harriet Hayden House and Coburn's Gaming House.

•Good Choices:

Natural Scenery: Blue Hills Trailside Museum, exhibits on wildlife rocks, minerals, plants, trails.

Nature and Man: Public Garden, formal gardens, behind the Common/ Franklin Park Zoo/ Arnold Arboretum, Jamaica Plain.

Science and Technology Computer Museum, hands on interactive exhibits of the latest in technology.

Historical and Cultural: Fort Warren, historic fort, Boston Harbor Islands State Park/ Nichols House Museum, Federal Style house/ Paul Revere House/ Harrison Gray Otis House/ John F Kennedy National Historic Site, J.F.K.'s birthplace, Brookline/ Charlestown Navy Yard, U.S.S. Constitution, U.S.S. Cassin Young, historic maritime artifacts, Charlestown.

Entertainment: Children's Museum of Boston/ John Hancock Observatory, view of Boston, "Aviation Radio," multimedia exhibits/ Massachusetts Bay Lines, boat trips.

Commercial: Christian Science Publishing Society, Mapparium and Multimedia Bible Exhibit/

Prudential Center, stores, offices, residential, observation deck.
Sports: Suffolk Downs Racetrack, East Boston.
Seasonal Events: Boston Marathon, Apr/ Patriots Day Celebration, Apr/ Harborfest, Jul.

Springfield

Fame: *Foliage; fairs and festivals; crafts and artisans.*

You must *visit the Basketball Hall of Fame; in the fall, travel the Mohawk Trail (Rte 2) to see the fall foliage.*

•Best Choices:

Naismith Memorial Basketball Hall of Fame
1150 W Columbus Av, 01105. (413)781-6500.

Exhibits delve into the history of Basketball through multi-media and "hands-on" exhibit. A memorial to the founder of the game, Dr James Naismith.
$5/adult; $3/sr citizen, child 8-14. 7/1-Labor Day, daily, 9-6. Rest of yr, daily, 10-5. Closed Thanksgiving, 12/25, 1/1.

Springfield Library and Museums
the Quadrangle, 220 State St, 01103. (413)739-3871.

Four museums and a library surround a tree-shaded green. The museums are George Walter Vincent Smith Art Museum, with collections of jade, bronzes, porcelain, cloisonne, armor and rugs; Springfield Science Museum, with a freshwater aquarium, planetarium, observatory and discovery room; Connecticut Valley Historical Museum, with displays pertaining to the history of the Connecticut Valley; and Museum of Fine Arts, with sculpture, Oriental, European and American paintings.
Donation requested.
Planetarium: $1/adult; $.50/child over 4. Tues-Sun, Noon-5. Closed Thanksgiving, 12/25, 1/1.

Indian Motorcycle Museum
33 Hendee St, 01104. (413)737-2624.

This museum has a fine collection of Indian Motorcycles and other Indian products, other brands of historic motorcycles, bicycles and over 2,000 toy motorcycles.
$2/adult; $1/child. Daily, 1-5. Closed Thanksgiving, 12/25, 1/1.

•Good Choices:

Natural Scenery: Brimfield State Forest, Steerage Rock, woods, ponds, Brimfield/ Arcadia Wildlife Sanctuary, marshes, woods, meadow, trails, East Hampton/

Massachusetts Audubon Society, trails, wildlife exhibits, green house, art gallery, Hampden/ Mt Tom State Reservation, mountain trails and scenery, Holyoke/ Look Memorial Park, zoo, recreation, Northampton.

Nature and Man: Northfield Mountain Recreation and Environmental Center, power station tour, mountain trails, environmental programs, Northfield/ Forest Park, recreation, scenery, entertainment, Springfield/ Stanley Park, gardens, arboretum, Westfield/ C Nash Dinosaurland, commercial dinosaur track quarry, South Hadley/ Bridge of Flowers, Shelburne Falls.

Historical and Cultural: Porter-Phelps-Huntington House, historic home, Hadley/ Wistariahurst Museum, opulent Victorian mansion, Holyoke/ Storrowton Village, early 19th century village, craft demonstrations, W Springfield.

Entertainment: Holyoke Childrens Museum, participatory activities, Holyoke/ Quinnituket II, boat trip, Northfield.

Seasonal Events and Festivals: Big Fourth, entertainment, fireworks, Jul/ Eastern States Exposition, largest fair in the East, pre-order tickets for affordable rate, Sept, W Springfield/ Glendi Greek Festival, dances, food, art, Sep/ Tri-County Fair, agricultural fair, entertainment, horse racing, Sep, Northampton.

Statewide attractions

•Best Choices:

Cape Cod National Seashore
c/o Superintendent, S Wellfleet 02663. (617)349-3785.

See dunes, beaches, woodlands, freshwater ponds and marshes, Cape Cod houses in 28,000 acre park. Guided walks, self-guided walks, interpretive exhibits, campfire programs, swimming, surfing, horseback riding, picnicking, fishing, hiking, shell fishing, biking. **$1/parking fee.** Daily, mid Apr-Nov.

Historic Deerfield Houses
The Street, Deerfield 01342. (413)774-5581.

12 historic houses are maintained by Historic Deerfield. Visitors trying to stay below $5 will have to pick and choose among Allen House, Asa Stebbins House, Ashley House, Dwight-Barnard House, Ebenezer Hinsdale Williams House, Frary House, Hall Tavern, Helen Geier Flynt Textile Museum, Henry Needham Flynt Silver and Metalware Collection, Sheldon-Hawks House, Wells-Thorn House, Wright House. 7/1-10/31: Mon-

Sat, 9:30-6; Sun, 11-6. 11/1-6/30:
Mon-Sat, 9:30-4:30; Sun, 11-4:30.

Lowell National Historical Park & Heritage State Park
Superintendent, 169 Merrimack St,
Lowell 01851. (617)459-1000.

In downtown Lowell. Lowell was
one of the first planned industrial
communities. It was an important
textile milling and manufacturing
center in the 19th century. The
Lowell National Historical Park includes mill buildings, a 5 1/2 mile
canal system, worker's houses and
gate houses. Guided walking tours,
barge and trolley tours. The
Heritage State Park, at 25 Shattuck
St, has waterpower exhibits that
demonstrate the use of waterpower
in the mills. Hands-on models.
Free. Reservations required.
Daily, 9:30-4:30. Closed
Thanksgiving, 12/25, 1/1.

Mayflower II
State Pier, Water St, Plymouth 02360.
(617)746-1622.

A reproduction of the type of ship
that brought the Pilgrims to the
shores of the New World. Costumed guides act as passengers and
crew and enact life aboard the ship.
$3/adult; $2/child 5-12. 4/1-
11/30, Daily, 9-5.

Salem
Chamber of Commerce, 32 Derby Sq,
Salem 01970. (617)744-0004.

Plan to spend at least one day visiting the town and its fascinating his-

toric sites. Among the places to
visit are the House of Seven
Gables (the house from Nathanial
Hawthorne's novel along with his
birthplace **$4**), Essex Institute
(museum and houses depicting
three centuries of New England his-
tory **$5/museum & 3 houses**),
Salem Maritime National Historic
Site (tours of wharves and
waterfront buildings of 17th-19th
centuries **Free.**), Peabody
Museum (nautical paintings and ar-
tifacts - a major collection **$3**),
Salem Witch Museum (**$3**), Witch
House (**$2**), Stephen Phillips
Memorial Trust (**$1.50**), Charter
Street Burying Ground (**Free.**).
Consider a walking tour of the city,
available from the Chamber of
Commerce office on Front St.
Most are open daily, 9-4:30.

Lexington
Chamber of Commerce Visitors Center,
1875 Massachusetts Av, Lexington
02173. (617)862-1450.

Lexington is the site of the first
clash of the Revolutionary War and
has been dubbed the "Birthplace of
American Liberty." Among the
sites to visit are the Historical
Society Houses, Lexington Battle
Green, Minuteman National Historical Park, Museum of our National Heritage, Revolutionary
Monument, Old Belfry and Old
Burying Ground. **$4.50/Houses;
$.75/Minuteman Park; Rest are
free.** Times vary. All open Mon-
Sat, 10-4; Sun, 1-4.

Norman Rockwell Museum
Main Street, Stockbridge 01262.
(413)298-3822

. Original Rockwell art from which
many of his famous Saturday Evening Post covers were taken. The
only permanent Rockwell display.
$3/adult; $1/child under 18.
Daily, 10-5. Closed Thanksgiving,
12/25, 1/1, last 2 wks of Jan.
Closed Tues Memorial Day-10/31

•Good Choices:

Natural Scenery: Bartholomew's
Cobble, hiking trails, natural his-
tory museum, Ashley Falls/ Great
Meadows National Wildlife
Refuge, Concord/ Ashumet Holly
Reservation & Wildlife Sanctuary,
Falmouth/ Pleasant Valley Wildlife
Sanctuary, representative of
Berkshires, Lenox/ Felix Neck
Wildlife Sanctuary, Martha's
Vineyard/ Broadmore Wildlife
Sanctuary, Natick/ Parker River Na-
tional Wildlife Refuge, New-
buryport/ Moose Hill Wildlife
Sanctuary, Sharon/ Wellfleet Bay
Wildlife Sanctuary, South
Wellfleet/ Ipswich River Wildlife
Sanctuary, Topsfield/ Norcross
Wildlife Sanctuary, rare
wildflowers, Wales.
Nature and Man: Capron Park,
zoo, rain forest, Attleboro/ Garden
in the Woods, extensive display of
native plants, Framingham/ Laugh-
ing Brook Educational Center and
Wildlife Sanctuary, trails, environ-
mental center, art gallery, zoo,
Hampden/ Blue Hills Trailside
Museum, history, wildlife of area,
Milton/ Northfield Mountain
Recreation and Environmental
Center, hydroelectric facility tour -
4/1-10/31, Northfield/ Drumlin
Farm, demonstration farm, South
Lincoln/ Berkshire Garden Center,
Stockbridge/ Walter D. Stone
Memorial Zoo, Stoneham/ Stanley
Park and Carillon, floral gardens,
covered bridge, arboretum, fountain, carillon, Westfield.
History: Harvard University, historic bldgs, no tours during school
vacations, Cambridge/ Massachusetts Institute of Technology,
guided tours, Cambridge/ Concord
Antiquarian Museum, period rms
and artifacts including belongings
of Paul Revere, Thoreau and Emerson, Concord/ Walden Pond Reservation, pond, replica of Thoreau
cabin, Concord/ Albert Schweitzer
Center, Schweitzer memorabilia,
wildlife sanctuary, walk, Great Bar-
rington/ Fruitlands Museum, buildings and artifacts relating to
Transcendentalist movement,
Shakers, American Indians/ Haver-
hill Historical Society, buildings,
period furnishings, Haverhill/
Holyoke Heritage State Park,
canals, mills, train ride, Holyoke/
Peter Foulger Museum, Nantucket,
farm life, craftsmen, Quakers,
paintings, Nantucket Island/
Western Gateway Heritage State
Park, railroad history, walking
tours, mini-train rides, North
Adams/ A & D Toy Train Village
and Railway Museum, 2,000 toy

trains, North Middleboro/ Plymouth Rock, Plymouth/ Pilgrim Hall, pilgrim artifacts, furniture, ship, Plymouth/ Saugus Iron Works National Historic Site, reconstructed iron works, blacksmith demonstrations, Saugus/ Sturbridge Auto Museum, Sturbridge/ Longfellow's Wayside Inn, restoration of inn, museum, chapel, gristmill, school, Sudbury.

Historic Houses: John Greenleaf Whittier Home, Amesbury/ Mary Baker Eddy Historic House, Amesbury/ Beverly Historical Society Museums: Batch House, Cabot House, John Hale House, Beverly/ Frederick Law Olmsted National Historic Site, 2 acre estate, Brookline/ Emerson House, Concord/ The Old Manse, Concord/ Orchard House, home of Louisa May Alcott, Concord/ William Cullen Bryant Homestead, Cummington/ Alden House, home of Pricilla & John Alden, Duxbury/ Whittier Homestead, Haverhill/ The Mount, estate and home of writer, Edith Wharton, Lenox/ Jeremiah Lee Mansion, Marblehead/ Adams National Historic Site: John Adams Birthplace, John Quincy Adams Birthplace, Quincy/ Josiah Quincy House, Quincy Historical Society, Quincy Homestead, Quincy/ Heritage Plantation, Sandwich/ Naumkeag, summer estate of J. Choate, furnishings, Chinese porcelain, formal gardens, Stockbridge/ Gore Place, mansion, Waltham.

Living History: Old Schwamb Mill, living history museum makes picture frames, Arlington/ Windfarm Museum, open-air museum, working farm, Martha's Vineyard.

Marine History: Nantucket Whaling Museum, Nantucket Island/ Whaling Museum, New Bedford/ Custom House Maritime Museum, Coast Guard and maritime history, Newburyport.

Art: Danforth Museum of Art, Framingham/ Hudson River School, paintings, Harvard/ De Cordova and Dana Museum and Park, significant 20th Century American art, sculpture garden, Lincoln/ Smith College Museum of Art, Northampton/ Reuss Audubon Galleries, large collection of Audubon lithographs, Stockbridge/ Sterling and Francine Clark Art Institute, Williamstown.

Religious La Salette Shrine, Statuary gardens, chapels, Christmas display, Attleboro/ Old Ship Meetinghouse, Hingham/ Bethlehem in Sturbridge, story of world's creation, Sturbridge.

Entertainment: Hyannis Harbor Tours, Apr-Nov, Hyannis/ Children's Museum at Holyoke, Holyoke/ Cape Cod Canal Cruises, Onset/ Children's Museum of Dartmouth, Dartmouth.

Commercial: Crane Museum, history of paper making, Dalton/ Cranberry World Visitors Center, everything about Cranberries, Plymouth/ Commonwealth Winery, Plymouth.

Michigan

Fame: *Upper and Lower Peninsulas, touched by four Great Lakes, a vacationland.*
You must *explore a sand dune, dine on a piece of Michigan cherry pie or fresh native whitefish.*

Detroit

Fame: *Cars, Motown music.*
You must *see Henry Ford Museum, tour an auto baron's home, eat Greek food while visiting Greektown, ride the People Mover.*

•Best Choices:

Detroit Zoological Park
10 Mile Rd at Woodward Av, Royal Oak 48068. (313)398-0903.

Animals appear in their natural habitats. One of the largest zoos in the U.S. **$3.50/adult; $1.50/child 5-12.** May-Oct, Mon-Sat, 10-5; Sun 10-6. Nov-Apr, Wed-Sun, 10-4.

People Mover
13 stations in business district. (313)224-2160.

New elevated automated transit system circles Detroit business district. **$.50.**

Cranbrook Institute of Science, Academy of Art Museum, Gardens

500 Lone Pine Rd, Bloomfield Hills 48013. (313)645-3323.

Former estate now a cultural and educational center. See mansion surrounded by 40 acres of gardens, contemporary art at the art museum, natural and physical sciences at Science Center, spectacular architecture and sculpture on grounds. **Science Center: $3/adult. Art Museum: $2.50/adult. Mansion: $2/adult. Gardens: $2/adult.** House: Apr-Oct, 4th Sun of mth, 2-4. Gardens: Jun-Aug, Mon-Fri, 10-5, Sun, 1-5. Science Center: Mon-Fri, 10-5; Sat, 10-10; Sun, 1-5. Art Museum: Tue-Sun, 1-5.

University Cultural Center
4735 Cass Av, Detroit 48202. (313)831-1811.

A cluster of municipal, state and private educational and cultural institutions concentrated in a few blocks. Included are Children's Museum, Detroit Historical Museum (stores and artifacts of Old Detroit), Detroit Institute of

Arts (100 galleries with world famous art treasurers), Detroit Science Center (conduct your own hands-on experiments), Your Heritage House (multi-cultural art exhibits). **Science Center: $4/adult; $2/sr citizen; $3/child 6-12. Rest are free.** All are open Wed-Sun, 1-4. Many are open other days and times.

Motown Museum
2648 W Grand Blvd, 48208. (313)875-2264.

Tour the recording studio where the careers of the Supremes, the Temptations, Michael Jackson, Diana Ross and Stevie Wonder were launched. **$2/adult; $1/student.** Fri, 11-5.

•Good Choices:

Nature and Man: Belle Isle Park: Belle Isle Aquarium, Belle Isle Nature Center, Belle Isle Zoo. **Science and Technology** Dossin Great Lakes Museum, Great Lakes shipping artifacts.

Historical and Cultural: Historic Fort Wayne, costumed guides, Detroit history/ Pewbic Pottery, ceramic museum, gallery, workshop/ Edsel and Eleanor Ford House/ The Fisher Mansion and Bhaktivedanta Cultural Center, magnificent estate, now Indian religious center/ Fair Lane, Henry Ford estate/ Meadow Brook Hall, mansion home of Alfred and Matilda Dodge Wilson.

Commercial: Detroit Free Press, tours/ Detroit Renaissance Center, World of Shops/ Eastern Market, open market - fresh produce/ Trappers Alley Festival Market Place, 80 shops & restaurants in festival atmosphere.

Sports: Detroit Tigers, bleacher seats.

Statewide Attractions

•Best Choices:

Bonner's Christmas Wonderland
25 Christmas Lane, Box 176, Frankenmuth 48734-0176. (517)652-9931.

Said to be the world's largest year-around display of Christmas decorations. Includes Christmas ornaments, nativity scenes, animated figures, Christmas trees. **Free.** Jun-12/25: Mon-Fri, 9-9; Sat, 9-7; Sun, 12-7. 12/26-May: Mon-Thurs, Sat, 9-5:30; Fri, 9-9; Sun, 1-5:30.

Sleeping Bear Dunes National Lakeshore
Box 277, Empire 49630. (616)326-5134.

Sand dune deserts, hardwood forests, swamps, many kinds of animals are all to be found on the lakeshore. Spectacular views from the top of Sleeping Bear Dune are of Lake Michigan in the west and

Glen Lakes in the east. **Free.** Mid May-early Nov.

Soo Locks Visitor Center and Observation Platform
U.S. Corps of Engineers, Sault Ste Marie 49783. (906)632-3301.

Both upper and lower parks parallel the locks and provide views. The upper park has 3 observation platforms, model and movie. **Free.** Best viewing Jun-Sept.

Pictured Rocks National Lakeshore
Superintendent, Box 40, Munising 49862. (906)387-2607.

Along Lake Superior shoreline nature has carved cliffs in multi-colored sandstone creating spectacular scenery which can be viewed from trails, roads or the lake. Historical walks, campfire programs in Summer. **Free.** May-Sept, daily; Oct-Apr, Sat-Sun.

Michigan Space Center
Jackson Community Campus, 211 Emmons Rd, Jackson 49201. (517)787-4425.

Geodesic dome houses Apollo 9 command module, space suits, lunar rover, orbiters, landers, rocket engines, lunar surveyor, moon rock. Other exhibits cover other space voyages, black hole, space capsule. **$3/adult; $2/sr citizen, student.** 5/26-9/1: Mon-Fri, 10-7; Sat, 10-5; Sun, noon-5. 3/31-5/15: Mon-Sat, 10-5; Sun, noon-5. 9/2-3/30: Tues-Sat, 10-5; Sun, noon-5.

•Good Choices:

Natural Scenery: Tunnel of Trees Drive, arboreal tunnel, Emmet County/ Seney National Wildlife Refuge, birds, wildlife, trails, movies, Germfask/ Gillette Nature Center, sand dunes, Grand Haven.

Nature and Man: Call of the Wild Museum, N American animals, Gaylord/ Blandford Nature Center, farmstead, working farm, fields, forests, ponds, Grand Rapids/ John Ball Park Zoo, Grand Rapids/ Carl G Fenner Arboretum, bison, deer, garden, science bldg, Lansing/ Chippewa Nature Center Museum, fields, woods, 1870 farm, museum, arboretum, Midland/ Dow Gardens, flowers, shrubs, Midland/ Hidden Lake Gardens, greenhouse, gardens, trails, Tipton.

Science and Technology Cook Energy Information Center, tour, video on nuclear power, Bridgman/ Robert T Longway Planetarium, Flint.

Historical and Cultural: Iron County Museum, outdoor complexes depict life in 1800s, Caspian/ Historic Fayette Townsite, ghost town, Fayette/ Alfred P Sloan, Jr, Museum, history, auto history, health, Flint/ De-Waters Art Center, Flint/ Gerald R Ford Museum, private and public life, Grand Rapids/ Charlton Park Village and Museum, Hastings/ Poll Museum of Transportation, Holland/ R.E. Olds Museum, antique autos, Lansing/ Historic White

Pine Village, reconstructed community, Ludington/ Old Fort Mackinac, 1780 fort, original buildings, costumed guides, Mackinac Island/ Fort Michilimackinac and Mackinaw Maritime Park, reconstructed fort, lighthouse, 1775 wooden sloop, Mackinaw City/ Old Mill Creek State Historic Park, site of 18th century industrial complex, Mackinaw City.

Marine Museums: Copper Harbor Lighthouse Boat Tour and Museum, Lake Superior history, Copper Harbor/ S.S. Keewatin, floating marine museum, Douglas/ Fort Michilimackinac and Mackinaw Maritime Park, reconstructed fort, lighthouse, 1775 wooden sloop, Mackinaw City/ Museum Ship Valley Camp, retired freighter tour, Sault Ste Marie.

Entertainment: Shrine of the Pines, furniture from tree stumps, roots, museum, nature trail, Baldwin/ Harbor Steamer Cruise, Grand Haven/ Harbor Trolley Ride, Grand Haven/ Dutch Village, gardens, windmills, dances, carvings, barn with live animals, Holland/ Queen of Saugatuck Boat Cruise, Saugatuck.

Commercial: Lakeside Vineyard Tour, Bridgman/ Delaware Copper Mine Tour, Copper Harbor/ Davisburg Candle Factory Tour, Davisburg/ General Motors AC Spark Plug Divn Tour, Flint/ G Heileman Brewing Company Tour, Frankenmuth/ Nickless-Hubinger Flour Mill, reconstructed working mill, Frankenmuth/ Adventure Copper Mine Tour, Greenland/ Arcadian Copper Mine Tour, Hancock/ De Klomp Wooden Shoe and Delft Factory Tour, Holland/ Wooden Shoe Factory Tour, Holland/ Iron Mountain Iron Mine Tour, Iron Mountain/ Boskydel Vineyard Tour, Leland/ St Julian Winery Tour, Paw Paw/ Warner Vineyards Tour, Paw Paw/ L Mawby Vineyards Tour, Traverse City.

Seasonal Events and Festivals: Holland Tulip Festival Parades, Mid May, Holland.

Minnesota

Fame: *A wealth of natural resources: lakes, rivers, woods, plains; outstanding arts in the Twin Cites of Minneapolis and St. Paul.*
You must *drive the North Shore Drive, if you're in the Lake Superior area; enjoy the lakes and parks in the area you're visiting; enjoy the theater and other arts in the metropolitan area.*

Minneapolis

Fame: *Riverfront development; lakes and parks; theaters and arts; shopping on the beautiful Nicollet Mall and on the Riverfront.*
You must *walk or drive the Great River Parkway, from Plymouth Av to Portland; see a play at the Guthrie Theater; take a tour of the city lakes and parks or shop on the Nicollet Mall, Riverplace - St Anthony Main.*

•Best Choices:

Minneapolis Institute of Arts
2400 Third Av S, 55404. (612)870-3046.

More than 70,000 works, including paintings, sculpture, photography, drawings, prints, period furnishings, from every culture and period. **$2/adult; $1/student; Free/sr citizen, child under 12.** Tues, Wed, Sat, 10-5; Thurs, Fri, 10-9; Sun, noon-5. Closed Thanksgiving, 12/25, 1/1, 7/4. Tours daily at 2 pm.

Walker Art Center
Vineland Place, 55403. (612)375-7600.

In Minneapolis Loop at Hennepin and Vineland. Permanent collection of 20th century American and international artists including painting, sculpture, photographs, drawings and prints. **Free.** Tues-Sat, 10-8; Sun, 11-5.

University of Minnesota Landscape Arboretum
Hwy 5, Chanhassen 55317. (612)443-2460. West of Chanhassen. Over 675 acres of cultivated plants, landscaped gardens, hills, lakes and ponds. Self-guided auto tour and many walking trails. **$2/adult; $1/child.** Daily, 8-sunset.

Bell Museum of Natural History
17th Av & University Av SE, 55455. (612)624-7083.

Permanent natural habitat groups with native plants and animals, hands-on Touch and See room, changing exhibits. **$2/adult; $1/sr citizen, child 3-16. Free on Thurs.** Tues-Sat, 9-5; Sun, 1-5.

Minneapolis Planetarium
300 Nicollet Mall, in Minneapolis Library 55401. (612)372-6644.

Regular shows range from tours of the night sky to the latest discoveries in space science. **$2/adult; $1/child under 13.** Mid Jun-Aug, Mon-Fri, 11 & 2; Thurs, 7:30 pm; Sat-Sun, 2. 9/1-6/14, Thurs, 7:30 pm; Sat, 11, 2, 3; Sun, 2, 3.

•Good Choices:
Natural Scenery: Minnehaha Falls, Minnehaha Park.
Nature and Man: Eloise Butler Wild Flower and Bird Sanctuary/ Lyndale Park and Garden Center, rose gardens, bird sanctuary/ St Anthony Falls - Upper Lock and Dam, observation deck, Apr-Nov/ Normandale Japanese Gardens, bridges, waterfall, trees, shrine, Normandale Community College.
Historical and Cultural: American Swedish Institute Museum, mansion with Swedish art, artifacts/ Hennepin County Historical Society Museum, 30 exhibit rms/ University Art Museum, American art 1900-1950, Univ of MN/ Murphy's Landing, 1800s village, Shakopee.
Entertainment: Como-Harriet Streetcar Ride, bet Lake Harriet and Lake Calhoun, 5/31-10/31/ Lake Harriet Bandshell Concerts, Summer/ Queen of the Lakes Cruise, Lake Harriet.
Commercial: Bachman's Florists Tour/ Farmers Market, May-Nov/ Federal Reserve Bank Tour/ Grain Exchange Tour/ Maid of Scandinavia Tour, cake decorating etc.
Sports: Hubert H. Humphrey Metrodome Tour/ Canterbury Downs Racetrack, Shakopee.
Seasonal Events and Festivals: Minneapolis Aquatennial, late July/ Renaissance Festival, 7 wknds beginning Mid Aug/ Sommerfest, mid Jul - mid Aug.

St. Paul

Fame: *Capital City, high above the Mississippi; beautifully restored old buildings mixed with contemporary; a cultural and arts center; world's longest publicly owned skyway.*
You must *visit a historic, restored house or building; visit the Ordway and, in the winter, take a skyway tour of the city.*

•Best Choices:
Skyway System
In downtown area.

Indoor walkway crosses streets and alleys while connecting department stores, shops, hotels, restaurants, office buildings, banks. Starting from the second floor of any participating building one may spend an entire day indoors, while dining, shopping and conducting business. **Free.** Daily, 6 am - 2 am.

Science Museum of Minnesota
30 E 10th St, 55101. (612)221-9876.

Displays on science, technology and natural history with many hands-on exhibits that children, and many adults, love to try. **$3/adult; $1.50/sr citizen; $2/child 3-12.** 6/9-9/2, Mon=Sat, 9:30-9; Sun, 11-9. 9/3-6/8: Closed Mon.

Como Park
N Lexington and Como Av. (612)489-1740.

Conservatory renowned for its floral displays, zoo, gardens, waterfalls, children's amusement park, lakeside pavilion, 18-hole golf course. **Free.** Daily, 10-6.

Minnesota Zoo
12101 Johnny Cake Ridge Rd, Apple Valley 55124. (612)432-9010.

Five exhibit trails with 1,300 animals and 800 plant species. Indoor, outdoor and nocturnal, tropical to northern areas. **$4/adult; $2/sr citizen; $1.50/child 6-16; $1/parking** Daily, 4/1-9/30, 10-6; 10/1-3/31, 10-4.

Fort Snelling State Historical Park
Jct I-494 and SR 55, 55111. (612)726-1171.

Take Ft Snelling exits from frwy 17 restored buildings in 19th century fort. Costumed guides recreate life in the fort while demonstrating arts and crafts. **$2/adult; $.75/child 6-16.** Daily, May-Oct.

•Good Choices:

Historical and Cultural: Alexander Ramsey House, home of 1st territorial governor/ Gibbs Farm Museum, farm life 100 yrs ago/ James J Hill House, mansion of rail baron/ Landmark Center, 19th century federal court now houses arts/ Minnesota State Capitol, tours/ St Paul Cathedral, modeled after St Peters in Rome/ Minnesota Museum of Art, contemporary and Asian art/ Sibley House, home of 1st State Governor/ Antie Clare's Doll Hospital and Museum, Oakdale.
Entertainment: Children's Museum at Bandana Square/ See the Ordway Music Theater/ Wm L. McKnight - 3M Omnitheater in Science Museum.
Commercial: Jacob Schmidt Brewing Company Tour/ Stroh Brewery Tour/ Farmers Market, Summer, Sat.
Seasonal Events and Festivals: St Paul Winter Carnival, early Feb/ Taste of Minnesota, 4 days includ-

ing 4th of July/ RiverFest, music groups & family fun, mid July/

Minnesota State Fair, 12 days ending Labor Day.

Statewide Attractions

•Best Choices:

Forest History Center
2906 Cnty Rd 76, Grand Rapids 55744. (218)327-4482.

Recreation of life in an old logging camp, with costumed staff representing lumberjacks and other workers. Also includes an interpretive center, Forest Service cabin and woodland trail. **$2/adult; $1/sr citizen, child 6-16.** 5/15-10/15: Tues-Sun, 10-5; 10/16-5/14: Tues-Sun, noon-4.

Mayo Medical Museum and Clinic Tours
200 First St SW, Rochester 55905. (507)284-3280 or (507)284-2653.

Museum has displays of the human body, diseases, injuries, treatments and medical technology such as heart-lung machine, artificial joints and kidneys. The clinic offers 90 minute tours describing both the medical treatments and the architecture and art in the 10-building complex. **Free.** Museum: Jun-Aug, Mon-Fri, 8-9; Sat, 9-5; Sun, 1-5. Sept-May, Mon-Fri, 9-9; Sat, 9-5; Sun, 1-5. Clinic Tours: Mon-Fri, 10 am and 2 pm.

Tower-Soudan Mine
Tower-Soudan State Park, Hwy 169, Soudan 55782. (218)753-2245.

Visitors don hard hats to take a tour of the oldest, deepest underground iron mine in the U.S. Also has an interpretive center on the surface. **$3/adult; $1.50/child. Vehicles must have $3/state park permit.** Memorial Day-Labor Day, Daily, 9-4.

North Shore Drive
Hwy 61, Duluth.

Follow Hwy 61 from Duluth to Grand Portage along the beautiful, scenic shore of Lake Superior. Many roadside parks line the drive.

The Depot
506 W Michigan St, Duluth 55802. (218)727-8025.

Renovated railroad depot with 4 levels of living history and arts exhibits, including depot square, a recreation of 1910 Duluth, railroad cars and locomotives, antique doll and toy collection, 200 yrs of clothing styles, fur-trading post. **$3/adult; $2.50/sr citizen; $1.50/student 6-17.** 5/31-10/15, daily, 10=5. 10/16-5/30, Mon-Sat, 10-5; Sun, 1-5.

•Good Choices:

Natural Scenery: Niagara Cave, Harmony/ Itasca State Park, headwaters of the Mississippi, Park Rapids/ Tamarack National Wildlife Refuge, waterfowl, wild animals, hiking, auto tours, Rochester/ Voyageurs National Park, lakes, rivers, wildlife, S International Falls/ Mystery Cave, Spring Valley/ Dalles of the St Croix, unusual rock formations, Taylors Falls/ Gooseberry Falls State Park, 5 waterfalls, lakes, forest, Two Harbors.

Nature and Man: Hill Annex Mine Tour, history of iron mining, Calument/ Duluth Zoological Gardens, Duluth/ Hull-Rust Mine, one of the largest open-pit iron mines in the world, Hibbing/ Split Rock Lighthouse, Two Harbors.

Science and Technology Palucci Space Theatre, astronomy, space exploration, environment, Hibbing.

History: Runestone Museum, runestone, Viking implements, Alexandria/ Canal Park Museum, history of Great Lakes shipping, Duluth/ Glensheen Mansion, Duluth/ Oliver H. Kelly Living History Farm, Elk River/ Grand Portage National Monument, reconstructed trading post, Grand Portage/ Hinkley Fire Museum, artifacts of forest fire, Hinkley/ Jeffers Petroglyphs, 2,000 historic Indian carvings, Jeffers/ Charles A Lindbergh House & Interpretive Center, Little Falls/ Chippewa City Pioneer Village, recreated 19th century town, Montevideo/ Heritage-Hjelmkost Interpretive Center, Viking ship, Red River Valley History, Moorhead/ North West Company Fur Post Reconstruction, living history, Pine City/ Pipestone National Monument, quarry for American Indian ceremonial pipes, Pipestone/ Mayowood Residence of Dr C Mayo, Rochester/ Julius C Wilkie Steamboat Center Museum, Winona.

Entertainment: Lumbertown, U.S.A., recreation of 1870s Minnesota, Brainerd/ Paul Bunyan Amusement Center, Brainerd/ Alpine Slide and Chairlift Ride, Lutsen/ Red Wing River Boat Excursions, Red Wing.

Commercial: Faribault Woolen Mill Tour, Faribault/ Deer Forest and Fantasy Land, deer, storybook character replicas, Nisswa/ Deer Town, deer, farm, stagecoach rides, Park Rapids/ Seneca Foods Corp Tour, Rochester.

Sports: United States Hockey Hall of Fame, Eveleth.

Mississippi

Fame: *The heart of the South.*
You must *visit a historic southern mansion, see a civil war battlefield, relax and enjoy southern hospitality.*

Biloxi and the Golf Coast

Fame: *World's longest manmade beach.*
You must *eat seafood harvested in local Gulf of Mexico waters.*

•Best Choices:

Beauvoir - Jefferson Davis Shrine

Box 200 W Beach Blvd, Biloxi 39531. (601)388-1313. On US 90. Historic last home of Confederate President Jefferson Davis, Confederate Museum, Davis Museum, cemetery with Tomb of Unknown Confederate Soldier, gardens, nature trail. $4/adults; $3/sr citizens, military; $2/children 6-16. Daily, 9-5, except Christmas.

Gulf Coast Research Laboratory, Marine Education Center and Aquarium

1650 E Beach Blvd, Biloxi 39530. (601)374-5550.

Foot of the Biloxi Bay Bridge, on US 90 at E end of Biloxi. 42,000 gallon main tank surrounded by 25 other containers of various sizes containing local species. Snake, alligator, seashell and other exhibits. $2/adults; $1/sr citizen, children

3-16. Mon-Sat, 9-4, except Thanksgiving, 12/25, 1/1.

National Space Technology Laboratories

NSTL 39520. (601)688-2321 or 688-2370.

Space shuttle complex where the main engines are test fired. Visitor's center features films, displays, moor rock display, space hardware, teacher resource center, live demonstrations, guided tours. **Free.** Daily, 9-5, except Christmas.

•Good Choices:

Natural Scenery: Gulf Islands National Seashore Davis Bayou Visitor Center, Ocean Springs.
Nature and Man: Seafood Industry Museum, Biloxi; Scranton Floating Museum (honoring fishing industry) Pascagoula. **Science and Technology** Keesler Air Force Base electronics and computer training center, Biloxi.
Historical and Cultural: Biloxi Lighthouse, Biloxi; Tullis-Toledano Manor, Biloxi; Mag-

noilia Hotel, Biloxi; Grass Lawn Summer Home, Gulfport; Old Spanish Fort & Museum, Pas

cagoula.
Commercial: Shearwater Pottery Workshop, Ocean Springs.

Jackson

Fame: *Capital City of Mississippi; Southern commercial center.*
You must *visit the Governor's Mansion, one of the few buildings in the city to survive the Civil War.*

•Best Choices:

Governor's Mansion
300 E Capitol St, 39201. (601)359-3175.

Restored Greek Revival mansion, home of Mississippi's governor's since 1842. Large grounds surround the house and the interior is decorated with 19th century decorative arts. **Free.** Tues-Fri, 9:30-11.

Jackson Zoological Park
2918 W Capitol St, 39209. (601)960-1577.

More than 500 animals on 35 acres of landscaped terrain. Miniature train ride. **$2/adult; $1/child 4-12.** Daily, summer, 9-6; winter, 9-5.

Mississippi Agriculture and Forestry Museum
Box 1609, 39211. (601)354-6113.

Farm and forest life in Mississippi is interpreted with exhibits, including a living history farm and small town, forest study area, general store, National Agriculture Aviation Museum. **$3/adult; $1/child 6-18.** Memorial Day-Labor Day, Mon-Sat, 10-7; Sun, 1-5. After Labor Day, Tues-Sat, 9-5; Sun, 1-5.

•Good Choices:
Nature and Man: Mynell Gardens, 6 acres of botanical gardens.
Science and Technology Russell C Davis Planetarium - Ronald McNair Space Theater, astronomy, light shows, cinema.
Historical and Cultural: Manship House/ The Oaks, Greek Revival cottage/ Smith Robertson Museum, black history.

Vicksburg

Fame: *Vicksburg is the site of the famous Civil War Battle "The Siege of Vicksburg."*

You must *tour the Vicksburg Military Park, see the antebellum homes and museums.*

•Best Choices:

Vicksburg National Military Park
3201 Clay St, 39180. (601)636-0583.

The battlefield of the Civil War siege with monuments and visitor's center with museum displaying artifacts, dioramas and film. **$3/car; $1/per person in bus or van.** Daily, 6/1-8/31, 8-6; 9/1-5/31, 8-5.

Biedenharn Candy Co Museum
1107 Washington St, 39180. (601)638-6514.

Restoration of the site where Coca-Cola was first bottled in 1894, including memorabilia. **$1.75/adult; $1.25/child under 12.** Mon-Sat, 9-5; Sun, 1:30-4:30.

Cairo Museum 3201 Clay St, 39180. (601)636-2199.
Union gunboat which was sunk during the Civil War has been raised and restored. Many artifacts from the sunken boat are displayed. Audiovisual program. **Free.** Daily, 9-5.

•Good Choices:
Science and Technology U.S. Corp of Engineers Waterways Experiment Station.
Historic: Old Court House Museum/ Yesterday's Children Antique Doll Museum/ The Vanishing Glory Movie of the Seige of Vicksburg/ Toys and Soldiers Museum.
Historic Homes: Anchuca/ Balfour House/ Cedar Grove/ The Corners/ Duff Green Mansion/ Grey Oaks/ Martha Vick House/ McRaven/ Tomil Manor.

Statewide attractions

•Best Choices:

Elvis Presley Birthplace Memorial Chapel
306 Elvis Presley Dr, Box 1339, Tupelo 38801. (601)841-1245.

The childhood home of the famous rock and roll singer. Chapel has unusual stained glass windows and panels. **$1/adult; $.50/child.** Mon-Sat, 9-5; Sun, 1-5.

Florewood River Plantation State Park
Box 680, Greenwood 38930. (601)455-3821 or 3822.

Living history presentations of lifestyle typical of antebellum cotton plantations. Museum exhibits. **$2.50/adult; $1.50/student.** Plantation open Mar-Nov. Museum open all yr. Tues-Sat, 9-5; Sun, 1-5.

Natchez Historic Homes
Natchez Pilgrimage Tours, Box 347,
Natchez 39120. (601)446-6631.

Natchez has almost 500 antebellum structures. Many contain original furnishings and are appropriately decorated for the period. During Spring and Fall Pilgrimages about 30 homes are open for tours. The following homes may be toured year around by individuals: Auburn, The Burn, Connelly's Tavern, D'Evereux, Dunleith, Hope Farm, Lansdowne, Linden, Longwood, Magnolia Hall, Melrose, Monmouth, Rosalie, Stanton Hall. **$4-6/adult; $1-3/child.**

•Good Choices:

Nature and Man: Wister Gardens, Belzoni/ Crosby Arboretum, Picayune/ Natchez Trace Parkway, Tupelo.

Historical and Cultural: Brices Cross Roads National Battlefield Site, Baldwyn/ Beauvoir, Jefferson Davis antebellum mansion, Biloxi/ Seafood Industry Museum, boat building, net making, fishing, Biloxi/ Historic Homes, Columbus/ Lauren Rogers Museum of Art, Laurel/ Jimmie Rodgers Museum, Meridan/ Merrehope restored house, Meridan/ Rowan Oak, William Faulkner Home, Oxford/ Waverly Mansion, West Point.

Missouri

Fame: *Ozark Mountains, Rivers, Mark Twain, Harry Truman, the Show Me State.*
You must *visit the beautiful Ozarks, take a riverboat cruise, visit a place associated with Mark Twin or Harry Truman, sample Missouri hospitality.*

Kansas City

Fame: *The city that is in two states (MO and KS); distribution point for a large agricultural area; a progressive city filled with tree-lined boulevards.*
You must: *eat a sirloin strip steak or barbecued brisket and ribs, two famous examples of Kansas City beef.*

•Best Choices:

Nelson-Atkins Museum of Art
4525 Oak St, 64111. (816)561-4000.

One of the most comprehensive art museums in the US with art that dates from 3,000 B.C. to the present and covers many styles and countries. It is noted for its superb oriental collection. **$2/adults; Free/teacher, student. Sun free for everyone.** Tues-Sat, 10-5; Sun, 1-5.

Liberty Memorial
100 W 26th St, 64108. (816)221-1918.

The only museum in the US devoted solely to the men and women who gave their lives in World War I. Includes Memory Hall with attractive murals and hand painted maps, Torch of Liberty, a 217 ft tower with a viewing platform that offers a panoramic view of the city. **Tower elevator: $.50/person.** Tues-Sun, 9:30-4:30.

Toy and Miniature Museum of Kansas City
5235 Oak St, 64112. (816)333-2055.

Exhibits from around the world, of miniatures, toys, dolls and dollhouses. Rooms are dedicated to certain types of toys. **$2.50/adult; $2/sr citizen; $1.50/child 5-12.** Wed-Sat, 10-4; Sun, 1-4.

Wornell House Museum
146 W 61st Terrace, 64113. (816)444-1858.

Restored 1858 plantation house, which was used as a hospital during the Civil War, now furnished with period furniture. Cooking demonstrations, formal herb garden, seasonal decorations. **$2/adult.** Tues-Sat, 10-4; Sun, 1-4.

Hallmark Cards Visitors Center and Kaleidoscope
Box 419580, 64141. (816)274-5672 or 8300.

On Hallmark Square, Crown Center, 25th and Grand. In the Visitors Center, craftspeople demonstrate engraving and printing processes, the making of greeting cards. Exhibits include audiovisuals and interactive displays. Kaleidoscope is a creative art experience for children 5-12. Children explore art by seeing, touching, imagining and creating their own art. **Free.** Mon-Fri, 9-5; Sat, 9:30-4:30.

•Good Choices:

Nature and Man: Kansas City Zoo.
Historical and Cultural: Kansas City Museum, history and science museum, planetarium/ Thomas Hart Benton Home & Studio State Historic Site.
Commercial: City Farmers Market, Sat, summer/ Kansas City Board of Trade, winter wheat and stock futures market.

St. Louis

Fame: *A city, with a rich history of settlers from many ethnic backgrounds, situated on the Mississippi and Missouri rivers. A diverse industrial and educational center.*

You must: *visit the Gateway Arch; sample some international cuisine at one of the city's many restaurants.*

•Best Choices:

The Gateway Arch
11 N 4th, 63102. (314)425-4465 or 982-1410.

Designed by Eero Saarinen, the stainless steel structure is 630 ft high, 75 ft higher than the Washington Monument. It houses the Museum of Westward Expansion, focusing on pioneer settlers. A tram carries visitors to the top of the arch inside a capsule tram, running on special tracks. At the top is an observation room with a 30 mile view of surrounding territory. **Arch: Free. Movies: $.50. Tram: $1.50.** Mem Day - Labor Day, Daily, 8-10. Rest of yr, Daily, 9-6.

Missouri Botanical Garden
4344 Shaw Av, 63110. (314)577-5100.

A beautiful and unique botanical garden, with many themed outdoor areas as well as several enclosed gardens with unusual plants from many regions of the world. **$1/adult; Free/sr citizen, child under 12.** Mem Day - Labor Day, Daily, 9-8; Rest of yr, Daily, 9-5.

Magic House
516 S Kirkwood Rd, 63122. (314)822-8900.

On Lindberg Blvd (Kirkwood Rd). A children's museum with 3 floors of participatory exhibits for "kids" of all ages. Match wits with a computer, leave a shadow on the wall, visit a touch tunnel. **$2.50/adult; $2/child 2-11.** Summer, Tues-Thurs, Sat, 10-6; Fri, 10-9; Sun, noon-6. Labor Day - Mem Day, Tues-Thurs, 3-6; Fri, 3-9; Sat, 10-6; Sun, noon-6.

St Louis Science Center
5100 Clayton Av, 63110. (314)289-4444.

Includes the McDonnell Planetarium, Museum of Science and Natural History, Medical Museum, Discovery Room with hands-on displays. **Exhibit Gallery: Free; Star Theater: $3; Discovery Room: $.50; Computer Connection: $1.** Summer: Mon-Tues, 9:30-5; Wed-Sat, 9:30-9; Sun, 11-5. Winter: Mon-Thurs, 9:30-5; Fri-Sat, 9:30-8; Sun, 11-5.

•Good Choices:

Natural Scenery: Rockwoods Reservation, oak hickory forest, Glencoe.

Nature and Man: St Louis Zoological Park.

Historical and Cultural: Eugene Field House & Toy Museum/ Laumeier Sculpture Park/ National Museum of Transport, locomotives, autos, trucks, aircraft/ St Louis Art Museum, Egyptian to modern/ St Louis Symphony Orchestra/ U.S.S. Inaugural, WWII minesweeper/ Jefferson Barracks Historic Park, Lamay.

Entertainment: Kramer's Marionnettes, adv reserv.

Commercial: Anheuser-Busch Brewery Tour/ Bardenheier Wine Cellars Tour/ Grant's Farm Tours/ Purina Farms Tour, Grey Summit/ Soulard Farmers Market.

Religious Concordia Lutheran Historical Institute/ Black Madonna Shrine & Grottos, Eureka.

Sports: National Bowling Hall of Fame and Museum/ St Louis Soccer Steamers/ St Louis Sports Hall of Fame.

Springfield

Fame: *Foothills of the Ozarks with scenery and lakes; Country Music Shows.*

You must: *see a country music show, enjoy the scenery.*

•Best Choices:

Museum of Ozarks' History
603 E Calhoun, 65802. (417)869-1976.

Restored 18-rm Victorian mansion built in 1892. Period furnishings are displayed with artifacts of the era. **$2/adult; $1.50/sr citizen; $1/child under 12.** Jun-Aug, Tues-Sat, 9:30-2:30; Sun, 1-4. Rest of yr, 11:30-4:30.

Springfield Art Museum
1111 E Brookside Dr, 65807. (417)866-2716.

Regional, national and European works of art are displayed in permanent and changing exhibits. **Free.** Tues-Sat, 9-5, Sun, 1-5. Jun-Sept, museum is also open Wed, 6:30-9:30 pm.

Exotic Animal Paradise
Rte 1, Box 270, Strafford 65757. (417)468-2016 or 468-2159.

12 mi E of Springfield. Drive through the 400 acre area on 9 1/2 mi of paved road to view herds of wild animals and rare birds roaming free. **$5/adult; $3/child under 12.** Daily, 8 to 1 hr before sunset.

•Good Choices:

Nature and Man: Crystal Cave/ Dickerson Park Zoo.

Historical and Cultural: Wilson's Creek National Civil War Battlefield.

Commercial: Bass Pro Shops, world's largest sporting goods store, aquariums, waterfall, indoor log cabin etc./ Moore-Dupont Wineries Tour.

Statewide Attractions

•Best Choices:

Mark Twain Home and Museum
208 Hill St, Hannibal 63401. (314)221-9010.

Mark Twain's boyhood home and other buildings have been restored with period furnishings, adjoining is a museum with Twain memorabilia. **$2/adult; Free/under 18.** Summer: Daily, 8-6. Spring, Fall: Daily, 8-5. Winter: 10-4.

Harry S. Truman Library and Museum
SR 24 and Delaware St, Independence 64050. (816)833-1400.

Harry S. Truman's career is depicted by historic and artistic objects, including many gifts from foreign governments, personal and official presidential papers. **$1.50/adult; Free/under 15.** Daily, 9-5, except Thanksgiving, 12/25, 1/1.

Mark Twain Cave
Box 913, Hannibal 63401. (314)221-1656.

1 mi S of Hannibal on Hwy 79. In this cave Becky Thatcher and Tom Sawyer were lost; and, the cave appeared in 4 other Twain books. The dry, lighted passageways stay at a temperature of 50 degrees. 55 min

guided tours. **$5/adult; $2.50/child 5-12.** Daily, 9-dusk. Closed Thanksgiving, 12/25.

•Good Choices:

Natural Scenery: Bridal Cave & Thunder Mountain Park, guided cave tours, nature walks, Camdenton/ Ha Ha Tonka State Park, caves, spring, Camdenton/ Swanlake National Wildlife Refuge, Canada geese, other wildlife, Chillicothe/ Ozark Caverns, Linn Creek/ Johnson's Shut-Ins Rocks State Park, unusual rock formations, river, Middlebrook/ Fantasy World Caverns, underground lake, waterfalls, deep canyons, Osage Beach/ Lake of the Ozarks State Park, lake, recreation, Osage Beach/ Mingo National Wildlife Refuge, hardwoods swamp, wildlife, waterfowl, plants, nature trail, Puxico/ Meramec State Park, 22 caves, Sullivan.

Science and Technology: Taum Sauk Pumped Storage Electrical Plant, observation deck, Hogan/ Osage Power Plant, tours, Lake Ozark.

Historical and Cultural: Arrow Rock State Historic Site, frontier settlement, Arrow Rock/ Harold Bell Wright Theater and Museum, film, art, artifacts, Branson/ Ft Osage Frontier Trading Post, reconstruction of frontier trading post, Buckner/ George Washington

Carver National Monument, birthplace, trail, cemetery, Diamond/ Winston-Churchill Memorial and Library in the United States, reconstructed historic London church, Churchill memorabilia, Fulton/ Missouri State Capitol Tour & State Museum, Jefferson City/ Bushwacker Museum, jail, Civil War, memorabilia, Nevada/ Memoryville, restored autos, storefronts, Rolla/ Drummond's Toy Museum, St Charles/ First Missouri State Capitol, St Charles/ Maramec Spring Park and Agricultural Museum, pioneer ironworks, farm artifacts, St James/ Patee House Museum, historic hotel, St Joseph/ Pony Express Museum, St Joseph/ St Joseph Museum, history of St Joseph, St Joseph.

Historic Houses: Daniel Boone Home, Defiance/ Garth Woodside Mansion, Hannibal/ Bingham-Waggoner Estate, Independence/ 1859 Marshal's Home, Jail & Museum, Independence/ Linwood Lawn Mansion, Lexington/ Victorianne Home, Lexington/ John J Pershing Boyhood Home, Laclede/ Laura Ingalls Wilder Home & Museum, Mansfield/ Jesse James Farm and Claybrook House, Kearney/ Historic Buildings: Amoureaux House, Bolduc House, Church of Ste Genevieve, Felix Valle Home, Green Tree Tavern, Guibourd-Valle House, Ste Genevieve/ Jesse James Home Museum, St Joseph.

Entertainment: Ozarks Auto Show, classic, antique, contemporary autos, Branson/ Twainland Express Tram Ride, Hannibal/ St Louis Iron Mountain and Southern Railway Trip, Jackson/ Mark Twain Clopper Horsedrawn Ride, Maywood.

Commercial: Montelle Vineyards and Winery Tour, Augusta/ The Abbey Winery, Cuba/ J.C. Penney Museum, Hamilton/ Cooperage Craft Center Demonstrations, Hermann/ Hermanhof Winery, Hermann/ Stone Hill Winery, Hermann/ Ferrigno Vineyards Tour, St James/ Buescher's Cob Pipes Demonstration, Washington/ McCormick Distilling Co Tour, Weston.

Religious: Morman L.D.S. Visitors Center, Independence.

Montana

Fame: *Glacier National Park, expansive plains leading to the Northern Rocky Mountains, Big Sky Country.*
You must *see Glacier National Park, ski the mountains.*

Statewide Attractions

•Best Choices:

Glacier National Park
West Glacier 59936. (406)88-5441.

A million acre wilderness containing over 200 mountain lakes, more than 50 living glaciers, hundreds of towering peaks and abundant wildlife at every turn. The Going-to-the-Sun Road winds through towering peaks and over the Continental Divide at Logan Pass. **$5/car.**

Alder Gulch
The Bovey Restoration, Box 338, Virginia City 59755. (406)843-5377.

Original buildings, dating from the Territorial days, filled with artifacts used when gold camps flourished. Alder Gulch is widely respected for the authenticity of the restoration. **Free.**

Charles M. Russell Museum
400 13th St N, Great Falls 59401. (406)727-8787.

One of the nation's finest collections of western art is displayed in the modern museum and gallery. Next door is the former home and studio of famous artist, Charles Russell. **$1.50/adult.** 6/1-Labor Day, Mon-Sat, 9-6; Sun, 1-5. Winter, Tues-Sat, 10-5; Sun, 1-5.

Museum of the Plains Indian
Box 400, Browning 59417. (406)338-2230.

Jct of Hwy 2 and 89. Exhibits of the art of the American Plains Indians, past and present. Permanent and traveling exhibitions. **Free.** Jun-Sept, daily. Oct-May, Mon-Fri

•Good Choices:

Natural Scenery: C.M. Russell National Wildlife Refuge, surrounding Ft Peck Reservoir/ Flathead Lake, between Kalispell and Polson/ National Bison Range Wildlife Refuge, Moise.
Nature and Man: Woodland Park, flower, rock gardens, Kalispell/ Aerial Fire Depot, training base for smoke jumpers, tours, Missoula/ Interagency Aerial Fire

Control Center, tour, W Yellowstone.

Historical and Cultural: World Museum of Mining and Hell Roarin' Gulch, mining town, mining artifacts, Butte/ Custer Battlefield National Monument, cemetery, visitor center, exhibits, Crow Agency/ Grant-Kohrs Ranch National Historic Site, historic ranch, house, barns, bunkhouse, Deer Lodge/ Towe Ford Museum, antique Ford cars, Deer Lodge/ Bannack State Park, ghost town, Dillon/ State Capitol, Helena/ Conrad Mansion, Norman style mansion, Kalispell/ Big Hole Battlefield National Monument, Nez Perce Indian - U.S. Troops battlefield, museum, Wisdom.

Entertainment: Last Chancer Tour Train, Helena.

Commercial: Montana-Dakota Utilities Co Industrial Tour, Sidney.

Nebraska

Fame: *Sandhill Country, Omaha Steaks, "Big Red:" University of Nebraska's football team.*

You must *visit the State Capitol; during the spring, along the Platte River, near Grand Island and Kearney, watch thousands of Sandhill Cranes perform their mating dance.*

Statewide Attractions

•Best Choices:

State Capitol Building
1445 K St, Box 94924, Lincoln 68509.
(402)471-3191, Ext 448 or 449.

This building has been called one of the architectural wonders of the world. The story of nature's gifts to man and Nebraska are interpreted through mosaic tiles, paintings, decorative arts and sculpture. Guided tours, audiovisual presentations. **Free.** Mon-Fri, 8-5; Sat and holidays, 10-5; Sun, 1-5. Closed Thanksgiving, 12/25, 1/1.

Stuhr Museum of the Prairie Pioneer
3133 W Hwy 34, Grand Island 68801.
(308)381-5316.

Jct of US 30 & 281, 4 mi N of I-80. 1908 railroad town of 60 restored buildings. Includes an operating steam train, farm machinery and vehicles, Stuhr-Stolley farm, 1859 cabin, Pawnee Indian earth lodge. **May-Sept: $5/adult; $2.50/student 7-16. Oct-**

116

Apr: $3/adult; $1.50/student 7-16. May-Sept, daily, 9-6. Oct-Apr, Mon-Sat, 9-5; Sun, 1-5; outdoor exhibits closed.

Arbor Lodge State Historical Park
Box 15, Nebraska City 68410. (402)873-7222.

At 2nd Av & Centennial Av. Mansion and surrounding acreage which was the home of Arbor Day founder, J Sterling Morton. Includes carriage house, Italian terraced garden, monument square, log cabin, Pine Grove and tree trail. **$1.50/adult; $.75/child 6-15.** 5/23-9/7, daily, 9-5. 9/8-10/31, 4/20-5/22, Daily, 1-5.

Fort Robinson
Box 304, Crawford 69339. (308)665-2852.

Restored US Army Post exhibiting military artifacts. Among the things you'll want to see are 1887 adobe officers' quarters, blacksmith, harness and wheelwright shops, veterinary office, post headquarters, stage coach and trail rides. **$1/adult; $.25/child.** May-Oct: Mon-Sat, 8-5; Sun, 1:30-5. Nov-Apr: Mon-Fri, 8-12.

Ak-Sar-Ben Thoroughbred Racing
Ak-Sr-Ben Field, Omaha 68106. (402)556-2305. (800)228-6001 out of state.

Exit N of I-80 at 60th or 72nd to about 63rd & Center. Considered one of the most beautiful and well-kept race tracks in the U.S. Trackside seating to private party room, air conditioned, art deco decor. **$2/adult gen admission.** 4/19-8/29, Wed-Fri, 4 pm; Sat, Sun, holidays, 2 pm.

Buffalo Bill's Scouts Rest Ranch State Historical Park
RR 1, North Platte 69101. (308)532-4795.

US 83 N to Hwy 30, go W 2 miles and follow signs. Cody's varied career is chronicled in his 18-rm mansion and his famous show barn, preserved to the finest detail. Rare film footage of the original wild west show shot by Thomas Edison is available for viewing. **$2/car.** Mem Day - Labor Day: Daily, 10-8. 4/1-Mem Day, Labor Day-11/1: Mon-Fri, 8-12, 1-5.

•Good Choices:

Natural Scenery: Fontenelle Forest Nature Center, 17 miles of wilderness trails, Bellevue/ Pine Ridge National Forest, canyons, buttes, forest, trails, Chadron/ Scotts Bluff National Monument, historic landmark, Oregon Trail museum, Gering/ Valentine National Wildlife Refuge, lakes, birds, wildlife, Valentine.
Nature and Man: State Museum and Mueller Planetarium, large fossils, natural history, anthropology, planetarium, Lincoln/ Henry Doorly Zoo, Omaha.

Science and Technology:
Strategic Air Command Museum,
aircraft, flight artifacts, Bellevue.
Historical and Cultural:
Plainsman Museum, log cabin,
homes, historic farm implements,
cars, toys, china, Aurora/ Boys
Town, tours/ Robert Henry
Museum and Historical Walkway,
home, Pony Express Station,
Cozad/ Hastings Museum, Hast-
ings/ Nebraska Art Collection,
Nebraska artists, Kearney/ New
State Museum of History, Lincoln/
University of Nebraska Museum,
Lincoln/ Pioneer Village and
Harold Warp Museum, 20 acre
complex of historic artifacts, Min-
den/ Mormon Pioneer Cemetery
and Visitors Center, graves, sculp-
ture, artifacts, Omaha/ Joslyn Art
Museum, ancient Greek, Egyptian,
European, American art Colonial
era to present, Omaha.
Entertainment: Spirit and Belle
of Brownville Cruise, Brownville.
Commercial: Old Market,
Omaha.
Sports: Fonner Park
Thoroughbred Racing, Grand Is-
land. **Seasonal Events and Fes-
tivals:** College World Series, Late
May or Early June, Omaha.

Nevada

Fame: *Gaming, spectacular desert scenery.*
You must *visit the strip in Las Vegas, visit Reno or visit a
ghost town.*

Statewide Attractions

•Best Choices:

Ghost Towns
Chamber of Commerce, 932 E St, Box
1635, Hawthorne 89415. (702)945-
5896.

Aurora, 35 mi SW. Mark Twain
looked for gold here. Now abandoned. Bodie, 43 mi SW. Once
known as a rough town, now a
state historic park. Rawhide, 41 mi
NE. Once a boomtown with copper, silver and gold mines. **Free.**

Lake Mead National Recrea-
tion Area
601 Nevada Hwy, Boulder 89005.
(702)293-8906.

4 mi E of Boulder on US 93. In-
cludes 30 miles of the Grand
Canyon, Lake Mead and Lake
Mohave, both man made lakes,
Hoover and Davis dams, beaches,
Joshua tree forests, desert and
mountains. Several paved roads are
available for driving tours. **Free.**
Open all year.

•Good Choices:

Natural Scenery: Lake Tahoe Nevada State Park, beautiful lake, sandy beaches, Crystal Bay/ Humboldt National Forest, forest, canyons, cliffs, old mining camps, Elko/ Lehman Caves National Monument, guided tours, Baker.
Science and Technology: Fleischmann Planetarium, Reno.
Historical and Cultural: Nevada State Museum, coins, guns, minerals, pioneer & mining memorabilia, Carson City/ Bowers Mansion, granite home, Carson City/ Nevada Northern Railway Museum, railway depot, short line railroad, Ely/ Las Vegas Art Museum, local, national, international artists, Las Vegas/ Imperial Palace Auto Museum, antique, classical autos, Las Vegas/ Bonnie Springs Old Nevada Mining Town, historic mining town, Las Vegas/ Sierra Nevada Museum of Art, international, national, regional artists, Reno/ The Castle, design of Normandy castle, Virginia City.
Ghost Towns: Delamar, near Caliente/ Searchlight, near Henderson/ Goodsprings, Sandy Valley Area, Rhyolite, Johnnie Mine, Leadfield, Carrara, Chloride Cliff, Lide, near Las Vegas/ Seven Troughs, Rochester, near Lovelock/ Goldfield, near Tonopah. **Entertainment:** Ponderosa Ranch and Western Theme Park, Crystal Bay/ Liberace Museum, Las Vegas/ Ripley's Believe It or Not Museum, Las Vegas.

New Hampshire

Fame: *the Granite State, mountains, seacoast, strong political involvement.*
You must *see the view from Mt. Washington on a clear day.*

Statewide Attractions

•Best Choices:

Franconia Notch State Park
Franconia 03580. (603)823-5563.

A valley between the Franconia and Kinsman Ranges in the white mountains with spectacular scenery. Look for Old Man of the Mountains, a face on the mountain carved by nature, the Basin, a deep glacial pool. Extra charge for the Flume a natural chasm, with waterfall, high granite walls, pool, films.

$2/adults. $5/Flume. Mem Day - Mid-Oct.

Portsmouth Harbor Cruises
64 Ceres St, Portsmouth 03801.
(603)436-8084.

Narrated harbor cruises, inland river cruises. **$4-10/adult; $4-6/children.** 6/13-10/31, Daily, 10-7.

•Good Choices:

Natural Scenery: Bear Brook Nature Center, nature trails, demonstrations, live exhibits, Allenstown/ Audubon Society, nature trails, programs, exhibits, Concord/ Rhododendron State Park, 16 acres of wild rhododendron, Jul 1-15, Fitzwilliam/ Paradise Point Nature Center, lake, shore line, natural history programs, exhibits, Hebron.
Nature and Man: Science Center of New Hampshire, live animals, games, activities, trails, Holdernesss/ Fuller Gardens, formal, Japanese gardens, North Hampton/ Lost River Reservation, gorge, rock formations, falls, boardwalks, river, Woodstock.
Science and Technology: Montshire Museum of Science, walk-through heart, fossils, Hanover/ Seabrook Station Educational Center, nuclear energy displays, aquarium, Seabrook.
Historical and Cultural: Canaan Historic District, late 18th-early 19th century rural community, Canaan/ Old Fort # 4, living history museum, 1740s, Charlestown/ Pierce Manse, Pres Franklin Pierce home, 6/1-9/4, Concord/ Saint Gaudens National Historic Site, sculptor's home, garden, studios, Cornish/ Museum at Lower Shaker Village, museum, village, Enfield/ Grand Manor, antique & classic car museum, Glen/ Currier Gallery of Art, European, American paintings, sculpture, decorative arts, Manchester/ New Hampshire Farm Museum, farmhouse, barns, agriculture tools, artifacts, Milton/ Port of Portsmouth Maritime Museum & Albacore Park, submarine tour, Portsmouth/ America's Stone Henge, astronomical stones, trails, viewing ramp, Salem.
Historic Houses: Robert Frost Homestead, Derry/ Gillman Garrison House, Cincinnati Hall, Exeter/ Daniel Webster Birthplace, Franklin/ Franklin PIerce Homestead, Hillsboro/ Abbot-Spalding House Museum, Nashua/ Barrett House, New Ipswich/ Samuel Morey House, Orford/ John Paul Jones House, Gov John Langdon Mansion, Jackson House, Moffatt-Ladd House, Rundlet-May House, Warner House, Wentworth Coolidge Mansion, Portsmouth/ Mary Baker Eddy Houses, Rumney & Groton/ Historic South Sutton, S Sutton.
Entertainment: Attitash-Alpine Slide, May-Sept, Bartlett/ Crossroads of America Model Railroad Museum, Bethlehem/ Rocks Estate, historic farm, modern dairy farm, Bethlehem/ Friendly Farm, farm animals, Dublin/ Ruggles

Mine, oldest mica, feldspar beryl mine in U.S., Grafton/ Clark's Trading Post & White Mt Central Railroad, train rides, museums, bear exhibit, 5/15-10/15, Lincoln/ White's Miniature Horse Petting Farm, miniature horse farm, other animals, 5/1-9/30, Pittsfield/ Polar Caves, tour, 5/16-10/15, Plymouth/ Children's Museum of Portsmouth, participatory exhibits, Portsmouth/ Frye's Measure Mill, wood-working mill, museum, Wilton.

Rides: Conway Scenic Railroad, 5/2-10/25, Conway/ Mt Cranmore Skimobile, late June - Oct, Conway/ Alpine Ridge, alpine slide & 8 other ways of sliding, June-Sept, Gilford/ Hampton Trolley Co Ride, 6/20-9/7, Hampton Beach/ Loon Mountain Recreation Area Aerial Ride, Jun-mid Oct, Lincoln/ Wildcat Mountain Gondola & Rec Area, 6/21-10/12, Pinkham Notch/ Olde Port Trolley Co, 6/20-Labor Day, Portsmouth & Hampton Beach.

Commercial: Anheuser-Busch Brewery, Merrimack/ Drakes Hill Sheep Farm, Northwood/ Hampshire Pewter Factory Tour, Wolfeboro.

Sports: Hinsdale Greyhound Racetrack, Hinsdale/ Rockingham Park, thoroughbred racing, Salem.

New Jersey

Fame: *the "Crossroads of the American Revolution," Atlantic City and 127 miles of coastline.*

You must *visit one of the state's many historical sites, the Broadwalk in Atlantic City or relax at the shore.*

Statewide Attractions

•Best Choices:

Morristown National Historical Park
Washington Place, Morristown 07960. (201)539-2085.

This park consists of three units covering sites directly connected with events of the Revolutionary War. The **Historical Museum and Library** contain memorabilia and papers related to the colonies and the Revolutionary War.

Fort Nonsense, Chestnut St, is the site of earthworks and probably of a fort built at General Washington's Order. **Jockey Hollow,** 6 mi SW of Morristown, contain sites occupied by the Continental Army, reconstructed soldier huts, Wick House, a reconstructed farm house and a wildlife sanctuary with hiking trails. **$.50/adult; Free/sr citizen,**

student under 16. Wed-Sun, 9-5. Closed Thanksgiving, 12/25, 1/1.

Cape May
Cape May County Chamber of Commerce, Cape May 08204. (609)465-7181.

This entire community has been designated a historic landmark. One of the nations oldest seaside resorts with Victorian buildings, summer houses, shops. Among the affordable things here are the beach, the promenade, hunting for "Cape May Diamond" rocks, taking a guided or self-guided tour, visiting historic Cold Spring Village.

Edison National Historic Site
Main St and Lakeside Av, West Orange 07052. (201)736-0550.

Laboratory includes library, machinery, chemicals, the first light bulb, photograph and motion picture equipment. Edison's home, Glenmont is restored as it appeared when Edison occupied it. **$.50/adult; Free/sr citizen, student under 16.** Wed-Fri, 9:30-3:30; Sat-Sun, 9:30-3:30. Closed Thanksgiving, 12/25, 1/1.

Old Barracks
Barracks St, Trenton 08608. (609)396-1776.

Colonial barracks that housed British, Hessian and Continental troops during the Revolution. Restored soldiers quarters, 18th century period rooms, antique exhibits, guides in period costumes. **$1/adult; $.50/child under 12.** Mon-Sat, 10-5; Sun, 1-5. Closed Easter, Thanksgiving, 12/24, 12/25.

State Museum
W State St, Trenton 08608. (609)292-6464.

A 3-building complex with a planetarium, auditorium and 3-floor main museum. Changing art, historical, cultural and natural science exhibits in the museum. Planetarium deals with space probes and duplicates motions of space vehicles. **Free.** Tues-Sat, 9-4:45; Sun, 1-5. Closed state holidays.

•Good Choices:

Natural Scenery: Barnegat Lighthouse State Park, beach, Barnegat Light/ Environmental Education Center, wildlife, trails, broadwalks, blinds, Basking Ridge/ Great Swamp National Wildlife Refuge, marsh, swamp habitat, wildlife, broadwalk, blinds, Basking Ridge/ Delaware Water Gap National Recreation Area, gap in Appalachians, restored village, craftsworkers, woods, river, trails, Columbia/ William L Hutcheson Memorial Forest, uncut hardwood forest - call for tour times, Rutgers, New Brunswick/ Edward B Forsythe National Wildlife Refuge, waterfowl, bays, channels, tidal marshes, Oceanville/ Gateway National Recreation Area, barrier beach peninsula, Sandy Hook Unit. **Nature and Man:** Space Farms Zoo and Museum, preserve with N American wildlife, museum with vehicles, Beemerville/ Bridgeton City Park, zoo, museum, recreation, Bridgeton/ Franklin Mineral Museum, minerals of area, replica mine, Franklin/ Statue of Liberty State Park, urban park facing the statue, Jersey City/ Frelinghuysen Arboretum, natural plantings, formal gardens, Morristown/ Trailside Nature and Science Center, human and natural history, planetarium, Mountainside/ Rutgers Display Gardens and Helvar Woods, 20 acre gardens, New Brunswick/ Skylands Botanical Gardens, Ringwood State Park, Ringwood/ Duke Gardens, 11 glass-enclosed gardens, Somerville/ Turtleback Zoo, West Orange/ Bergen County Wildlife Center, pond, flowers, herb garden, native animals, trails, Wyckoff.

Science and Technology: US Army Communications Electronics Museum, Fort Monmouth/ Submarine USS Ling, tours, Hackensack.

Historic: Batsto Village, sawmill, gristmill, historic ironworks, Wharton State Forest, Batsto/ Clinton Historical Museum, water wheel, restored buildings, Clinton/ Allaire State Park, historic ironworks, village, Allaire/ Fort Lee Historic Park, Revolutionary War fort, film, exhibits, Fort Lee/ Monmouth Battlefield State Park, Revolutionary War battlefield, film, nature center, Freehold/ Wheaton Village and Museum of American Glass, 1888 glassmaking community, Millville/ Historic Speedwell, ironworks, Morristown/ Princeton University, tours, Princeton/ City of Salem, historic buildings/ Aviation Hall of Fame of New Jersey, Teterboro/ Washington Crossing State Park, site where Washington crossed the Delaware, Trenton.

Historic Houses: James Fenimore Cooper House, Burlington/ Grover Cleveland Birthplace State Historic Site, Caldwell/ Walt Whitman Home State Historic Site, Camden/ Boudinot Mansion State Historic Site, Elizabeth/ Kuser Farm Mansion, Hamilton/ Smithville Mansion, Mount Holly/ Rockingham State Historical Site, Princeton/ Thomas Clarke House, Princeton/ Ringwood Manor, Ringwood State Park, Ringwood/ Wallace House State Historic Site, Somerville/ Trent House, Trenton/ Dey Mansion, Wayne.

Art: Montclair Art Museum, American painting, sculpture, Montclair/ Newark Museum, American paintings, sculpture, decorative arts, Newark/ Jane Voorhees Zimmerli Art Museum, western art, Rutgers, New Brunswick.

Entertainment: See the Broadwalks, Atlantic City/ Cape May Court House Information Center, find historic homes, outdoor attractions, Cape May Court House/ Miniature Kingdom, scale-model community, Washington.

Religious Catholic Cathedral of the Sacred Heart, Newark/ Shrine of the Immaculate Heart of Mary, Washington.

Commercial: Broadwalk, Atlantic City/ Renault Winery, Egg Harbor City/ Flemington Cut Glass Co

Glass Cutting Demonstrations, Flemington.

Sports: Meadowlands Race Track, East Rutherford/ Golf House Museum, US Golf Association, Far Hills.

New Mexico

Fame: *Indian and Hispanic arts and culture.*
You must *visit Santa Fe, Carlsbad Caverns.*

Statewide Attractions

•Best Choices:

Carlsbad Caverns
3225 National Parks Hwy, Carlsbad 88220. (505)785-2232.

25 mi SW of Carlsbad on US 62/180. There are 21 miles of surveyed chambers and corridors, 750 ft underground. The complete self-guided tour covers about 3 miles and takes close to 3 hrs. You'll see huge rooms and small chambers, delicate and massive formations as you explore this internationally famous cavern. **$5/adult; $3/student under 16.** 6/1-8/15, daily, 7:30-3:30. 8/16-5/31, daily, 8:30-2.

Santa Fe

The history of the city dates back to 1610 and the downtown historic district is worth a day of explora-

tion. Among the notable affordable attractions in Sante Fe are Mission of San Miguel of Santa Fe, Place of the Governors, Museum of International Folk Art, Museum of Fine Arts, Museum of New Mexico, Our Lady of Light Chapel, Cathedral of St. Francis, Loretto Chapel with famous staircase, State Capitol. On a drive out of town there are many more fascinating places to explore.

Taos Pueblo
2 1/2 mi N of Taos Plaza, Taos.

One of the tallest and most famous of the pueblos. The people who live here are very conservative and religiously very devout. Visitors must get permission to bring a camera into the area and permission to take individual pictures. There is an additional charge for

124

parking a car and for a camera. $3/adult. Mon-Fri, 9-5; Sat, Sun, holidays, 9-3.

Old Town Albuquerque
1 blk N of 2000 blk of Central Av, at Rio Grande Blvd, Albuquerque.

The original Spanish settlement of the city, this area is now filled with shops and galleries offering many arts, crafts and foods. Indian vendors bargain with visitors.

•Good Choices:
Natural Scenery: White Sands National Monument, white sand dunes, walks, visitor center, Alamogordo/ Rio Grande Nature Center State Park, wildlife refuge, Albuquerque/ Capulin Mountain National Monument, 10,000 yr old volcanic cinder cone, Capulin/ Valley of Fires State Park, ancient lava flow, Carrizozo/ Las Vegas National Wildlife Refuge, prairieland, wildlife, driving trail, Las Vegas/ Bitter Lake National Wildlife Refuge, grassland, wildlife, Roswell/ Gila National Forest, forest, rangeland, recreation, 75 mile drive, Silver City/ Bosque del Apache National Wildlife Refuge, auto tour, Nov-Feb best, Socorro.
Nature and Man: Rio Grande Zoological Park, Alburquerque/ Living Desert State Park, native animals, plants, Carlsbad/ Pancho Villa State Park Botanical Garden, Columbus/ City of Rocks State Park, massive rock formations, Demino.

Science and Technology: Space Center, space craft, launch vehicles, Alamogordo/ Perpetual Ice Caves, Grants/ Bradbury Science Hall, history of nuclear and other energy resources, Los Alamos/ Very Large Array Radio Telescope, exhibits, tours, Socorro.
Historical and Cultural: Albuquerque Museum, history, art, science, Albuquerque/ Confederate Air Force Flying Museum, WWII planes, Hobbs/ Indian Pueblo Cultural Center, museum, arts, crafts, Albuquerque/ Roswell Museum and Art Center, SW artists, historical artifacts, Roswell/ Millicent Rogers Museum, Spanish, Indian, pioneer articles, Taos/ Historic Houses: Ernest L Blumenschein Home, La Hacienda de Don Antonio Severino Martinez, Kit Carson Home and Museum, Taos/ Ft Union National Monument, ruins of 3 forts, adobe ruins, Watrous.
Religious: Mission of St Francis of Assisi, Taos.
Pueblos: Acoma Pueblo, Acoma/ Aztec Ruins National Monument, Aztec/ Bandelier National Monument Pueblo and Cliff Ruins, Los Alamos/ Salinas National Monument Pueblos, Mountainair.
Entertainment: Scandia Peak Chairlift, summer, Albuquerque.
Commercial: Anderson Valley Vineyards, Albuquerque/ Ortega's Weaving Shop, Espanola/ Chino Copper Mine, Silver City.
Seasonal Events and Festivals: International Balloon Fiesta, Oct, Albuquerque/ New Mexico State Fair, Sept, Albuquerque.

New York

Fame: *Mountains: Catskills and Adirondacks. Ocean: Atlantic. Cities:*
You must *enjoy some of the scenic beauty of outstate New York.*

Buffalo - Niagara Falls

Fame: *The falls; scenic beauty; fall foliage; Buffalo chicken wings.*
You must: *see the falls and, of course, eat some chicken wings.*

•Best Choices:

Maid of the Mist Boat Ride
Prospect Point, Niagara Falls. (716)284-4233.

Half-hour boat tour of all three falls, which passes at the foot of the falls and enters Horseshoe Basin. **$5/adult; $2.50/child 6-12.** 5/15-10/15, daily, 9:15-8.

Buffalo Zoological Gardens
Delaware Park, Amherst & Parkside Av, Buffalo 14214. (716)837-3900.

Natural environments are recreated for animals, including a tropical rain forest, gorilla habitat and Asian forest. **$2.50/adult; $1/student 11-16; $.50/child 4-10; free/sr citizen.** Daily, 10-4:30.

Artpark
Box 371, Lewiston 14092. (716)754-9001.

A state park for the performing arts. Visitors can observe specialists of visual and performing arts from artist-in-residence program. Free outdoor activities include crafts, sculpture, workshops, cooking, performers and storytelling. **Free park admission. $2.50/parking. $4-18/theater tickets.** Memorial Day - Labor Day. Closed Mon.

Goat Island and Cave of the Winds
Niagara River, between U.S. and Canadian Falls. (716)282-8979.

Goat Island is a 70 acre park that offers magnificent views of both falls. The Cave of the Winds trip begins on the island. Guides lead visitors, in waterproof garments, on wooden walkways through the spray at the foot of the U.S. falls. **Cave: $3/adult; $2.50/child 5-11.** Memorial Day - 10/15: Daily, 9-9.

Albright-Knox Art Gallery
1285 Elmwood Av, Buffalo 14222.
(716)882-8700.

An internationally renown collection of 18th, 19th and 20th century U.S. and European paintings, sculpture from 3000 B.C. **$2/suggested donation.** Tues-Sat, 11-5; Sun, noon - 5. Closed Thanksgiving, 12/25, 1/1

•Good Choices:

Natural Scenery: Niagara Falls: Whirlpool State Park, view gorge, rapids.

Nature and Man: Buffalo: Buffalo and Erie County Botanical Gardens. Niagara Falls: Aquarium of Niagara Falls/ Prospect Park, museum, theater, garden/ Prospect Point Observation Tower, 282 ft structure/ Schoellkopf Geological Museum, history of falls, geological garden, trail/ Wintergarden, glass enclosed garden.

Science and Technology: Buffalo: Buffalo Museum of Science. Niagara Falls: Niagara Power Project Visitor Center, movies, models, diorama.

Historical and Cultural: Buffalo: Naval and Servicemen's Park, WWII boats and equipment/ Theodore Roosevelt Inaugural National Historic Site, Greek Revival structure. Niagara Falls: Old Fort Niagagra/ The Turtle, Native American Center for the Living Arts.

Entertainment: Niagara Falls: Viewmobile.

Commercial: Buffalo: Allentown Historic Preservation Site/ QRS Music Rolls Industrial Tour.

New York City

Fame: The largest city in the U.S.; the business and entertainment capital of the nation.

You must: see the Statue of Liberty.

•Best Choices:

Statue of Liberty National Monument
Liberty Island. (212)269-5755.

Reached by boats from Battery Park, S tip of Manhattan Island. This huge statue was presented to the U.S. by France in 1884 and was traditionally the first sight seen by immigrants or visitors sailing into the harbor. **Boat fare: $3.25/adult; $1.50/child under 11.** Daily, 9-4. Closed 12/25.

United Nations
First Av between 42nd and 48th Sts. (212)754-7713.

The buildings were designed and decorated by the world's leading architects and decorators. "First come, first served" for meetings of the General Assembly and Councils. **Tours: $4.50/adult; $4/sr citizen; $2.50/student.** Daily, 9:15-4:45.

Brooklyn Botanic Garden
1000 Washington Av, Brooklyn. (718)622-4433.

52 acres, including Rose Garden, Japanese Garden, Herb Garden, Fragrance Garden. **$.25/wknds for Japanese Garden. Rest free.** Tue-Fri, 8-4:30; Sat-Sun, 10-6.

Bronx Zoo
Fordham Rd and Southern Blvd, Bronx. (212)367-1010.

Famous for rare mammals, birds and reptiles. Also includes a children's zoo, camel ride and safari monorail. **Apr-Oct, $3.75/adult; $1.50/child 2-13. Nov-Mar, $1.50/adult; $.75/child 2-13. Free/sr citizen.** Daily, 10-5.

The Cloisters
Fort Tryon Park, Manhattan. (212)923-3700.

A branch of the Metropolitan Museum of Art devoted to medieval art and architecture. Includes French cloisters, paintings, statues, tapestries and stained glass windows. **$4.50/adult; $2.25/sr citizen, student. Includes admission to Met Museum of Art.** Tues-Sun, 9:30-4:45.

Metropolitan Museum of Art
82nd St and 5th Av, Manhattan. (212)535-7710.

One of the world's great museums with hundreds of world-famous masterpieces. Many outstanding collections. **$4.50/adult; $2.25/sr citizen, student. Includes admission to Cloisters.** Wed-Sun, 9:30-5:15; Tues, 9:30-8:45.

World Trade Center
Church St between Vesey and Liberty, Manhattan. (212)466-7397.

A 16 acre complex of offices and plaza. Enclosed 107th floor observation deck and rooftop promenade, world's highest open air viewing platform. **$2.95/adult; $1.50/sr citizen, child.** Daily, 9:30-9:30.

Stock Exchanges
New York Exchange, 20 Broad St. (212)623-5167. American Exchange, 86 Trinity Pl. (212)306-1000. Manhattan.

Visitors Gallery with narrated explanation of activity on floor. **Free.** Mon-Fri, 9:20-4.

Staten Island Ferry
Manhattan to Staten Island.

A terrific bargain, the 20 minute ride gives you a spectacular view of the Statue of Liberty and the harbor. While on Staten Island you may visit several interesting and affordable attractions, including

Richmondtown, children's museum and zoo. **$.25/person. Return trip free.** Daily.

South Street Seaport Museum
Foot of Fulton St at East River, Manhattan. (212)669-9400.

An 11 block area is being restored to exhibit the city's maritime history. Mariners will want to visit the museum ships docked at piers 15 and 16: Wavertree, 1885 full-rigged ship; Lettie G. Howard, 1893 fishing schooner; Ambrose, 1907 lightship; Peking, 1911 four-masted bark. **$4/adult; $3/sr citizen; $2/child 4-12.** Mon-Fri, 11-4; Sat-Sun, 11-5. Closed Thanksgiving, 12/25, 1/1.

•Good Choices Manhattan:

Science, Technology, Space: American Museum of Natural History, history of mankind, animal, plant life/ Battery Park, view of Statue of Liberty, New York Harbor/ Central Park, woods, lakes, skating rinks, pool/ Con Edison Energy Museum, history of electricity/ Hayden Planetarium/ Intrepid Sea-Air-Space Museum, aircraft carrier houses 4 museums/ Museum of Holography, holographic art.

Art Museums: Asia Society Galleries, Asian art/ Cooper-Hewitt Museum, decorative art/ Frick Collection, paintings, antiques/ Japan House, traditional, contemporary Japanese art/ Museum of American Folk Art/ Museum of Modern Art, art from 1880s to present/ National Academy of Design, paintings, sculpture, graphic arts/ Solomon R Guggenheim Museum, 19th, 20th century art/ Studio Museum in Harlem, master to emerging black artists/ Whitney Museum of Modern Art, 20th century art.

Historic: Federal Hall National Memorial, first capitol/ Jewish Museum, Judaica, archaeology, art/ Museum of Broadcasting, thousands of radio and TV broadcasts/ Museum of the City of New York, history of the city/ Police Museum, police memorabilia.

Historic Houses: Dyckman House, only Dutch farmhouse still on Manhattan/ Hamilton Grange National Memorial, Alexander Hamilton's home/ Morris Jumel Mansion, historic house, gardens/ Theodore Roosevelt Birthplace National Historic Site.

Areas: Chinatown at Mott, Pell and Doyers Sts/ Garment District, 6th AV to 8th Av, 30th St to 39th St/ Greenwich Village from 14th St to Houston St, Washington Sq to Hudson River/ SoHo, bounded by Broadway, 6th Av, Houston and Canal St.

Buildings: Cathedral Church of St. John's the Divine/ Empire State Building/ Lincoln Center for the Performing Arts/ New York Public Library/ Radio City Music Hall/ Rockefeller Center/ St Patrick's Cathedral/ St Paul's Chapel/ Temple Emanu-El/ Trinity Church.

Entertainment: Free tickets to TV shows at NYC Visitors Bureau.

Commercial: New Amsterdam Brewery and Taproom Tours.
Seasonal Events and Festivals: Lincoln Center Out-Of-Doors, Summer/ Opera Under the Stars, Summer - Central Park/ Philharmonic Under the Stars, Summer - Central Park/ Rockefeller Center Noontime Entertainment, Summer/ Shakespeare in the Park, Summer - Central Park/ South Street Seaport Street Entertainment, Summer/ World Trade Center Noontime Entertainment, Summer.

•Good Choices Bronx, Brooklyn, Queens, Staten Island:

Nature and Man: Bronx: New York Botanical Garden, one of the largest gardens in the world/ North Wind Undersea Museum, marine life, submarines/ Wave Hill, estate, gardens. Brooklyn: New York Aquarium/ Prospect Park, zoo, lakes. Queens: Flushing Meadows-Corona Park, zoo, art museum, recreation.. Staten Island: Staten Island Zoo.

Historical and Cultural: Bronx: Edgar Allen Poe Cottage. Brooklyn: Brooklyn Museum, art from Egypt, North, South, Central America. Queens: Queens Museum, fine arts, young artists. Staten Island: Conference House, historic house, gardens/ Richmondtown Restoration, outdoor, living history.

Entertainment: Brooklyn: Brooklyn Children's Museum, participatory exhibits. Staten Island: Staten Island Children's Museum, rotating participatory exhibits.

Statewide Attractions

•Best Choices:

Roosevelt - Vanderbilt National Historic Sites
Hyde Park 12538. (914)229-9115.

The Home of Franklin D. Roosevelt, the Franklin D. Roosevelt Library and Museum and the Vanderbilt Mansion are closely connected and one admission encompasses the three sites. The Eleanor Roosevelt National Historic Site can only be reached by a shuttle bus from the Home of FDR and includes a guided tour of cottages, outbuildings and gardens.
Admission 3 sites: $2/adult; free/sr citizen, under 16. Shuttle bus: $1.95/adult; $1.10/child 4-15. All are open daily, 4/1-10/31, 10-5. Hours vary during rest of yr.

National Baseball Hall of Fame and Museum
Main St, Cooperstown 13326. (607)547-9988.

Museum details the history, development and great movements of baseball with artifacts, photographs, tapes and daily movies. Hall of Fame has plaques honoring the all-time greats. **$5/adult; $2/students 7-15.** Daily, 5/1-10/31, 9-9. Rest of yr, 9-5.

Corning Glass Center
Corning 14830. (607)974-8271.

Museum of Glass portrays the history of glassmaking through over 20,000 glass objects chronologically displayed from 1500 BC to the present. Hall of Science has demonstrations and films on glass making and use today, including fiber optics. In the Steuben Glass factory, artists hand fashion Steuben crystal objects. **$2.50/adult; $2/sr citizen; $1.25/6-17. Family rate.** Daily, 9-5. Closed Thanksgiving, 12/24, 12/25, 1/1.

Watkins Glen State Park
Franklin St, Watkins Glen 14891.

Climb or take a taxi to the top of this spectacular glen which drops about 700 ft in 2 miles. There are cataracts, rapids, waterfalls and magnificent rock formations. The glen is illuminated at night. "Timespell," a 45 minute show that uses panoramic sound, laser images and special effects to trace the 45 million century history of the gorge, is presented nightly for an extra charge. **$2.50/parking fee.**

Timespell: $4/person. 5/15-10/15, Daily, 8-10.

Vanderbilt Mansion and Planetarium
Littleneck Rd, Centerport 11721. (516)261-5656.

Spanish Revival mansion with original furnishings of William K. Vanderbilt. More than 17,000 marine, wildlife exhibits. Planetarium with sky shows, astronomy, science exhibits, observatory. **$4/adult; $3/sr citizen, student 8-12.**

•Good Choices:

Natural Scenery: Adirondack Mountains Park/ Taughannock Falls State Park, falls, glen, Ithaca/ Ausable Chasm, scenic gorge, Keeseville/ Letchworth State Park, Genesee River Gorge, museum, Portageville/ Allegany State Park, trails, hills, recreation, Salamanca.
Nature and Man: Bayard Cutting Arboretum, evergreens, shrubs, wild flowers, Bay Shore/ Ross Park Zoo, Binghamton/ Jones Beach State Park, Jones Beach, swimming, roller skating rink, court games, Jones Beach/ Planting Fields Arboretum, greenhouses, gardens, trees, Oyster Bay/ Fort Rickey Game Farm, zoo, Rome/ Whiteface Mountain Summit, reached by Whiteface Mountain Veterans Memorial Highway, White Plains.

Science, Technology, Space and Air: Old Rhinebeck Aerodrome, antique planes, Rhinebeck/ Brookhaven National Laboratory of Nuclear Science, guided tours, Riverhead.

Historic: New York State Capitol, tours, Albany/ New York State Museum, Albany/ Senate House State Historic Site, 1st NY state senate, Kingston/ National Women's Hall of Fame, Seneca Falls.

Living History: Old Bethpage Village Restoration, Bethpage/ Museum Village in Orange County, Monroe/ Muscoot Farm Park, Pound Ridge.

Special Interest Museums: Town Marine Museum, whaling, fishing, underwater archeology, Amagansett/ Musical Museum, Clinton/ Farmers' Museum, Cooperstown/ American Museum of Fire Fighting, Hudson/ International Museum of Photography, Rochester/ National Museum of Horse Racing, Saratoga Springs.

Historic Houses: Historic Cherry Hill, Albany/ Schuyler Mansion State Historic Site, Albany/ Sagtikos Manor, Bay Shore/ Constable Hall, Boonville/ Granger Homestead, carriage museum, Canandaigua/ Sonnenberg Gardens, Canandaigua/ Fenimore House, Cooperstown/ 2890 House Museum, Corland/ Boscobel Mansion, Garrison/ Boldt Castle, Heart Island/ Sunnyside, home of Washington Irving, Tarrytown/ Elizabeth Cady Stanton Home, Seneca Falls.

Military: Washington's Headquarters Historic Site, Newburgh/ Fort Stanwix National Monument, Rome/ Fort Ticonderoga, Ticonderoga/ West Point Military Academy, West Point/ West Point Museum, West Point.

Art: Governor Nelson A Rockefeller Empire State Plaza, offices, shopping, arts, Albany/ The Rockwell Museum, Corning/ The Hyde Collection, Glens Falls/ Strong Museum, Rochester.

Commercial: Brotherhood Winery, Goshen/ Taylor-Great Western-Gold Seal Winery, Hammondsport/ Gold Seal Vineyards, Hammondsport/ Windmer's Wine Cellars Industrial Tour, Naples/ Hudson Valley Wine Co. Tour, New Paltz/ Widmark Farms, bees and bears, New Paltz/ Barton Garnet Mines Corp, North Creek/ Eastman Kodak Co, Rochester/ Chevrolet-Pontiac-Canada Plant Industrial Tour, Tarrytown/ F. X. Matt Brewing Company Tour, Utica.

North Carolina

Fame: *Cape Hatteras National Seashore, Blue Ridge Parkway, Appalachian Folk Art, Biltmore Estate at Asheville, Heritage U.S.A. at Charlotte.*
You must *drive the Blue Ridge Parkway, hike a mountain trail, visit the seashore and see a demonstration of folk art.*

Statewide Attractions

•Best Choices:

Cape Hatteras National Seashore
from Nags Head to Ocracoke.

70 miles of undeveloped seashore along islands connected by a free ferry and free bridge. You'll see huge vistas of sand and water without any commercial interruptions. Visitor centers are at Whalebone Junction Information Center, Cape Hatteras Lighthouse and Pea Island National Wildlife Refuge. **Free.** Whalebone Junction is open Mem Day - Labor Day, 8-5/ Lighthouse, daily 9-5, except 12/25.

Blue Ridge Parkway
Great Smoky Mountains National Park.

A 470 mile rd connecting Great Smoky Mountains National Park in N Carolina and Tennessee with Shenandoah National Park in Virginia. It is designed to leisurely follow the crest of several ranges. Among the points of interest are Parkway Craft Center, Milepost 294 near Blowing Rock/ Linn Cove Viaduct, Milepost 307/ Linville Falls Recreation Area, Milepost 316/ Museum of N Carolina Minerals, Milepost 331 near Spruce Pine/ Craggy Gardens, Milepost 364.6 NE of Asheville/ Folk Art Center, at Milepost 382, near Asheville/ Mount Pisgah, Milepost 409/ Richland Balsam, Milepost 431/ and Waterrock Knob, Milepost 451.2 near Balsam. Although the road is open year around, sections may be closed due to icy winter conditions. Best viewing is May-Oct, best visiting of attractions is 10-5.

Discovery Place
301 N Tryon St, Charlotte 28202. (704)372-6261.

Hands on exhibits include a tropical rain forest, aquarium, Science Circus, life center and four other exhibit areas. Films, lectures, multimedia presentations and live demonstrations. **$3/adult; $2/sr citizen, student 6-18; $1/child 3-5.** Jun-Aug, Mon-Sat, 9-6; Sun, 1-6. Sept-May, Mon-Fri,9-5, Sat, 9-6, Sun, 1-6.

North Carolina Museum of Art
2110 Blue Ridge Blvd, Raleigh 27607. (919)833-1935.

The art is displayed chronological-ly, from Ancient Egypt, Greece and Rome, Pre-Columbian through present day. Eight art schools are represented. Permanent and chang-ing exhibits. **Free.** Tues-Sat, 10-5; Fri, 10-9; Sun, noon-5. Closed major holidays.

North Carolina Museum of History
109 E Jones St, Raleigh 27601. (919)733-3894.

In the Archives, History and Library Bldg. Permanent exhibits include North Carolina history, from the Roanoke Island Colonies to the present, transportation, decorating trends, fashion, folk art, firearms. Changing exhibits and guided tours. **Free.** Tues-Sat, 9-5; Sun, 1-6. Closed major holidays.

•Good Choices:

Natural Scenery: Mount Mitchell State Park, includes Mt Mitchell summit, Asheville/ Blowing Rock, odd stone formations, tower/ Whitewater Falls Scenic Area, falls, cascades. Cashiers/ Chimney Rock Park, rock monolith, Chim-ney Rock/ Croatan National Forest, forest, wildlife, swamp/ Hanging Rock State Park, mountains, streams, waterfall, Danbury/ Cliffs of the Neuse State Park, Goldsboro/ Great Smoky Moun-tains National Park/ Bottomless Pools, Lake Lure/ Linville Gorge, falls, mountains, Linville Falls/ Nantahala National Forest, trails, scenic drives/ Pisgah National Forest, falls, fish hatchery, trails. **Nature and Man:** North Carolina Zoological Park, Asheboro/ Western N Carolina Nature Center, plant, animal exhibits, Asheville/ Morehead Planetarium, Cashiers/ North Carolina Botanical Garden, native plants, Cashiers/ Charlotte Nature Museum and Kelly Planetarium, child oriented, Char-lotte/ North Carolina Museum of Life and Science, nature, space, Durham/ Schiele Museum of Natural History and Planetarium, Gastonia/ Natural Science Center, participatory exhibits, planetarium, zoo, Greensboro/ N Carolina Aquarium-Fort Fisher, marine animals, Kure Beach/ N Carolina Aquarium-Roanoke Island, marine animals, Manteo/ N Carolina Museum of Natural Sciences, na-tive animals, Raleigh/ Greenfield Park and Gardens, Wilmington/ Orton Plantation Gardens, Wil-mington/ Tote Em in Zoo, Wil-mington/ Nature Science Center, physical, natural science, par-ticipatory exhibits, Winston-

Salem/Tanglewood, recreation park, Winston-Salem.

History: Cherokee Indian Cyclorama Wax Museum, Cherokee/ Museum of the Cherokee Indian, Cherokee/ Moores Creek National Battlefield, Revolutionary battlefield, near Currie/ Guilford Courthouse National Military Park, Revolutionary War battlefield, Greensboro/ Caswell-Neuse State Historic Site, museum, Confederate naval vessel, Kinston/ Fort Fisher State Historic Site, Confederate battlefield, Kure Beach/ Elizabeth II State Historic Site, reproduction of 400 yr old vessel, Manteo/ Bentonville Battleground State Historic Site, Civil War battlefield, Newton Grove.

Auto, Train, Boat: North Carolina Maritime Museum, Beaufort/ Rear View Mirror Classic Car Museum, Nags Head/ U.S.S. N Carolina Battleship Memorial, Wilmington/ Wilmington Railroad Museum, Wilmington.

Art: Asheville Art Museum, 20th century American, Civic Center, Asheville/ Duke University Museum of Art, medieval, Renaissance, Greek, Roman, Durham/ Greenville Museum of Art, 20th century American, Greenville/ Southeastern Center for Contemporary Art, SE artists, Winston-Salem.

Historic Houses: Thomas Wolfe Memorial State Historic Site, Asheville/ Zebulon B Vance Birthplace State Historic Site, Asheville/ Beaufort Restoration Area, Beaufort/ Somerset Place State Historic Site, Creswell/ Bennett Place State Historic Site, Durham/ Carl Sandburg National Historic Site, Flat Rock/ Charles B Aycock Birthplace State Historic Site, Goldsboro/ Newbold White House, Hertford/ High Point Museum, High Point/ Liberty Hall, Kenansville/ The Carson House, Marion/ James K Polk Memorial State Historic Site, Pineville/ Chinqua-Penn Plantation House, Reidsville/ Vance House, Statesville/ Blount-Bridgers House, Tarboro/ The Burgwin-Wright House and Garden, Wilmington/ Hope Plantation, Windsor/ Reynolds House and Gardens, Winston-Salem/ Airlie, Wrightsville Beach.

Restored communities: Historic Bath Site, Bath/ Duke Homestead State Historic Site, Durham/ Historic Edenton, Edenton/ Fort Raleigh National Historic Site/ Historic Halifax State Historic Site, Halifax/ Town Creek Indian Mound State Historic Site, precolonial buildings, Mount Gilead/ New Bern Historic Buildings, tour map, also Tyron Palace, New Bern/ Historic Bethabara Park, 1st Moravian settlement in state, Winston-Salem/ Old Salem, Winston-Salem.

Mountain Crafts: Biltmore Industries & Museum, Asheville/ Maco Crafts, Franklin.

Minerals: Colburn Mineral Museum, Civic Center, Asheville/ Reed Gold Mine State Historic Site, Concord/ Cowee Ruby Mines,

Franklin/ Franklin Gem & Mineral Museum, Franklin.
Religious: Field of the Woods, 23 devotional areas, Murphy/ Home Moravian Church, Winston-Salem.
Entertainment: Children's Museum, Rocky Mount/ Captain J N Maffitt River Cruises, Wilmington.
Commercial: North Carolina Mutual Life Insurance Co Industrial Tour, Durham/ Cannon Village Visitor Center, Kannapolis/ Potter's Museum, Seagrove/ CP & L Brunswick Energy Visitors Center, Southport/ Duplin Wine Cellars, Warsaw/ Stroh Brewery Co., Winston-Salem.
Sports: PGA World Golf Hall of Fame, Pinehurst.

North Dakota

Fame: *The Peace Garden State, the Roughrider State.*
You must *visit Medora to see the badlands and Theodore Roosevelt National Park or visit the Peace Garden.*

•Best Choices:

International Peace Garden
Rt 1, Box 116, Dunseth 58329. (701)263-4390.

12 mi N of Dunseth. 2,300 acres of gardens dedicated to international peace, set in the beautiful Turtle Mountains on the border between Manitoba and N Dakota. Formal gardens, arboretum, floral clock, hiking paths, arts and crafts. **$4/car 5/15-9/15.** Open year around.

Theodore Roosevelt National Park
Medora 58645. (701)623-4466.

Comprised of a south unit, near Medora, and a north unit, near Watford City. 70,400 acre park in the bad lands of N Dakota, with abundant wild life including buffalo, elk, deer, coyote, prairie dog and wild turkey. Take a scenic drive, hike, bike or trail ride. Erosion has carved the land into spectacular formations with many beautiful colors. **$3/car.** Open year around but best viewing is May - Oct.

Bonanzaville, U.S.A.
Box 719, West Fargo 58078. (701)282-2822.

1/2 mi E of I-94, Exit 85. Pioneer village and museum with 47 buildings representative of the pioneer experience. Museum houses one of the most complete Indian collections in the midwest. **$3/adult; $1/student 6-16.** 5/30-10/30, Mon-Fri, 9-5, Sat-Sun, 1-5.

•Good Choices:

Natural Scenery: Tewaukon National Wildlife Refuge, birds, mammals, Cayuga/ Sully's Hill National Game Preserve, bison, deer, elk, Devils Lake/ Lake Ilo National Wildlife Refuge, waterfowl, Dunn Center/ Audubon National Wildlife Refuge, waterfowl, upland game birds, Garrison/ Arrowwood National Wildlife Refuge, deer, waterfowl, upland game birds, Jamestown/ Des Lacs National Wildlife Refuge, deer, coyotes, waterfowl, upland game birds, Kenmare/ Loswood National Wildlife Refuge, prairie wetlands, grouse, Kenmare/ J Clark Salyer National Wildlife Refuge, waterfowl, upland game birds, Minot/ Upper Souris National Wildlife Refuge, waterfowl, shorebirds, Minot/ Long Lake National Wildlife Refuge, water, shore birds, Moffit.

Nature and Man: Dakota Zoo, Bismarck/ Gunlogson Arboretum, museum, nature trail, wildlife, Cavalier/ Roosevelt Park and Zoo, Minot.

Historical and Cultural: Ft Abercrombie State Historic Site, reconstructed pioneer fort, Abercrombie/ N Dakota Heritage Center, state history, Bismarck/ State Capitol, guided tours, Bismarck/ Ft Totten Historic Site, original Indian war fort, museum, Devils Lake/ Myra Museum and Campbell House, pioneer artifacts, restored buildings, Grand Forks/ N Dakota Museum of Art, U of ND Memorial Union, Grand Forks/ Frontier Village, Jamestown/ Pioneer Village, Kenmare/ Ft Abraham Lincoln State Park, Mandan lodges, restored infantry post, Mandan/ Great Plains Museum, history of plains, Mandan/ Pioneer Village and Museum, historic structures, museum, Minot/ Geographical Center Pioneer Village, restored pioneer buildings, antique farm implements, Rugby/ Ft Union Trading Post, restored fur trading center, Williston.

Commercial: Bulova Watch Co, Rolla/ Coal Creek Electrical Generating Station Tours, Wahpeton.

Seasonal Events and Festivals: United Tribes International Pow Wow (Thurs-Sun after Labor Day), Bismark.

Ohio

Fame: *Theme parks; festivals, largest of which is the Ohio State Fair.*
You must *visit an Amish community in Holmes and surrounding counties; visit Lake Erie and islands; visit the Ohio State Fair, at Columbus, in August.*

Cincinnati

Fame: *Cincinnati Reds, Floating Restaurants, Kings Island, Cincinnati Zoo.*
You must: *try Cincinnati Chili, see a white Bengal tiger at the zoo.*

•Best Choices:

Cincinnati Zoo
3400 Vine St, 45220. (513)281-4700.

Rated the second best in the country and a pioneer in natural habitats. white Bengal tigers, lowland gorillas, insectarium and the children's zoo are among the top displays. **$3.75/adult; $1.50/sr citizen, child under 12.** Summer, daily, 9-6. Rest of yr, daily, 9-5.

Cincinnati Arts Museum
Eden Park, 45202. (513)721-5204.

I-71, Exit 2 to Eden Park. One of the top general art museums in the nation and one of the oldest art museums that survey the visual arts of almost all major civilizations over the past 5,000 yrs.

$2/adult; $1.50/college student; $1/sr citizen, student 12-18; $.50/child 3-11. Tues-Sat, 10-5; Sun, 1-5.

•Good Choices:

Natural Scenery: Mount Airy Forest, flowers, dwarf evergreens.
Nature and Man: Cincinnati Museum of Natural History and Planetarium/ Krohn Conservatory, includes tropical flowers, plants, Eden Park.
Historical and Cultural: Cincinnati Fire Museum/ John Hauck House/ Taft Art Museum, Old Masters, Renaissance dishes/ Warren County Historical Society Museum, SW Ohio, prehistoric - 19th century/ Basilica of the Assumption, replica of Notre Dame.
Entertainment: Carew Tower Observatory, Cincinnati's tallest bldg.
Commercial: Goodwill Industries Tour/ Meier's Wine Cellars/ Oldenberg Brewery Tour.

Sports: Cincinnati Reds/ College Football Hall of Fame, Kings Mills/ Riverfront Stadium tours/ River Downs Racetrack.
Seasonal Events and Festivals: Appalachian Festival, May/ A Taste of Cincinnati, May/ Octoberfest Zinzinnati, Sept/ Riverfest, Sept/ International Folk Festival, Nov/ Winterfest, Nov/ International Festival of Lights, Nov.

Statewide Attractions

•Best Choices:

Roscoe Village
331 Hill St, Coshocton 43812. (614)622-9310.

On SR 16, 83 at jct US 36. Restored 1830s Ohio & Erie Canal town with homes and businesses. Five exhibit bldgs, flower gardens, seasonal horse-drawn trolley, canal boat rides. Craft demonstrations, displays of daily life on canal. **Village: free. Exhibit tour: $4.50/adult; $2.25/student 8-18.** Summer, daily, 10-6; Spring, Fall, 11-5.

U.S. Air Force Museum
Springfield St, Wright-Patterson Air Force Base 45433-6518, Dayton. (513)255-3284.

SR 4 to Harshman Rd, S to Springfield St, lt to entrance. Said to be the world's largest and oldest military aviation museum. About 200 aircraft and missiles, plus many family oriented and historical aeronautical displays. **Free.** Mon-Fri, 9-5, Sat-Sun, 10-6. Closed 12/25.

Pro Football Hall of Fame
2121 George Halas Dr NW, Canton 44708. (216)456-8207.

Exhibition area, action movies, theatre, library presents pro football history, teams and individual stars. **$4/adult; $2/sr citizen, $1.50/5-13.** Memorial Day - Labor Day, 9-8. Rest of yr, 9-5.

Neil Armstrong Space Museum
Bellefontaine St and I-75, Wapakoneta 45895. (419)738-8811.

I-75 business, Exit 111. Balloon flights and early Wright Bros airplanes to Earth Orbiter and Gemini VIII. An infinity rm and astrotheatre give visitors the feeling of traveling through space. **$2/adult; $1.50/sr citizen; $1/6-12.** 3/1-11/30: Mon-Sat, 9:30-5; Sun, holidays, noon-5. Closed Thanksgiving.

Warthers
331 Karl Av, Dover 44622. (216)343-7513.

1/4 mi E of I-77 on SR 211. Intricately handcarved working steam engines in ivory, ebony and walnut, tracing the history of steam power. Also includes reproduction of Dover steel mill, plier tree, railway equipment, Swiss gardens, working knife shop, button collection. **$3.50/adult; $2/student 6-17.** Daily, 9-5. Closed Thanksgiving, 12/25, 1/1, Easter.

•Good Choices:

Natural Scenery: Paint Valley Skyline Drives, spectacular scenery, Bainbridge/ Seven Caves, Bainbridge/ Zane Caverns, Bellefontaine/ Aullwood Audubon Center, wildlife refuge, educational farm, Dayton/ Hocking Hill State Park, caves, cliffs, birds, forest, Logan/ Bruker Nature Center, swamp, pine forest, prairie, Troy/ Ohio Caverns, West Liberty/ Wilderness Center, Inc, forest, prairie, marshes, Wilmot.

Nature and Man: Lake Erie Science & Nature Center, live animals, planetarium, programs, Bay Village/ City of Cleveland Greenhouse, outdoor gardens, showhouse, Rockefeller Park, Cleveland/ Cleveland Metroparks Zoo, Cleveland/ Columbus Zoo, Columbus/ Franklin Park Conservatory, glass enclosed exotic plants, Columbus/ Cox Arboretum, botanical collections, Dayton/ Dayton Museum of Natural History, live animals, planetarium, Dayton/ Kingwood Center, woodlands, greenhouses, gardens, Mansfield/ Malabar Farm State

Park, conservation demonstration farm, Mansfield/ Holden Arboretum, gardens, fields, plants, woods, Mentor/ Dawes Arboretum, forest, plants, Newark/ Bob Evans Farms, museum, log buildings, wild & domestic animals, recreation, Rio Grande/ Crosby Gardens, flowers, greenhouse, Toledo/ Toledo Zoo, Toledo/ Agricultural Research and Development Center, arboretum, gardens, etc, Wooster/ Mill Creek Park, scenic natural areas, golf course, playground, ballfield, gardens, Youngstown.

Science and Technology: Cleveland Health Education Museum, health and the human body, Cleveland.

Historical: McKinley Museum of Historical Science, history, science, planetarium, Canton/ Hayes Presidential Center, mansion, estate, private & public papers of Pres Rutherford B. Hayes, Fremont/ Old Water Mill, grinds flour, Garrettsville/ Buckeye Furnace, historic iron ore furnace, Jackson/ Slate Run Living Historical Farm, historic working farm, Lithopolis/ Ohio River Museum and W P Snyder Towboat, steam boat era memorabilia, steam powered tow boat, Marietta/ Great Lakes Historical Society Museum, history of Great Lakes navigation, Vermilion/ National Road-Zane Grey Museum, history of 1st national highway, Zane Grey's belongings, Zanesville.

Historic Houses: Perkins Mansion, Akron/ Stan Hywet Hall and Gardens, Akron/ Adena, Chillicothe/ J E Reeves Home and Museum, Dover/ Chateau Laroche, Loveland/ President Harding Home and Museum, Marion/ Lawnfield, home of President Garfield, Mentor/ Wildwood Manor House, Toledo.

Special Interest Museums: The Cambridge Glass Museum, Cambridge/ Degenhart Paperweight and Glass Museum, Cambridge/ Western Reserve Historical Society, auto, aviation and historical Museums, Cleveland/ Conneaut Historical Railroad Museum, Conneaut/ Carillon Historical Transportation Park, Dayton/ Museum of Ceramics, East Liverpool.

Villages: Sauder Farm and Craft Village, Archbold/ Historic Lyme Village, Bellevue/ Amish Heritage Village Tour, Berlin/ Ohio Village, Columbus/ Auglaize Village, Defiance/ Walcott House Museum Complex, Maumee/ Schoenbrunn Village State Memorial, New Philadelphia/ Indian Museum of Lake County, Painesville/ Piqua Historical Area, Piqua/ Sharon Woods Village, Sharonville/ Zoar Village, Zoar.

Art: Akron Art Museum, European, American art, 19th century to present, Akron/ Cleveland Museum of Art, European Masters, Oriental art, Cleveland/ Columbus Museum of Art, European, American, Oriental art, 16th - 20th century, Columbus/ Dayton Art Institute, European, Oriental, pre-Columbian art, Dayton/ Toledo Museum of Art, ancient Egypt - 20th century, Old Masters, Toledo.

Rides: Trolley Tours of Marietta, Marietta/ Valley Gem Steamboat, Marietta/ Hocking Valley Scenic Railway, Nelsonville/ Put-in-Bay Tour Train, Put-in-Bay/ Toledo River Cruise, Toledo/ Mystic Belle-Rick Sterling Boat Charters, Vermilion/ Lorena Sternwheeler, Zanesville.

Commercial: Goodwill Industries Tour, Akron/ Goodyear World of Rubber, Akron/ Quaker Square, Akron/ D Picking & Co. Tour, copper products, Bucyrus/ Pickwick Standardbred Horse Farms, Bucyrus/ Boyd's Crystal Art Glass Co. Factory Tour, Cambridge/ Mosser Glass, Inc. Tour, Cambridge/ Bucyrus Historic German Village, Columbus/ Anheuser-Busch Brewery Tour, Columbus/ Hall China Co Tour, East Liverpool/ Louis Jindra Winery, Jackson/ Chalet Debonne Vineyards, Madison/ Lonz Winery, Middle Bass Island/ Heini's Cheese Place, Millersburg/ Valley Vineyards, Morrow/ Endres Floral Co Tours, New Philadelphia/ Hoover Historical Center, North Canton/ Mon Ami Wine Co. Tour, Port Clinton/ Heineman Winery Tour and Crystal Cave, Put-in-Bay/ Robinson-Ransbottom Pottery Co. Tour, Roseville/ Sickles Cut Glass Co. Tour, St. Clairsville/ Firelands Winery Tour, Sandusky/ Maxwell Crystal Demonstrations, Tiffin/ General Motors Assembly Division Tour, Warren/ Alpine-Alpa Cheese Factory Tour, Wilmot.

Sports: Sioto Downs Harness Racetrack, Columbus/ Beulah Park Thoroughbred Racing, Grove City/ College Football Hall of Fame, Kings Mills/ Ohio Baseball Hall of Fame, Maumee/ Raceway Park

Pari-Mutual Harness Racing, Toledo.
Seasonal Events and Festivals: Air Force Festival of Flight, Sept, Dayton/ Erie County Vineyard Days, Sept, Erie County/ Pumpkin Show, Oct, Circleville.

Oklahoma

Fame: *Native American Indians, oil wells.* **You must** *visit an Indian pow wow. There are over 200 pow wows a year in Oklahoma.*

Statewide Attractions

•Best Choices:

Indian City USA
Box 695, Adadarko 73005. (405)247-5661.

2 1/2 mi SE of Anadarko on SR 8. A huge outdoor museum featuring authentic villages, pictures the daily lives, religions and cultures of seven Indian tribes. Indoor exhibits of clothing, photos and artifacts. **$5/adult; $4/child 6-11.** Summer, daily, 9-6. Winter, daily, 9-5. Closed Thanksgiving, 12/25, 1/1.

National Cowboy Hall of Fame and Western Heritage Center
1700 NE 63rd St, Oklahoma City 73111. (405)478-2250.

A national memorial to the people who pioneered the west, exhibits western lore from 17 western states. Includes paintings and sculpture by Russell, Remington, Moran and Fraiser, the National Rodeo and Western Performers Hall of Fame, John Wayne's Kachina doll collection and re-created western town. **$4/adult; $1.50/child 6-12.** Memorial Day - Labor Day, daily, 8:30-6. Rest of yr, daily, 8:30-5. Closed Thanksgiving, 12/25, 1/1.

Gilcrease Institute of American History and Art
1400 Gilcrease Museum Rd, Tulsa 74127. (918)582-3122.

Collection of art, rare books, documents and artifacts explains the development of the American West from the pre-Columbian era through the 19th Century. The art collection contains works by Remington, Russell, Audubon, Catlin, Moran and many others. **Free.**

Mon-Sat, 9-5, Sun, 1-5. Closed
12/25.

Kilpatrick Center

2100 NE 52nd St, Oklahoma City
73111. (405)427-5461.

NE 52nd and Martin Luther King
Av. A cultural, educational and
recreational facility containing two
museums and six galleries. In-
cluded are Center of the American
Indian, International Photography
Hall of Fame and Museum,
Kirkpatrick Planetarium, Ok-
lahoma Air Space Museum, Om-
niplex Science Museum and
Sanamu African Gallery. **Adult ad-
missions in order named above:
Free, $1, $1.50, $2.50, $2.50,
Free.** Mon-Sat, 10-5; Sun 12-5.
Closed Thanksgiving, 12/25.

Woolarock Ranch and Museum

Rt 3, Bartlesville 74003. (918)336-
0307.

---

14 mi SW of Bartlesville on SR
123. A 3,500 acre wildlife refuge
where a variety of wild animals
can be seen. The museum displays
art and artifacts tracing the development of man in Southwestern U.S.
$2/adult; Free/child under 16.
Tues-Sun, 10-5. Closed Mon, 7/4,
Thanksgiving, 12/25, 1/1.

•Good Choices:

Natural Scenery: Alabaster
Caverns, natural gypsum cave,
Alva/ Salt Plains National Wildlife
Refuge, salt flats, wildlife, nature
walk, Cherokee/ Tenkiller State
Park, Gore/ Wichita Mountains
Wildlife Refuge, Lawton/ Chick-
asaw National Recreation Area,
woods, streams, buffalo, Sulpher/
Talimena Scenic Drive, between
Mena, AR and Talihina, OK/ Rob-
bers Cave State Park, Wilburton.
Nature and Man: Forest Heritage
Center, trees, forest industry ar-
tifacts, trails, Broken Bow/
Alabaster Caverns State Park, gyp-
sum cave, Freedom/ Oklahoma
City Zoo, Oklahoma City/ Tulsa
Zoological Park, Tulsa.
History: Will Rogers Memorial,
Rogers memorabilia, dioramas,
movies, Claremore/ Tom Mix
Museum, Mix memorabilia,
Dewey/ Oklahoma Territorial
Museum, Oklahoma 1890-1907,
Guthrie/ Oklahoma State Museum
and Historical Society, Oklahoma
history, Oklahoma City/ State
Capitol, Oklahoma City/ Pawnee
Bill Ranch, original ranch house,
buildings, buffalo, Pawhuska.
Indian Culture: Southern Plains
Indian Museum and Crafts Center,
history, culture of S Plains Indian,
Anadarko/ Cherokee Courthouse,
restored Cherokee Nation court-
house, councilhouse, Gore/ Spiro
Mounds Archeological State Park,
Indian mounds, interpretive center,
Spiro/ Chickasaw Council House
and Museum, restored 1st council-
house, Tishomingo.
Historic Homes: Frank Phillips
Home, Bartlesville/ Peter Conser
Home, Heavener/ Norman and

Cleveland County Historical Museum, house of early 1900s, Norman/ Oklahoma Heritage Center, Oklahoma City/ Overholser Mansion, Oklahoma City/ Marland Mansion and Estate, Ponca City.

Historic Villages & Military Posts: Old Town Museum Complex, early western town, Elk City/ Ft Gibson Military Park, reconstructed buildings, Ft Gibson/ Har-Ber Village, reconstructed 19th century village, Grove/ Fort Sill Military Reservation and National Historic Landmark, restored Old Post buildings, Lawton/ Cherokee Heritage Center, 17th century living history Cherokee village, Tahlequah.

Special Interest Museums: J M Davis Gun Museum, guns, saddles, musical instruments, Claremore/ Oklahoma Firefighters' Museum, Oklahoma City.

Art: Oklahoma Art Center, Southwestern, American, international art, Oklahoma City/ Oklahoma Museum of Art, 15th to 20th century, garden, Oklahoma City/ Mabee-Gerrar Museum and Art Gallery, 18th century to present, Shawnee/ Philbrook Art Center, 18th & 19th century, American Indian art, Tulsa.

Science and Technology: Enterprise Square, computers, audiovisual show, game playing explain economics, Oklahoma City.

Commercial: Phillips Petroleum Co Exhibit Hall, Barlesville/ Frankoma Pottery Plant Tour, Sapulpa/ Shawnee Milling Co. Tour, Shawnee.

Sports: National Softball Hall of Fame, Oklahoma City.

Seasonal Events and Festivals: International Finals Rodeo, Jan, Tulsa/ Azalea Festival, Apr, Muskogee/ Medieval Fair, Apr, Norman/ Easter Pageant, Easter Eve, Lawton/ Festival of the Arts, Oklahoma City/ Mayfest, May, Tulsa/ Tulsa Pow Wow, July, Tulsa/ State Fair of Oklahoma, Oct, Oklahoma City.

Oregon

Fame: *Vineyards, orchards, gardens, forests, mountains, ocean.*
You must *visit Crater Lake National Park.*

Statewide Attractions

•Best Choices:

Crater Lake National Park
Box 7, Crater Lake 97604. (503)594-2211.

SR 62, N of Klamath Falls. Famous for its natural beauty, lava cliffs surround deep, brilliantly blue Crater Lake, the deepest in the U.S. Among points of interest are mountain trails, high peaks, volcanic craters, forested slopes, 570 species of plants, wildflowers, wild animals and scenic drives. **$2/car.**

Oregon Caves National Monument
19000 Caves Hwy, Cave Junction 97523. (503)592-3400.

SR 46, 20 mi E of Cave Junction. The cave, deep in the heart of Mount Elijah, has many chambers and many features. The park itself covers 480 acres of mountain forest with many trails. The 75 min cave tour is strenuous. **$4.75/adult; $2.50/child 6-11.** Daily, Summer, 8-7; Spring, Fall, 9-5; Winter, 10:30-3:30.

Bonneville Lock and Dam
Bonneville 97014. (503)374-8820.

The dam has created a deep lake that extends 45 miles to The Dalles. Off I-84, Exit 40, is the Bradford Island Visitor Center, with 5 floors of displays, including a theater and an underwater viewing rm where fish can be seen. Best viewing is between Mar and Nov. **Free.** Memorial Day-7/4, daily, 8-6; 7/5-Labor Day, 8-8; rest of yr, 9-5. Closed Thanksgiving, 12/25, 1/1.

Oregon Art Institute
1219 SW Park, Portland 97205. (503)226-2811.

Park at Jefferson. European paintings and sculpture from the Renaissance to the present, 19th and 20th century American pieces, artwork by Indians of the Pacific NW, Asian, pre-Columbian, West African art and changing contemporary art exhibits. **$2.50/adult; $1.50/sr citizen, student; free/under 12.** Tues-Thurs, 11-7; Fri, 11-9:30; Sat-Sun, noon-5.

Washington Park
W Burnside, Portland 97210. (503)223-1321.

---

145 acres includes International Rose Test Garden, Shakespeare Garden, Japanese Gardens and a beautiful view of Portland. **$2.50/adult; $1.25/sr citizen, student.** 4/15-9/15, Daily, 10-6; 9/16-4/14, Daily, 10-4.

•Good Choices:

Natural Scenery: Cascade Lakes Highway, forest, lakes, Bend/ Hells Canyon National Recreation Area, rugged canyon, forest, river/ John Day Fossil Beds National Monument, colored formations, wildlife, hiking, at Dayville, Mitchell or Clarno/ Lakeview Nature Trail, plants, wildlife, Lakeview/ The Cove Palisades State Park, 3 canyons, Madras/ Owyhee Lake, lake, spectacular cliffs, Ontario/ John Inskeep Environmental Learning Center, wildlife, bird exhibit, Oregon City/ Columbia River Highway, gorge, cliffs, waterfalls, Portland/ Umpqua Lighthouse State Park, shoreline, dunes, Reedsport.

Wildlife Refuges: Malheur National Wildlife Refuge, Burns/ Upper Klamath National Wildlife Refuge, Chiloquin/ National Wildlife Refuge, Hermiston/ Lower Klamath National Wildlife Refuge, Klamath Falls/ Audubon Society of Portland, wildlife sanctuary, Portland/ Mountain National Antelope Refuge, Lakeview/ Umatilla National Wildlife Refuge, Umatilla.

Forests: Deschutes National Forest, mountains, forest, cave/ Mount Hood and Mount Hood National Forest, mountain, forest/ Ochoco National Forest, forest, rocks, wildlife/ Rogue River National Forest, scenery, hiking/ Siskiyou National Forest, wilderness, fishing, hiking/ Siuslaw National Forest, shoreline, crabbing, fishing/ Umatilla National Forest, Blue Mountains, fishing/ Umpqua National Forest, wildlife, forest/ Wallowa-Whitman National Forest, mountains, rivers, trails/ Willamette National Forest, mountains, wilderness/ Winema National Forest, mountains to basin.

Nature and Man: Shore Acres State Park, estate with botanical parks, Charleston/ Crystal Hoyt Arboretum, coniferous, deciduous trees, Portland/ World Forestry Center, forestry recreation & education, Portland/ Petersen's Rock Gardens, many rock structures, Redmond/ Palmerton Arboretum, plants, shrubs, trees, Rogue River.

Marine plants, animals: Aquarium, Depoe Bay/ Sea Lion Caves, observe sea lions yr around, Florence/ Undersea Gardens, underwater viewing of marine plants, animals, Newport/ Seaside Aquarium, native marine life, Seaside/ The Dalles Dam, tours, train ride, fish ladder, The Dalles/ McNary Lock and Dam, locks, fish ladder, viewing room, Umatilla.

Animals: West Coast Game Park, animal petting parks, Bandon/ Oregon High Desert Museum, otter feedings, birds-of-prey, Western art, films, Bend/ Woodland Wildlife Park, deer, lions, cougars, bears, Cave Junction/ Washington Park Zoo, Portland/ Western Deer Park and Arboretum, wildlife, birds, trees, Sheridan.

Flowers: Springs Rhododendron Gardens, best in Apr-May, Portland/ Leach Botanical Park, estate, flowers, plants, Portland/ Sunken Rose Garden, Portland/ Hendricks Park Rhododendron Garden, Eugene.

Science and Technology: Willamette Science and Technology Center, participatory biology, computer, physics, planetarium, Eugene/ Oregon Museum of Science and Industry, aviation, space, industrial, animals, Portland/ Tera One, energy conservation, Portland/ Trojan Visitors Nuclear Energy Information Center, nuclear, alternative energy, Rainier.

Historic: Columbia River Maritime Museum, NW coast maritime history, lightship Columbia, Astoria/ Fort Clatsop National Memorial, Lewis & Clark expedition, Astoria/ Cascade Locks and Marine Park, historic locks, marina, museum, Cascade Locks/ Dolly Wares Doll Museum, Florence/ Indian Forest, recreation of N American Indian dwellings, deer, buffalo, Florence/ Children's Museum, artifacts of Indians and settlers, Jacksonville/ Champoeg State Park, Oregon history, house, cabin, Newberg/ Portland Police Historical Museum, Portland/ Mission Mill Village, historic buildings, woolen mill, Salem.

Historic Houses: Captain Flavel House, Astoria/ Caples House, Columbia City/ Beekman House, Jacksonville/ John McLoughlin House National Historic Site, Oregon City/ Bybee Howell Houe, Portland/ John Palmer House, Portland/ Pittock Mansion, Portland/ Deepwood Estate, Salem.

Art: Lawrence Gallery, NW artists, Gleneden Beach/ Favell Museum of Western Art and Indian Artifacts, Klamath Falls.

Entertainment: Sumpter Valley Railroad, steam train ride, Baker/ Sand Dunes Frontier, dune buggy rides, miniature golf, Florence/ Oregon Vortex, odd magnetic forces, Gold Hills/ Ripley's Believe It or Not Museum, Newport/ Children's Museum, Portland/ Enchanted Forest, storybook characters, haunted house, mining town, Salem/ Wonder Works Children's Museum, The Dalles.

Commercial: Hidden Springs Winery Tour, Amity/ Coquille Valley Dairy Cooperative, Bandon/ Strahm's Lilies, Inc Tour, Brookings/ U S Coast Guard Chetco River Station Tour, Brookings/ House of Myrtlewood Factory Tour, Coos Bay/ Tualatin Vineyards Tour, Forest Grove/ Hood River Vineyards Tours, Hood River/ Luhr Jensen & Sons Fishing Lures Tours, Hood River/ Valley View Vineyard Tours, Jacksonville/

Weyerhaeuser Co Hardboard Factory Tour, Klamath Falls/ Nehalem Bay Wine Co Tour, Nehalem/ Harris Pine Mills Tour, Pendleton/ Pendleton Woolen Mills Tour, Pendleton/ Pendleton Woolen Mills Tour, Portland/ Bjelland Vineyards Tours, Roseburg/ Hillcrest Vineyard Tours, Roseburg/ Honeywood Winery, Salem/ Tillamook Cheese Factory, Tillamook/ Henry Winery, Umpqua. **Seasonal Events and Festivals:** Rose Festival, June, Portland/ Pendleton Round-Up, Sept, Pendleton.

Pennsylvania

Fame: *The Keystone State: Second of the original 13 colonies, with a strong political tradition but also a keystone of culture, farming and industry.*

You must: *visit Pennsylvania Dutch country, explore the state's covered bridges, sample the local wine or enjoy the history of our country with a visit to Independence National Park.*

Philadelphia

Fame: *Home of the Liberty Bell and Independence Hall, where the Declaration of Independence and the Constitution were developed.*
You must: *visit Independence National Historical Park.*

•Best Choices:

Independence National Historical Park
Visitor Center, 3rd & Chestnut St, 19106. (215)597-8974.

This park has been dubbed "America's most historic square mile" because it contains 26 sites that are historically significant to anyone in the U.S. Included are Jacob Graff House, where Thomas Jefferson drafted the Declaration of Independence, Independence Hall and Liberty Bell Pavilion. Start at the visitor center to get a map, walking tour guide and information on the sites and current activities. **Free.** Daily, 9-5.

Franklin Institute Science Museum
20th St & Ben Franklin Pkwy, 19103. (215)448-1200.

Four floors of participatory exhibits. World's largest public observatory, Boeing 707, giant walk-through heart, computers, demonstrations, planetarium. **$4.50/adult; $3.50/child 4-12; $3/sr citizen.** Mon-Sat, 10-5; Sun, noon-5.

Fairmount Park
Visitor Center, 16th and JFK Blvd. (215)686-2176.

Access at any point along E River Dr. World's largest municipally owned park,with more than 8,900 acres. Contains 2 outdoor perform-ing arts centers; Boathouse Row, Victorian era boathouses; Japanese Tea House; Colonial era mansions open for tours; picnic and sports recreation areas. One hundred miles of jogging, bike and bridal paths, sailboat, canoe, bike rental. A trolley leaves the visitor center to tour the grounds with on and off privileges. **$3/adult; $2/student 13-18; $1/sr citizen.** Tours Wed-Sun, 10-4.

Philadelphia Museum of Art
26th St & Ben Franklin Pkwy, 19130. (215)763-8100.

In Fairmont Park. The third largest art museum in the U.S. with more than 500,000 works on display. Paintings and sculpture from all schools, period rooms, oriental art, decorative arts, permanent collec-tion of arms and armor. **$4/adult; $2/sr citizen, student under 18.** Wed-Sun, 10-5. Closed holidays.

Academy of Natural Sciences
19th St and Ben Franklin Pkwy, 19103. (215)299-1000.

Features "Discovering Dinosaurs," a new permanent exhibit featuring more than a dozen dinosaur specimens, interactive displays and activities; "Outside In," a child's nature center; gems and minerals, wildlife dioramas, live animal programs. **$4.50/adult; $4/sr citizen, military; $2.50/child 3-12.** Mon-Fri, 10-4, Sat, Sun, holidays, 10-5. Closed Thanksgiv-ing, 12/25, 1/1.

•Good Choices:

Natural Scenery: Schuylkill Val-ley Nature Center, trails, nature museum/ Tinicum National En-vironmental Center, freshwater tidal wetland, wildlife.

Nature and Man: Bartram's Gar-dens, former estate/ Morris Ar-boretum, trees, shrubs/ Pennsylvania Horticultural Society, 18th century garden/ Philadelphia Zoological Gardens.

Historic: American Swedish Museum, Swedish-American memorabilia/ Arch Street Meeting House, 1804 Quaker meeting house/ Atwater Kent Museum, his-tory of Philadelphia/ Christ Church, many historic people wor-shipped here/ City Hall Tours/ Elfreth's Alley, narrow street lined with restored houses, museum/ Fireman's Hall, historic fire fighting equipment/ Franklin Court, 5 houses, newspaper office, post office restored to Ben Franklin's era/ Free Library of Philadelphia, exhibits, concerts, films, lectures/ Germantown, museum of costumes, needlework, silver, textiles, toys/ Mummers Museum, history of Mummers/ National Archives Branch, exhibits, archives, tours/ Old Ft Mifflin, living history Rev War fort/ Penn's Landing, museum, historic ships, sculpture garden/ Tomb of the Unknown Revolutionary War Soldier/ U S Mint, tours/ University Museum, archaeology, anthropology.

Historic Houses: Betsy Ross House/ Edgar Allen Poe National Historic Site/ Glen Foerd Estate/ Powel House.

Art: Afro-American Historical and Cultural Museum, art, history of black culture/ Fabric Workshop, museum of 20th century textiles, demonstrations/ Institute of Contemporary Art/ Norman Rockwell Museum, includes all Post covers/ Pennsylvania Academy of the Fine Arts, American art, 1750 to present/ Philadelphia Art Alliance, paintings, sculpture, arts, crafts/ Rodin Museum, largest collection of Rodin outside Paris.

Entertainment: Centipede Candlelight Tours, nighttime tours of historic areas/ Please Touch Museum for Young Children/ South Street-Society Hill Night Life District.

Commercial: Christian Schmidt Brewing Co, tour/ Reading Terminal Farmers Market/ Head House Square Shopping Area.

Sports: Garden State Park Thoroughbred Racing/ Philadelphia Park Thoroughbred Racing.

Seasonal Events and Festivals: Mummers Parade, Jan 1/ Philadelphia Open House, May/ Devon Horse Show, Memorial Day Wknd/ Freedom Wk, late Jun-July 4/ Thanksgiving Day Parade/ Army-Navy Football Game, last Sat Nov or 1st Sat Dec.

Pittsburgh

Fame: *City framed by three rivers; former industrial city that has become a tech center, and was recently dubbed "most livable city" by a researcher.*

You must: *see the city from a riverboat, ride the Duquesne or Monongahela Inclines and visit the "nation's largest dinosaur collection" at the Carnegie.*

•Best Choices:

Inclines
Duquesne Incline, lower station W Carson St opposite the fountain, upper station 1220 Grandview Av, (412)381-1665; **Monongahela Incline,** station W Carson at Smithfield St, (412)231-5707.

Travel on a cable car from the South Side to the top of Mt Washington to get an excellent view of the rivers and the city. **One way fare: $.60-.75/adult; $.30-.35/child 6-12.** Mon-Sat, 5:30 am - 12:30 am; Sun, holidays, 8:45 am - midnight.

Phipps Conservatory
Schenley Park, 15213. (412)255-2375.

2 1/2 acres of gardens under glass. There are 13 houses with plants and flowers from around the world. **Flower Shows: $2/adult; $.75/child. Rest of yr: $1/adult; $.50/sr citizen, child.** Flower shows, Spring, Fall, Christmas: Daily, 9-5, 7-9. Summer, Winter: Daily, 9-5.

The Carnegie
4400 Forbes Av, 15213. (412)622-3313.

Cultural complex consisting of library, music hall, museum of natural history and museum of art, given to the city as a gift by Andrew Carnegie in 1895. Carnegie Library has over 4 million items and is one of the nation's best. Museum of Art has masterpieces dating from French Impressionists to contemporary works. Museum of Natural History is known for its huge dinosaur collection, minerals and gems, dioramas, fossils and North American Indian artifacts. **$3/adult; $1/student.** Tues-Thurs, Sat, 10-5; Fri, 10-9; Sun, 1-5. Closed holidays.

Hartwood Acres
215 Saxonburg Blvd, 15238. (412)767-9200.

Recreation of an English country estate, with Gothic Tudor mansion, formal gardens and stable complex. **$2.50/adult; $1.50/sr citizen; $1/child 1-14.** Varying hours, call for tour times. Closed Thanksgiving, 12/25, 1/1.

Buhl Science Center
Allegheny Square, 15212. (412)321-4302.

Participatory science and technology exhibits. Visit the Computer Learning Lab, Planetarium and Laserium. **$3.50/adult; $1.75/child 3-18.** Spring, Summer: Sun-Fri, 1-5; Sat, 10-5. Rest of yr, hrs vary, call for times.

•Good Choices:

Natural Scenery: Beechwood Farms Nature Reserve, fields, ponds, woods, bird observation rm. **Nature and Man:** Pittsburgh Aviary & Conservatory, birds, plants in natural settings/ Pittsburgh's New Zoo/ Point State Park, Allegheny, Monongahela, Ohio Rivers converge. **Historical and Cultural:** Cathedral of Learning, design by artists & architects from many nations, Univ of Pittsburgh/ Frick Art Museum, early Renaissance thru

18th century/ Ft Pitt Museum, Point State Park.
Entertainment: Pittsburgh Children's Museum.

Commercial: Pittsburgh Brewing Co Tour/ Station Square Shopping Area.

Statewide Attractions

•Best Choices:

Gettysburg National Military Park
Visitor Center, SR 134, Gettysburg 17325. (717)334-1124.

Scene of one of the most definitive battles of the Civil War and of Lincoln's Gettysburg address. Monuments and historic sites are scattered throughout the park. **$2/adult; $1.50/sr citizen; Free/under 15.** Summer, daily, 8-6; Rest of yr, daily, 8-5.

Valley Forge National Historic Park
Valley Forge 19481. (215)783-1000.

A 3,000 acre memorial to the brave soldiers of the Continental Army who camped here from December 19, 1977, to June 19, 1778. Many died but those who survived the cold, shortages and poor sanitation became a well trained force. Exhibits, film, memorials, self-guided tour. **Free.** Daily, 8:30-5. Closed 12/25.

Longwood Gardens
Box 501, Kennett Square 19348. (215)388-6741.

The former estate of Pierre S. du Pont, there are 350 acres of outdoor gardens, including lakes, woodland, formal gardens and fountains. There are also 3 1/2 acres of heated greenhouses and conservatory. **$5/adult; $1/student 6-14.** 4/1-10/31, daily, 9-6. 11/1-3/31, daily, 9-5.

Eisenhower National Historic Site
Gettysburg 17325. (717)334-1124.

Accessible by a shuttle bus from Gettysburg Military Park Visitor Center. The 230 acre Eisenhower farm has been carefully preserved. Much of the original house plus the president's paintings, gifts and memorabilia are on display. **$1.25/adult; $.70/student under 16.** Daily, 8:30-4:30.

Wheatland
1120 Marietta Av, Lancaster 17603. (717) 392-8721.

Restored Federal mansion home of President James Buchanan. Period rooms contain original furniture and objects. Costumed guides conduct tours. **$3.25/adult; $2.25/student; $1.25/under 12.** Apr-Nov,

Daily 10-4:15. Closed Thanksgiving.

Hersey's Chocolate World
US 322,422, next to Hershey Park, Hershey 17033. (717)534-4900.

This entire town was built by chocolate: Hershey's chocolate. Here a tour shows you the steps of chocolate production from cacao bean plantations in the tropics to a factory in Hershey. **Free.** 6/6-Labor Day, daily, 9-6:45; 3/30-6/5, Labor Day-12/31, 9-4:45; rest of yr, Mon-Sat, 9-4:45, Sun, noon-4:45

•Good Choices:

Natural Scenery: Allegheny National Forest, virgin forest, Allegheny Reservoir, marina/ Audubon Wildlife Sanctuary, birds, Audobon's paintings, Audubon/ Hawk Mountain Sanctuary, migrating birds-of-prey, Eckville/ Presque Isle State Park, wildlife refuge, conservation area, Erie/ Pennsylvania's Grand Canyon, get map from Chamber of Commerce at Wellsboro.
Nature and Man: Glenwood Municipal Park and Zoo, Erie/ Gettysburg Game Park, 30 species, Fairfield/ Gettysburg Land of Little Horses, miniature horses, tours, programs, Gettysburg/ Claws 'N Paws Wild Animal Park, 65 species, shows, Hamlin/ Lost River Caverns and the Gilman Museum, 5 chamber cave, natural history, minerals, Hellertown/ Hershey Gardens, 6 themed gardens, 4/1-11/15, Hershey/ Crystal Cave, cave, miniature golf, museum, nature trail, Kutztown/ Tyler Arboretum, woods, fields, gardens, rhododendrons, Lima/ Swiss Pines Gardens, Japanese gardens, Malvern/ Elmwood Park Zoo, Norristown/ Fallingwater, stone, concrete, waterfall, designed by Frank Lloyd Wright, Ohiopyle/ Walnut Acres, organic farm, cannery, bakery, mill, Penns Creek/ Indian Caverns, Spruce Creek/ Woodward Cave, Woodward.
Science and Technology: Susquehanna Energy Information Center and Riverlands, energy conservation explained through computers, displays, audiovisual, Berwick/ Erie Planetarium, Erie/ Museum of Scientific Discovery, hands-on science center, Harrisburg/ North Museum, planetarium, natural history, children's discovery rm, Lancaster/ Three Mile Island Park and Observation Center for Nuclear Station Site, exhibits, tours, Middletown/ Planetarium, Reading.
History: Eighteenth-Century Industrial Area, tannery, mill, colonial trades, demonstrations, Bethlehem/ Sun Inn, colonial tavern, Bethlehem/ Carlisle Barracks and Omar N Bradley Museum, military memorabilia, Carlisle/ Newlin Mill Park, gristmill, buildings, Concordville/ Cornwall Iron Furnace, buildings, shops, displays, Cornwall/ Allegheny Portage Railroad National

Historic Site, museum, 19th century railroad, crafts, Cresson/ Lee's Headquarters and Museum, Civil War history, Gettysburg/ National Civil War Wax Museum, Gettysburg/ State Capitol, tours, Harrisburg/ State Museum of Pennsylvania, history of PA, Harrisburg/ Hershey Museum of American Life, history of Hershey, Indian, assorted artifacts, Hershey/ Lancaster Walking Tour, tour of city with guide, Lancaster/ Lancaster Valley Museum, early PA rural life, Lancaster/ Compass Inn Museum, restored 19th century tavern, outbuildings, Laughlintown/ Stoy Museum, reconstructed 18th century businesses, Lebanon/ Packwood House Museum, 19th century inn, Lewisburg/ Washington Crossing Historic Park, site where Washington crossed the Delaware, historic buildings, wildflowers/ Greene County Historical Museum, Victorian mansion, store, artifacts, steam locomotive, Waynesburg.

Historic Battlefields, Forts: Fort Roberdeau, reconstructed Revolutionary War fort, Altoona/ Brandywine Battlefield Park, Revolutionary War battlefield, Chadds Ford/ Fort Necessity National Battlefield, replica of Revolutionary War fort, Fayetteville.

Historic Farms: Peter Wentz Farmstead, 1758 working farm, Center Point/ Pennsylvania Dutch Farm, typical Amish farm, Mount Pocono/ Quiet Valley Living Historical Farm, 1765 Pennsylvania German farm, tours, demos, Stroudsburg.

Historic Villages: Olde Economy Village, Ambridge/ Colony Village and Pocono Mineral Museum, Canadensis/ Ephrata Cloister, restoration of communal religious colony, 1732-1934, Ephrata/ Historic Fallsington, Fallsington/ Historic Hanna's Town, Greensburg/ Eckley Miners' Village, Hazleton/ Hopewell Furnace National Historic Site/ Curtin Village, Milesburg/ Amish Village, Strasburg.

Historic Homes: Baker Mansion, Altoona/ Daniel Boone Homestead, Baumstead/ Old Bedford Village, Bedford/ Columbus Chapel - Boal Mansion and Museum, Boalsburg/ Thomas Massey House, Broomall/ Harriton House, Bryn Mawr/ John Chad House, Chadds Ford/ Hibernia Mansion, Coatesville/ Wright's Ferry Mansion, Columbia/ Linden Hall, Dawson/ Fonthill Museum, Doylestown/ Pearl S Buck Estate, Dublin/ Hope Lodge, Fort Washington/ Graeme Park, Horsham/ Asa Packer Mansion, Jim Thorpe/ Harry Packer Mansion, Jim Thorpe/ Amish Farm and House, Lancaster/ Amish Homestead, Lancaster/ Hans Herr House, Lancaster/ Rock Ford, 18th century plantation, Lancaster/ Heisey Museum, Lock Haven/ Mount Hope Estate and Winery, Manheim/ Baldwin-Reynolds House, Meadville/ Grey Towers, Milford/ Pennsbury Manor, Morrisville/ Donegal Mills Plantation, Mount Joy/ Pottsgrove Mansion, Pottstown.

154

Specialized Museums: Railroaders Memorial Museum, Altoona/ Lehigh Valley Antique Fire Museum, Bethlehem/ Boyerstown Museum of Historic Vehicles, Boyertown/ Chambersburg Volunteer Fireman's Museum, Chambersburg/ Watch and Clock Museum of the National Watch and Clock Collectors, Inc, Columbia/ Pennsylvania Lumber Museum, Coudersport/ Firefighters Historical Museum, Erie/ Swigart Museum of Antique Automobiles, Huntingdon/ Lancaster Newspapers Newseum, Lancaster/ Pennsylvania Dutch Folk Culture Center, Lenhartsville/ Forbes Road Gun Museum, Ligonier/ Mary Merritt Doll Museum, Reading/ Drake Oil Well Museum, history of oil wells, Titusville.

Art: Allentown Art Museum, 15th - 18th century European, 18th - 20th century American, Allentown/ Brandywine River Museum, American paintings, Wyeth family, Chadds Ford/ Westmoreland Museum, American art, Greensburg/ Reading Art Gallery, art, science, arboretum, Reading/ Sordoni Art Gallery, 19th - 20th century American, Wilkes-Barre.

Entertainment: Clyde Peeling's Reptileland/ Pioneer Tunnel Coal Mine and Steam Lokie Coal Mine Tour, Ashland/ Koziar's Christmas Village, Bernville/ Canal Boat Rides, Easton/ The Conflict, Civil War multi-media documentary, Gettysburg/ Inclined Plane Ride, Johnstown/ East Broad Top Railroad Ride, Orbisonia/ Seldom Seen Valley Mine, St Boniface/ Strasburg Railroad Co Ride, Strasburg/ Trackless Train Ride, Uniontown/ Hiawatha Riverboat Tours, Williamsport.

Commercial: Stroh Brewery Tour, Fogelsville/ Phillips Lancaster County Swiss Cheese Co Observation Rm, Intercourse/ Buckingham Valley Vineyards and Winery Tour, Lahaska/ Farmers Market, Lancaster/ Lancaster County Winery, Ltd, Lancaster/ Bomberger's Bologna Tour, Lebanon/ Buffalo Valley Winery Tour, Lewisburg/ Candy Americana Museum and Demonstrations, Lititz/ Sturgis Pretzel House, Lititz/ Winery at Nissley Vineyards Tour, Marietta/ Bube's Brewery Tour, Mount Joy/ L E Smith Glass Co, Mount Pleasant/ Bucks County Vineyards and Winery, New Hope/ Palmyra Bologna Co Tour, Palmyra/ Straub Brewery Tour, St Marys/ Michter's Distillery Tour, Schaefferstown/ Rodney C Gott Museum and Harley-Davidson Assembly Plant Tour, York.

Rhode Island

Fame: *The smallest state in the union, the ocean state; only a 45 minute drive from one end to the other, it has more than 400 miles of shoreline.*
You must: *visit the Newport Mansions and feast at an authentic Rhode Island Clambake.*

Statewide Attractions

•Best Choices:

Newport Mansions
Preservation Society of Newport County, 118 Mill St, Newport 02840. (401)847-1000.

Hunter House, 54 Washington St, colonial mansion, built in 1748, National Historic Landmark. **$4.**
Kingscote, Bellevue Av, charming Victorian cottage built in 1839. **$4.**
Chateau-sur-Mer, Bellevue Av, example of lavish Victorian architecture, built in 1852. **$4.** *Marble House*, Bellevue Av, sumptuous Newport cottage, completed in 1892, for William K. Vanderbilt. **$4.50.** *The Breakers*, Ochre Point Av, built in 1895 for Cornelius Vanderbilt, resembles 16th century northern Italian Palace. **$4.50.** *The Elms*, Bellevue Av, built in 1901, modeled after the Chateau d'-Asnieres, near Paris. **$4.** *Rosecliff*, Bellevue Av, built in 1902, designed by Stanford White after the Grand Trianon at Versailles. **$4.** 5/2-11/2, daily, 10-5.

Slater Mill Historic Site
Roosevelt Av, Pawtucket 02860. (401)725-8638.

Birthplace of the American Industrial Revolution, the restored buildings include Old Slater Mill, 1793, Sylvanus Brown House, 1758, and Wilkinson Mill, 1810. Also includes a reconstructed 16,000 lb water wheel, dam and power canal. **$2.50/adult; $1/child.** 6/1-9/1: Tues-Sat, 10-5; Sat-Sun, 1-5. 3/1-5/31, 9/2-12/21: Sat-Sun, 1-5.

Blithewold Mansion, Gardens & Arboretum
Ferry Rd, Bristol 02809. (401)253-2707.

Thirty-three acres of landscaped, grounds, gardens and plants. 45 rm, turn-of-the-century mansion, formerly summer residence of Pennsylvania coal magnate, Augustus VanWickle. **Grounds: $2/adult; $.50/child. Grounds and Mansion: $4/adult; $2/child.** Grounds:

all yr, daily, 10-4. Mansion: 4/18-10/31, Tues-Sun, 10-4.

Children's Museum of Rhode Island

58 Walcott St, Pawtucket 02860.
(401)726-2591.

Participatory exhibits include Great Grandmother's Kitchen, My Way, Your Way, The Great Puzzle Room, Shape Up. Located in 1840 Pitcher-Golf Mansion. **$2.50** Sept-Jun: Wed-Thurs, 1-5; Fri-Sat, 10-5. Jul-Aug: Tues-Sat, 10-5; Sun, 1-5.

Hammersmith Farm

Ocean Drive, Newport 02840.
(401)846-0420 or 846-7346.

Oceanside 28-rm, shingle style cottage, on 50 acre estate, with rolling pastures and beautifully landscaped gardens. Summer home of the Auchincloss family for 4 generations, the reception following the wedding of Jacqueline Bouvier and John F Kennedy was held here. **$4.50/adult; $1.50/child.** Memorial Day - Labor Day, daily, 10-7. 4/1 - Memorial Day, Labor Day - 11/11, daily, 10-5. Mar, Nov, Sat-Sun, 10-5.

•Good Choices:

Natural Scenery: Mohegan Bluffs and Southeast Lighthouse, Block Island/ Colt State Park, picturesque shoreline drive, Bristol/ Norman Bird Sanctuary, fields, swamp, woods, trails, Middletown/ South County Beaches, South County Tourism Council, Narragansett/ Ocean Drive, Atlantic coast, Newport.

Nature and Man: Coggeshall Farm Museum, 18th century working farm, Bristol/ Green Animals Topiary Gardens, sculpted trees and shrubs, Portsmouth/ Roger Williams Park and Zoo, woods, gardens, drives, zoo, Providence.

Historic: Rhode Island Historical Farm, historic working farm, Johnston/ South County Museum, history of Rhode Island, Narragansett/ Fort Adams State Park, Naragansett Bay defenses, 1799-1945, reproduction of Colonial ship, Newport/ Benefits Street Mile of History, walking tour, Providence Preservation Society, Providence/ Meeting House of the First Baptist Church in America, established by Roger Williams, Providence.

Historic Houses: Whitehall, Middletown/ Astors' Beechwood Mansion, Newport/ Belcourt Castle, Newport/ Samuel Whitehorne House, Newport/ Wanton-Lyman-Hazard House, Newport/ Smith's Castle, Wickford.

Art: Newport Art Museum and Art Association, changing exhibits, Newport/ Rhode Island Watercolor Society, changing exhibits of water colors, Pawtucket/ Rhode Island School of Design Museum, classic art from Ancient Greece & Rome, European, American art, Middle ages to present, Providence.

Entertainment: Enchanted Forest, children's rides, Hopkinton/ Oldport Harbor Tours, Newport/ Crescent Park Carousel, Providence/ Flying Horse Carousel, Westerly.
Commercial: Sakonnet Vineyards Tour, Little Compton/ Prudence Island Vineyards Tour, Prudence Island.

Sports: Surfing Lessons, Narran-gansett/ International Tennis Hall of Fame and Museum, Newport.
Seasonal Events and Festivals: Medieval Faire, Aug, The Monastery, Cumberland/ Seafood Festival, Aug, Charlestown/ Christmas in Newport, Dec, New-port.

South Carolina

Fame: *Historic cities and towns, sandy beaches.*
You must: *visit a beach, Hopeland Gardens, or Old Charleston.*

Charleston

Fame: *A 300-year-old city with preserved and restored old homes and a reputation for cultivated manners.*
You must: *take a walking tour of Old Charleston, see the beautiful gardens and magnificent old homes.*

•Best Choices:

Charles Towne Landing
1500 Old Towne Rd, 29407-6099. (803)556-4450.

SC 171 between I-26 and US 17. A park on the site of the first permanent English settlement in SC. Visitors may ride a mini-train past the reconstructed earthworks and palisade, wander through a beautiful English park gardens, enter a forest in which animals roam freely behind camouflaged barriers,

board the replica of a 17th century trading vessel. **$4/adult; $2/sr citizen, child.** Daily, Jun-Aug, 9-6. Rest of yr, 9-5.

Charleston Museum
360 Meeting, 29403. (803)722-2996.

This museum dates back to 1773 and is the oldest in the US. Collections include more than 500,000 objects, covering history, anthropology, decorative arts, from all over the world but with most emphasis on S Carolina. **$3/adult; $1/child.** Daily, 9-5.

•Good Choices:
Nature and Man: Cypress Gardens, lake with cypress, azaleas, camellias, daffodils.
History and Art: The Battery, palmettos, live oaks, historic can-

nons, war relics/ Gibbs Art Gallery, American paintings/ Old Exchange and Provost Dungeon, historic building, self-guided tour, film. **Historic Homes:** Siken Rhett Mansion/ Calhoun Mansion/ Edmonston-Alston House/ Heyward-Washington House/ Joseph Manigault House/ Nathaniel Rus

sell House/ Boone Hall Plantation. **Churches and Synagogues:** Beth Elohim, birthplace of reform Judaism in US/ Huguenot Church, one of last Hugenot churches in US.

Entertainment: The Charleston Adventure, multimedia introduction to city/ Dear Charleston, film presentation of city.

Statewide Attractions

•Best Choices:

Hopeland Gardens and Thoroughbred Hall of Fame
Box 1177, Aiken 29802. (803)649-7700.

8 mi S of Aiken off I-20. The grounds of a former estate contain 14 acres of gardens, with azaleas, Japanese Iris, Day Lilies and many other flowers. There is also a Touch and Scent Trail for the visually impaired. A restored carriage house contains the memorabilia of national champion thoroughbreds and equine art exhibits. **Free.** Gardens: Daily, 10 - dusk. Hall of Fame: Oct-Jun, Tues-Sun, 2-5.

Brookgreen Gardens
US Hwy 17 S, Murrells Inlet 29576. (803)237-4218.

3 mi S of Murrells Inlet on US 17. A unique blend of beautiful gardens and impressive 18th and 19th century American sculpture. The

grounds include a wildlife park with an aviary, cypress swamp and nature trails. **$4/adult; $1/child 6-12.** Daily, 9:30-4:45.

Greenville County Museum of Art
420 College, Greenville 29601. (803)271-7570.

Houses largest Andrew Wyeth collection outside of artist's own holdings. Includes paintings by other noted U.S. painters, and American art ranges from ancient Indian artifacts to 20th century. **Free.** Tues-Fri, 9-5; Sat-Sun, 2-5.

Historic Pendleton
Pendleton District Historical & Recreational Commission, Box 565, Pendleton 29670. (803)646-3782.

An important district of culture, government and business in the 18th century, the entire town and adjoining area is on the National Register of Historic Places. Points of interest include farm museum, toy museum, two house museums and visitor center. **Rates of attractions are $1 to $5.** Apr-Oct.

•Good Choices:

Natural Scenery: Cape Roman National Wildlife Refuge, undeveloped barrier islands, Awendaw/ Savannah National Wildlife Refuge, marshes, rivers, creeks, wildlife, drive, Hardeeville/ Sea Pines Forest Preserve, Newhall Audubon Preserve, Hilton Head Plantation Whooping Crane Conservancy, Hilton Head Island/ Carolina Sandhills National Wildlife Refuge, forest, field, pond, wildlife, McBee/ Santee National Wildlife Refuge, waterfowl, walking trail, Santee/ Francis Beidler Forest in Four Holes Swamp, swamp, virgin cypress, tupelo trees, boardwalk, Summerville/ Sumter National Forest, mountains, forest, river, flowers.

Nature and Man: Cheraw Fish Hatchery and Aquarium, Cheraw/ Horticulture Gardens, arboretum, greenhouse, gristmill, Clemson University, Clemson/ Riverbanks Zoological Park, zoo, gardens, Columbia/ Kalmia Gardens, flowers, swamp, walking trails, Hartsville/ Little Mountain Zoological Park, Inman/ Edisto Gardens, swamp, oaks, cypress, dogwood, flowers, Orangeburg/ Glencairn Gardens, flowers, pond, fountain, Rock Hill/ Swan Lake Iris Gardens, lawns, lake, pines, flowers, Sumter.

Science and Technology: World of Energy, story of energy, aquarium, Clemson/ Nuclear Information Center, nuclear energy exhibits, Hartsville/ I P Stanback Museum and Planetarium, Orangeburg/ Museum of York County, natural history, planetarium, Rock Hill.

History: Historic Camden, reconstruction of 1780 village, Camden/ Historic district, self-guided tour, Cheraw/ Fort Jackson Museum, history of Ft Jackson, Columbia/ State House, tours, Columbia/ Cowpens National Battlefield, Revolutionary War battlefield, exhibits, auto trail/ Fort Sumter National Monument, opening shots of Civil War were fired here, tours/ Historic District tours, Georgetown/ Andrew Jackson State Park, museum, log schoolhouse, Lancaster/ Lexington County Museum Complex, 1830s lifestyles, Lexington/ Ninety Six National Historic Site, Revolutionary War battlefield, Ninety Six/ Old Dorchester State Park, ruins of 18th century village, Summerville.

Historical Homes: John Mark Verdier House, Beaufort/ John C Calhoun Mansion, Clemson University, Clemson/ Hampton-Preston Mansion and Garden, Columbia/ Woodrow Wilson Boyhood Home, Columbia/ Hopsewee Plantation, Georgetown/ Hampton Plantation State Park, McClellanville/ Walnut Grove Plantation, Spartanburg.

Art: Columbia Museum, Renaissance, Baroque, European,

American paintings, Columbia/
McKissick Museum, changing ex-
hibits, Columbia/ Florence
Museum, Oriental, Western art,
Florence/ Sumter Gallery of Art,
contemporary art, Sumter.
Entertainment: Ripley's Believe
It or Not Museum, Myrtle Beach.

Commercial: Anderson Jockey
Lot and Farmers Market, flea
market, produce, Anderson/ State
Farmers Market, Columbia/
George W Park Seed Co Display
Plots, Greenwood/ Truluck
Vineyards, Lake City.
Sports: Stock Car Hall of Fame,
Darlington.

South Dakota

Fame: *Weather: If you don't like it, just wait 5 minutes until it changes; Black Hills and Mt. Rushmore.*
You must: *visit Mt. Rushmore, eat an Indian taco.*

Statewide Attractions

•Best Choices:

Mount Rushmore National Memorial
Black Hills, Keystone 57751. (605)574-2515.

The faces of four presidents, Washington, Jefferson, Lincoln and Theodore Roosevelt, have been carved in a 6,000 ft mountain, in the Black Hills. The sculptor, Gutzon Borglum, began the work in 1927, and it was completed in 1941. **Free.**

Badlands National Park
Box 6, Interior 57750. (605)433-5361.

Follow the Badlands Loop, SR 240, which leaves I-90 at Exit 110, at Wall, and Exit 131, at Cactus

Flat. The erosion of wind and water has cut through clay and sandstone hills to form cliffs, ridges, ravines, buttes and spires striped with variegated ribbons of color. **$1/vehicle.**

Needles Highway
Custer State Park, Box 70, Custer 57730. (605)255-4464.

A 14 mile highway that winds through the Black Hills, past needle-like spires, around hairpin curves and through narrow tunnels. Watch for wandering bison. **Park fee: Daily, $2/person. 3 day: $6/vehicle.** Memorial Day - Labor Day.

Homestake Gold Mine
Main and Mill St, Lead 57754.
(605)584-3110.

A gold mine that has been in operation since 1876 and is one of the largest producing mines in North America. Guided 1 1/2 hr tours show surface workings and explain gold production. **$2.50/adult; $2/student 13-17; $1.50/child 6-12.** May-Oct, Mon-Fri, 8-4. Closed holidays.

Black Hills Passion Play
Box 489, Spearfish 57783. (605)642-2646.

An amphitheater, with a mountain backdrop, is the setting for the famous dramatization of the last 7 days of the life of Christ are presented each summer. **$5-10/adult; $2.50-5/Child under 12.** Sun, Tues, Thurs, 6/7-8/30.

•Good Choices:

Natural Scenery: Black Hills National Forest, forest, wildlife, visitor center/ Custer State Park, bison, forest, wildlife, visitor center, Custer/ Sylvan Lake, lake, rock formations, Custer/ Bear Butte State Park, volcanic rock, Sturgis/ Waubay National Wildlife Refuge, lakes, woods, marshes, grass, wildlife, Waubay.
Nature and Man: McCrory Gardens, flowering annuals, SD State Univ, Brookings/ Mammoth Excavation Site, mammoth bones, museum, visitor center, Hot Springs/ Badlands Petrified Gardens, petrified logs, stumps, Kadoka/ Black Hills Petrified Forest, petrified logs, museum, Rapid City/ Black Hills Reptile Gardens, snakes, other reptiles, gardens, Rapid City/ Marine Life Aquarium, Rapid City/ Museum of Geology, rocks, minerals, ores, fossils, Rapid City/ Great Plains Zoo, Sioux Falls/ D C Booth Historic Fish Hatchery, restored hatchery, house, museum Spearfish/ Bramble Park Zoo, Watertown/ Gavins Point National Fish Hatchery and Aquarium, Yankton.
Caves: Jewel Cave National Monument, Custer/ Rushmore Cave, Keystone/ Bethlehem Cave, Piedmont/ Stagebarn Crystal Cave, Piedmont/ Black Hills Caverns, Rapid City/ Crystal Cave Park, Rapid City/ Wonderland Cave Natural Park, Rapid City/ Wind Cave National Park, Hot Springs.
Dams: Fort Randall Dam, exhibits, guided tours, Pickstown/ Oahe Dam and Reservoir, guided tours, Pierre/ Gavins Point Dam and Power, guided tours, Yankton.
Historical and Cultural: Smith-Zimmermann State Museum, history of SD, Dakota State College, Madison/ Friends of the Middle Border - Museum of Pioneer Life, history of Dakota Territory, Mitchell/ Prehistoric Indian Village, study of 1,000 yr old village, guides, Mitchell/ State Capitol, Pierre/ Chapel in the Hills, exact copy of Norwegian church, Stav-

kirke, Rapid City/ Ellsworth Air Force Base, guided tour, Rapid City/ Dakota Territorial Museum, restored pioneer buildings, memorabilia, Yankton.

Special Interest Museums: Enchanted World Doll Museum, Mitchell/ Pioneer Auto Museum and Antique Town, Murdo.

Historic Gold Mines: Broken Boot Gold Mine, guided underground tours, Deadwood/ Big Thunder Gold Mine, underground tours, Keystone.

Historic Homes: Surveyors' House and Ingalls Home, June-Sept, Deadwood/ Mellette House, Watertown/ Cramer-Kenyon Heritage Home, Yankton.

Art: Crazy Horse Memorial, world's largest statue, Custer/ Western Woodcarvings, animated woodcarvings, Custer/ Rushmore-Borglum Story, works of G Borglum, story of Mt Rushmore, Keystone/ Oscar Howe Art Center, works of Sioux artist, Mitchell/ Black Hills Gold, observe jewelry making, Rapid City/ Sioux Indian Art Museum, works of Native American artists, Rapid City/ Civic Fine Arts Museum, local, regional, international artists, Sioux Falls.

Wax Museums: Ghosts of Deadwood Gulch, Western Heritage Wax Museum, Deadwood/ Parade of Presidents Wax Museum, Keystone/ Prairie Village, Madison/ Wild West Historical Wax Museum, Wall.

Entertainment: "Trial of Jack McCall for the Murder of Wild Bill Hickok" play, Deadwood/ Evans Plunge, world's largest natural warm water indoor swimming pool, Hot Springs/ Rushmore Aerial Tramway, Keystone/ Terry Peak Chairlift, Lead/ Corn Palace, interior & exterior are covered with corn, Mitchell/ Rotary Story Book Island, children's park, Rapid City/ Matthews' Opera House, old-time melodramas, Spearfish.

Commercial: Landstrom's Original Black Hills Gold Creations, view jewelry making, Rapid City/ Sioux Pottery and Crafts Tours, Rapid City/ Wall Drug Store, Wall.

Tennessee

Fame: *Great Smoky Mountains National Park; Nashville, the Country Music Capital of the World; Memphis, birthplace of the blues and known for its barbecued foods.*
You must: *hike a trail in the Great Smoky Mountains National Park, listen to Tennessee music in a Nashville "honky-tonk," or eat barbecued pork ribs in Memphis.*

Statewide Attractions

•Best Choices:

Great Smoky Mountains National Park
Superintendent, GSM National Park, Gatlinburg 37738. (615)436-5615.

Sugarlands Visitor Center, 2 mi S of Gatlinburg. The park encompasses over 500,000 acres of wilderness. Combined with unspoiled forests are outdoor museums of pioneer life, such as Cades Cove, Oconaluftee Pioneer Farmstead and Roaring Fork. More than 800 miles of hiking trails. **Free.** Campgrounds are open year around.

American Museum of Science and Energy
300 S Tulane AV, Oak Ridge 37830. (615)576-3200.

One of the world's largest energy shows. Displays include models, movies, demonstrations, devices, gadgets and machines and hands-on experiments. **Free.** Jun-Aug, daily, 9-6. Rest of yr, daily, 9-5. Closed Thanksgiving, 12/25, 1/1.

Rocky Mount State Historic Site
Johnson City 37601. (615)538-7396.

A log farmhouse and other buildings, constructed in 1770, have been restored. Costumed guides conduct living history tours and demonstrate pioneer skills. The Overmountain museum portrays the history of the region. **$4/adult; $2.50/student.** Mar-Dec, 10-5; Sun, 2-6. Rest of yr, Mon-Fri, 10-5. Closed Thanksgiving 12/5-1/5.

Mud Island
Downtown Memphis. (901)576-7241.

A 50 acre island in the Mississippi River, reached by pedestrian bridge or monorail. A museum presents the story and history of the Mississippi with unusual exhibits such as a steamboat, Union gunboat, towboat, Indian artifacts and the River Walk, a 5-block long, scale model of 1,000 miles of the river. Also here are restaurants, shops and amphitheater. **$4/adult; $2.50/sr citizen, child 4-11.** Daily, spring - summer. Fall and winter schedule varies.

Lookout Mountain Incline Railway
3917 St Elmo Av, Chattanooga. (615)821-4224.

One of the steepest incline railways in the world, climbs straight up the side of Lookout Mountain, reaching a grade of 72.7 percent. Glass-roofed trains. Observation deck at top of mountain. **Round trip: $4.50/adult; $2.75/child 6-12.** Memorial Day - Labor Day, daily, 8:30-8:20. Rest of yr, daily, 9-6.

Hermitage
I-40 E, Nashville. (615)889-7050.

12 mi E of Nashville on I-40, Old Hickory exit. Home of President Andrew Jackson, built in 1819. Built on 425 acres of land, includes mansion and furnishings, museum, gardens, church, tombs and Tulip Grove, which was the home of Andrew Jackson Donelson, nephew of President Jackson. **$3.75/adult; $1.25/child 6-13.** Daily, 9-5. Closed Thanksgiving, 12/25.

•Good Choices:

Natural Scenery: Big South Fork National River and Recreation Area, gorges, rocks, river, lush vegetation, NE Tennessee/ Nature Center at Reflection Riding, auto trail, trees, flowers, shrubs, pools, Chattanooga/ Cherokee National Forest, gorges, mountains, trees, streams, waterfalls, trails, wildlife, E Tennessee/ Lichterman Nature Center, wildlife sanctuary, greenhouse, nature trails, Memphis/ Tennessee National Wildlife Refuge, waterfowl, turkeys, deer, auto tour, Paris.

Nature and Man: Bays Mountain Park, nature center, exhibits, barge trips, planetarium, Kingsport/ Knoxville Zoological Park, Knoxville/ Students' Museum - Akima Planetarium, participatory exhibits, minerals, aquariums, Knoxville/ Memphis Botanic Garden and Goldsmith Civic Garden Center, flowers, Japanese garden, conservatory, Memphis/ Memphis Zoo and Aquarium, Memphis/ Wonder Cave, Monteagle/ Tennessee Botanical Gardens and Fine Arts Center, gardens, greenhouses, 19th - 20th century art. sculpture, Nashville/ University of Tennessee Arboretum, trees, shrubs, flowers, Oak Ridge/ Tuckaleechee Caverns, Townsend.

Science and Technology: Raccoon Mountain Pumped Storage Plant, power generating plant, Chattanooga/ Kingston Steam

Plant, electric generating plant, Kingston/ Cumberland Science Museum, natural & physical sciences, children's curiosity corner, Nashville.

History: Confederama, Civil War exhibits, Chattanooga/ American Historical Wax Museum, celebrated people, Gatlinburg/ Andrew Johnson National Historic Site, homestead, tailor shop, cemetery, Greeneville/ Jonesborough History Museum, Jonesborough from pioneers to present, Jonesborough/ Memphis Pink Palace Museum, Memphis history, planetarium, Memphis/ Cannonsburgh Village, restored village, Murfreesboro/ Fort Nashborough, reproduction of Indian Wars fort, Nashville/ State Capitol, Nashville/ Tennessee State Museum, history of state, operating gristmill, Nashville/ Natchez Trace Parkway, Shady Grove to near Jackson, MS/ Museum of Appalachia, mountain village, Norris/ Children' Museum of Oak Ridge, hands-on cultural exhibits, Oak Ridge/ Historic Rugby, restored buildings, Rugby/ Falls Mills, working gristmill, Winchester.

Civil War Battlefields: Chickamauga and Chattanooga National Military Park, Chattanooga/ Fort Donelson National Battlefield, Civil War field, Dover/ Stones River National Battlefield, Murfreesboro/ Shiloh National Military Park.

Historic Houses: James K Polk Ancestral Home, Columbia/ Carter House, Franklin/ Cragfont, Gallatin/ Rock Castle, Hendersonville/ Armstrong-Lockett House and W P Toms Memorial Gardens, Knoxville/ Confederate Memorial Hall, Knoxville/ Governor William Blount Mansion, Knoxville/ James White's Fort, Knoxville/ Historic Fontaine House, Memphis/ Oaklands Mansion, Murfreesboro/ Beele Meade Mansion, Nashville/ Belmont Mansion, Nashville/ Travellers' Rest, Nashville/ Sam Davis Home, Smyrna.

Art: Hunter Museum of Art, 19th - 20th century American, Chattanooga/ Knoxville Museum of Art, changing exhibits, Knoxville/ Dixon Gallery and Gardens, 18th - 19th century Impressionists, gardens, Memphis/ Memphis Brooks Museum of Art, 13th - 20th century, European, American, Memphis/ University Gallery, African and Egyptian art, Memphis State Univ, Memphis/ Tennessee Botanical Gardens and Fine Arts Center, 19th - 20th century American, gardens, Nashville/ Oak Ridge Community Art Center, regional, national, international, Oak Ridge/ Appalachian Center for Crafts, exhibits, demonstrations, sales gallery, Smithville.

Religion: Christus Gardens, Gatlinburg/ Upper Room Chapel and Museum, Nashville/ "Smoky Mountain Passion Play" and "Damascus Road," plays, Townsend.

Special Interest Museums: Houston Museum, pitchers, mugs, pressed glass, Chattanooga/ National Knife Museum, Chattanooga/

Casey Jones Home and Railroad Museum, Jackson/ George Jones' Car Collectors Hall of Fame, Nashville/ Carbo's Police Museum, Pigeon Forge.

Entertainment: Raccoon Mountain Flight Park, simulated hang-gliding flights, Chattanooga/ Transportation to the top of Mount Harrison: aerial tramway, chairlift, sky lift, Gatlinburg. Movie and Music Stars: Stars: over Gatlinburg, movie star wax museum, Gatlinburg/ House of Cash, Johnny Cash memorabilia, Hendersonville/ Bill Monroe Bluegrass Hall of Fame, Hendersonville/ Ferlin Husky Wings of a Dove Museum, Hendersonville/ Marty Robbins Memorial Showcase, Hendersonville/ Loretta Lynn's Dude Ranch and Museum, Hurricane Mills/ Carl Perkins Music Museum,

Casey Jones Village, Jackson/ Country Music Wax Museum, Nashville/ Waylon's Private Collection, Nashville/ Jim Reeves Museum, Nashville/ Music Valley Wax Museum of the Stars, Nashville/ Cars of Stars, Nashville.

Commercial: Chattanooga Choo Choo and Terminal Station, original train, shops and restaurants, Chattanooga/ ProGroup, Inc, tour manufacturer of golf equipment, Chattanooga/ Highland Manor Winery Tour, Jamestown/ Iron Mountain Stoneware Tour, Laurel Bloomery/ Jack Daniel's Distillery, Lynchburg/ Standard Candy Company Tour, Nashville/ Pigeon Forge Pottery Demonstrations, Pigeon Forge/ George A. Dickel Distilling Co. Tours, Tullahoma.

Texas

Fame: *Lone Star State; Cowboys; Cattle; Oil Wells; so large that 15 of the 50 states could fit within its borders.*
You must: *sample some Texas chili and see a field of bluebonnets in bloom.*

Dallas and Fort Worth

Fame: *Country-western music and Texas beef; Nieman-Marcus, in Dallas, and the historic stockyards district, in Fort Worth.*
You must: *dine on Texas barbecue, sample sophisticated downtown Dallas and friendly downtown Fort Worth, then turn your radio to a* country-western station and drive out of town to see rural Texas.

•Best Choices:

State Fair Park
US 67/80, E of Dallas. (214)565-9931.

The site of the Texas State Fair in Oct, this area is a city park during the rest of the year. It has many attractions, including the Dallas Aquarium, Garden Center, Hall of State, Music Hall, Museum of Natural History, Science Place and Cotton Bowl. **Science Place: $1/adult; $.50/sr citizen, child under 11. Others are free.** Most are open Mon-Sat, 9-5; Sun, 12-5. Call for specific attractions. Closed 1 wk in early Oct, before the fair.

Amos Carter Square
West of downtown at jct of Lancaster Av and Camp Bowie Blvd.

Will Rogers Memorial Center is surrounded by many interesting attractions including Amos G. Carter Museum of Western Art, Casa Manana Theater-in-the-Round, Fort Worth Art Museum, Kimball Art Museum, Museum of Science and History, Noble Planetarium and William Edrington Scott Theater. **Charge for theaters and planetarium. Rest are free.** Most are open Mon-Sat, 10-5; Sun 1-5. Call for specific attractions.

•Good Choices:
Natural Scenery: Fort Worth: Nature Center and Refuge, wildlife, trails.

Nature and Man: Dallas: Dallas Zoo/ Thanks-Giving Square, chapel, waterfall, landscaping. Fort Worth: Botanic Gardens/ Water Gardens, with fountains, channels, cascades, pools and geometric sculpture/ Zoological Park.
Historical and Cultural: Dallas: Biblical Arts Center, nondenominational, paintings, sculptures, icons, artifacts/ Bryan Cabin, 1st log cabin/ Dallas Museum of Art, pre-Columbian, European, American/ John F Kennedy Memorial, site of assasination/ Owens Art Center, Spanish, American art, Southern Methodist Univ/ Old City Park, restored buildings/ Telephone Pioneer Museum of Texas. Fort Worth: Log Cabin Village, restored pioneer homes.
Entertainment: Dallas: Reunion Tower of Dallas Observation Deck. Fort Worth: Forest Park, recreation, rides.
Commercial: Dallas: Farmers Market. Fort Worth: Historic Stockyard District, shopping and dining/ Sundance Square, shopping and dining.
Seasonal Events and Festivals: Dallas: Cotton Bowl Festival, Jan/ National Championship Indian Powwow, Sept. Fort Worth: Southwest Exposition, Fat Stock Show, Jan-Feb/ Chisholm Trail Roundup, June.

San Antonio

Fame: *The Alamo; an area heavily influenced by many different cultures from a colorful past.*

You must: *eat Tex-Mex food, visit the Alamo, a mission and Market Square.*

•Best Choices:

The Alamo
center of town, Alamo Plaza.

Mission San Antonio de Valero, established in 1718, was the first of five Spanish missions founded in San Antonio. It became a fortress for the famous battle of 187 defenders against the forces of Santa Ana and 5,000 troops. The battle took the life of of over 1,500 Mexican soldiers and all of the defenders. Two museums. **Free.** Mon-Sat, 9-5:30; Sun and holidays, 10-5:30. Closed 12/24, 25.

Institute of Texas Culture
HemisFair Plaza. (512)226-7651.

Features 26 ethnic and cultural groups that helped to settle Texas. Exhibits are supplemented by demonstrations of music, food, festivals. Multi-media show 3 times daily. **Free.** Tues-Sun, 9-5. Closed Thanksgiving, 12/25.

San Antonio Museum of Art
200 W Jones Av, 78215. (512)226-5544.

Six building complex of renovated brewery, features art of the Americas. Pre-Columbian, American Indian, Spanish Colonial, 18-20th Century U.S. painting and sculpture, photography. **$3/adult; $1.50/sr citizen;** $1/child 6-12. Free Thurs, 3-9. Tues-Sat, 10-5; Thurs, 10-5; Sun, noon-5.

•Good Choices:

Nature and Man: Botanical Gardens, formal gardens, native plants, exotic, tropical/ Brackenridge Park, Japanese gardens, bridges, walks, pools/ San Antonio College Planetarium/ San Antonio Zoological Gardens and Aquariums.

Historical and Cultural: La Villita, restored Mexican village/ McNay Art Institute, 20th century paintings/ Plaza Theater of Wax, historic & famous/ Texas Star Trail, historical walking tour/ Witte Museum, natural history and history.

Historic Houses: General Cos House/ Jose Navarro State Historic Site/ Spanish Governor's Palace/ Steves Homestead.

Missions: Nuestra Senora de La Purisima Concepcion/ San Francisco de la Espada/ San Jose y San Miguel de Aguayo/ San Juan Capistrano.

Specialized Museums: Buckhorn Hall of Horns/ Hangar 9 - Museum of Flight Medicine/ Hertzberg Circus Collection/ San Antonio Museum of Transportation.

Entertainment: Tower of the Americas Observation Deck.

Commercial: Market Square; River Walk.

Seasonal Events and Festivals: Livestock Exposition and Rodeo,

Feb/ Texas Independence Day and Flag Celebration, Mar/ Fiesta San Antonio, Apr/ Fiesta Navidena, Dec.

Statewide Attractions

•Best Choices:

Big Bend National Park
Park Superintendent, Brewster 79834. (915)477-2291.

The park encompasses 708,221 acres. The visitor can travel from the Rio Grande, with spectacular canyons and jungle-like flood plain, through the Chihuahuan Desert to Chisos Mountains, with their cool woodlands. More than 1,100 plant types, hundreds of birds and other animals, many of them very rare, are found in the park. There are paved roads, graded dirt roads, short nature walk trails, longer primitive trails and guided walks. Interpretive programs are given daily. Information is available at visitor contact stations. Park headquarters is at Panther Junction. **$5/car; $2/person without car.** Headquarters open summer, 8-7; winter, 8-5.

Lyndon B. Johnson Space Center
AP-5, Houston 77058. (713)483-4321.

25 mi SE of Houston; 3 mi E of I-45 on NASA Road 1. Headquarters of the U.S. manned space program. At the visitor orientation center see lunar rocks, photos from Mars, movies of space flights and orbital rendezvous. Exhibits include spacecraft, a full-scale Skylab and examples of space-technology spinoff. **Free guided tours.** Daily, 9-4. Closed 12/25.

Lyndon B. Johnson National Historical Park
Superintendent, Box 329, Johnson City 78636. (512)868-7128.

Information Center, 2 blks S of US 290. Consists of two separate units, both homes of the former president. Across the street from the visitor center is a frame structure where Lyndon Johnson lived while attending school. One block W is an old ranch complex called Johnson Settlement, owned by the president's grandfather and great-uncle, 1867-72. **Free.** Daily, 9-5. Closed 12/25, 1/1.

Permian Basin Petroleum Museum
1500 I-20 W, Midland 79701. (915)683-4403.

Explains the formation of oil, the oil industry and the Permian Basin. Includes historic photos, paintings, models, hardware, AV shows, actual oil-well cores, walk-through diorama of the ocean floor as it was 230 million years ago. Experience a simulated wild well blowout. **$2/adult; $1/child 6-11.** Daily, Mon-Sat, 9-5; Sun, 2-5. Closed Thanksgiving, 12/24, 12/25.

•Good Choices:

Natural Scenery: Aransas National Wildlife Refuge, wild whooping cranes, many other wild animals, Austwell/ Hagerman National Wildlife Refuge, waterfowl, shorebirds, Denison/ Scenic Drive, magnificent view from mountain overlook, US 80 to N Piedras St, El Paso/ Hueco Tanks State Historical Park, rock formations, caves, pictographs, hiking, El Paso/ Guadalupe Mountains National Park, mountains, canyon, accessible by hiking trail/ Santa Ana National Wildlife Refuge, great birdwatching, hiking, McAllen/ Natural Bridge Caverns, New Braunfels/ Padre Island National Seashore, barrier island, sand dunes.

Nature and Man: Don Harrington Discovery Center Planetarium, Amarillo/ Zilker Park, gardens, restored buildings, pool, train, hiking, biking trails, Austin/ Palo Duro Canyon State Park, ancient geological formations, railroad, drives, bridal paths, hiking trails, Canyon/ Lake Meredith Aquatic and Wildlife Museum, dioramas depict animal habitats, aquarium, Fritch/ Houston Arboretum and Nature Center, native plants, wildlife,

hiking trails, Houston/ King Ranch Headquarters, 12 mile self-guided drive around ranch buildings, Kingsville/ Lajitas Museum and Desert Garden, native plants, geological, archeological, art, Lajitas/ Natural Bridge Wildlife Ranch, exotic wildlife, New Braunfels/ Municipal Rose Garden, Tyler.

Caves: Cascade Caverns, Boerne/ Longhorn Cavern State Park, Burnet/ Inner Space Cavern, Georgetown.

Zoos, aquariums: Nelson Park Zoo, Abilene/ Gladys Porter Zoo, Brownsville/ El Paso Zoo, El Paso/ Houston Zoological Gardens and Kipp Aquarium, Houston/ Caldwell Zoo, Tyler/ Texas Zoo, Victoria.

Science and Technology: Edison Plaza Museum, electricity, Beaumont/ Crosbyton Solar Power Project, Crosbyton/ W J McDonald Observatory, Ft Davis.

History: Lyndon B Johnson Library and Museum, boyhood, presidential, retirement memorabilia, papers, presidential gifts, Austin/ State Capitol, tours, Austin/ Sam Rayburn Library, duplicated Capitol office, memorabilia, Bonham/ Tigua Indian Reservation and Pueblo, visitor program, arts, crafts center, musueum, restaurant, El Paso/ Fort Davis National Historic Site, restored 19th century frontier fort, Fort Davis/ Admiral Nimitz State Historical Park, Pacific War museum, History Walk, Japanese garden, art gallery, Fredricksburg/

The Elissa, 1877 merchant ship, Galveston/ San Jacinto Battleground State Historic Park, Mexican War battlefield, museum, Battleship Texas, Houston/ Atalanta, G J Gould's private rail car, Jefferson/ Judge Roy Bean Visitor Center, restored saloon, courtroom, billiard hall, cactus garden, Langtry/ Museum of Texas Tech University, arts, humanities, social, natural sciences, planetarium, Lubbock/ Square House Museum, Texas history, Panhandle.

Missions: El Paso Self-guided Mission Tour, Visitors Bureau, El Paso/ Goliad State Historical Park, restored mission, interpretive displays, Goliad.

Historic Villages: Buffalo Gap Historical Village, Abilene/ Panhandle-Plains Historical Museum, Canyon/ Pioneer Village, Corsicana/ Magoffin Home State Historic Site, El Paso/ Washington-on-the-Brazos State Historical Park, historic townsite, Navasota/ Millard's Crossing, Nocogdoches.

Historic Homes: Governor's Mansion, Austin/ John Jay French Museum, Beaumont/ Sam Rayburn House, Bonham/ Eisenhower Birthplace, Denison/ Pioneer Museum, Fredericksburg/ Ashton Villa, Galveston/ Bishops Palace, Galveston/ 1839 Williams Home, Galveston/ Bayou Bend, Houston/ Sam Houston Park, Houston/ Sam Houston Memorial Museum and Park, Huntsville/ House of the Seasons, Jefferson/ Highland Mansion, Marlin/ Maxey House State Historical Structure, Paris/ Fulton Mansion State Historic Structure, Rockport/ Varner-Hogg Plantation Historical Park, West Columbia.

Special Interest Museums: Gladys City-Spindletop Boomtown, oil, Beaumont/ Railroad Museum, Galveston/ Confederate Air Force Flying Museum, Harlingen/ Classic Car Showcase and Wax Museum, Kerrville/ East Texas Oil Museum, Kilgore/ Old Clock Museum, Pharr/ Texas Ranger Hall of Fame, Fort Fisher Park, Waco.

Art: Archer M Huntington Art Gallery, 20th century art, Austin/ Museum of Oriental Culture, art from Tang, Sung, Ming dynasties, Japanese exhibits, Corpus Christi/ Contemporary Arts Museum, 20th century art, Houston/ Museum of Fine Arts, American, European, Far Eastern, Houston/ Cowboy Artists of America Museum, living Western artists, Kerrville/ Museum of the Southwest, Southwestern art, culture, Midland.

Entertainment: "Texas," outdoor drama, Pioneer Amphitheatre, Canyon/ Alamo Village Movie Location, Brackettville/ "Viva! El Paso!," musical history, El Paso/ Treasure Isle Tour Train, Galveston/ Port of Houston Turning Basin, Houston Ship Channel, Houston/ Bayou Queen Riverboat Cruise, Jefferson/ Surrey Ride Tour, Jefferson.

Commercial: General Motors Assembly Division Tours, Arlington/ Blue Bell Creamery Ice Cream Plant Tour, Brenham/ Val Verde

Winery Tour, Del Rio/ Stroh Brewing Company Tour, Longview. **Sports:** Babe Didrikson Zaharias Memorial Museum, Beaumont/ National Cowgirl Hall of Fame, Hereford/ Astrodome, Houston.

Utah

Fame: *International headquarters of the Mormon Church, the Great Salt Lake.*
You must: *visit Temple Square and the Great Salt Lake, see some of Utah's spectacular natural scenery.*

Statewide Attractions

•Best Choices:

Temple Square
center of Salt Lake City.

Bounded by N, S, W Temple Sts and Main St. Contains the famed Mormon Temple, Salt Lake Tabernacle, Museum, Genealogical Library, Assembly Hall, Seagull Monument, 2 visitor centers. Tours every 15 mins, free parking. **Free.** Daily, 9-9. Tabernacle choir performances, Thurs evening and Sun.

Great Salt Lake State Park
SR 108, Ogden. (801)942-6673.

17 mi W of Salt Lake City. The second saltiest body of water, after the Dead Sea. The park has sandy beaches, areas for boating and sailboarding. **Free.**

Zion National Park
Superintendent, Springdale 84767.
(801)772-3256.

SR 9, W of Zion. One of the most rugged, startling areas in the world. Zion Canyon is a deep, narrow chasm with other canyons branching from it. Erosion and volcanic activity have created fantastic rock formations in spectacular colors. **$5/vehicle or $2/person.** Open yr around. Peak season is Apr-Oct; some portions closed in winter.

Bryce Canyon National Park
Superintendent, Bryce Canyon 84717.
(801)834-5322.

A 56 mile square park with forests of ponderosa pine, spruce, fir and aspen leading to the overlook. The canyon itself, is filled with fantastic, sculptured, multi-colored pinnacles, spires and cliffs which seem to change color as the sunlight shines from different angles. **$5/vehicle or $2/person.** Open all yr. Peak Season is Apr-Oct; some portions closed in winter

•Good Choices:

Natural Scenery: Timpanogos Cave National Monument, cave, rock formations, views, American Fork/ Natural Bridges National Monument, rock formations, paved drive, hiking trail, Blanding/ Cedar Breaks National Monument, canyon, colorful rocks, trees, trails, nature walks, Cedar City/ Dinosaur National Monument, dinosaur fossils, exhibits, hiking trails, boat trips, Dinosaur/ Arches National Park, natural arches, hiking trails, paved road, nature walks, Moab/ Canyonlands National Park, rock formations, canyons, pictographs, desert plants, Moab/ Manti-LeSai National Forest, canyons, rock formations, Indian ruins, forests, meadows, scenic drives, trails, Monticello and Price/ Rainbow Bridge National Monument, largest natural bridge, reached by boat, Page/ Capitol Reef National Park, rock formations, petroglyphs, unpaved drive, trails, guided walks, Torray.

Nature and Man: Hardware Elk Ranch, wild elk are fed, Jan-Mar, Logan/ Hogle Zoological Garden, Salt Lake City.

Historical and Cultural: Golden Spike National Historic Site, site where Union Pacific met Central Pacific railroads, train exhibits, Brigham City/ Territorial Statehouse State Park, pioneer, Indian artificats, garden, Fillmore/ Ronald V Jensen Historical Farm and Man and His Bread Museum, recreated farm, history of agriculture, Logan/ State Capitol, tours, Salt Lake City/ Old Deseret Pioneer Village, living history, restored buildings, Salt Lake City/ Wheeler Historical Farm, living history farm, Salt Lake City/ Utah Field House of History State Park, fossils, archeology, geology, Dinosaur Gardens, Vernal.

Historic Houses: Bingham Young Winter Home, St George/ Lion House and Beehive House, Salt Lake City/ Governor's Mansion, Salt Lake City.

Mormon Temples: Brigham City/ Logan/ Manti/ Ogden/ Provo/ St George.

Art: Kimball Art Center, local, national artists, Park City/ Utah Museum of Fine Arts, ancient Egypt, 19th century French, American, 20th century American, Univ of Utah, Salt Lake City.

Commercial: Cache Valley Dairy Tours, Amalga/ Pepperidge Farms Plant Tour, Logan/ Kennecott Bingham Copper Mine Observation Area, Midvale.

Vermont

Fame: *Fall foliage, winter skiing, maple syrup, cheddar cheese.*
You must: *visit Shelburne Museum, in Shelburne; sample maple syrup, cheddar cheese, ice cream after watching it being made.*

Statewide Attractions

•Best Choices:

Billings Farm and Museum
Woodstock 05091. (802)457-2355.

This is a working dairy farm that demonstrates life on a Vermont farm 100 years ago. You may have a chance to help milk a cow, churn butter or pet a calf. **$4/adult; $2/student 6-17; free/child under 6.** Mid-May - late Oct, daily, 10-5.

Rock of Ages Granite Quarry
Barre 05641. (802)476-3119.

See world's largest granite quarry, watch miners quarry the blocks, then observe the manufacturing process, watch craftsmen creating artistic sculptures. A railroad train tour is available to take you right into the quarries. **Free. Optional train ride: $1.95/adult; $.50, child 5-12.** 6/1-10/15, daily, 8:30-5. Trains: Mon-Fri.

Vermont Wildflower Farm
Rt 7, Charlotte 05445. (802)425-3500.

Acres of wildflowers bloom from spring through the fall. Winding pathways, displays, slide shows, self-guided tours. gift shop. **$2/adult; $1.50/sr citizen.** Daily, 10-5.

Ben & Jerry's Ice Cream Factory Tour
Waterbury 05676.

Rte 100. Media show, guided factory tour, sample of ice cream. Interesting and funny. **$1/adult donation which goes into charitable foundation.** Mon-Sat, 9-4

•Good Choices:

Natural Scenery: Groton State Forest, lake, ponds, forest, trails, Barre/ Green Mountain Audubon Nature Center, representative Vermont habitats, ponds, swamp, brook, river, marsh, trails, Burlington/ Lake Champlain, recreation/ Mount Mansfield State Forest, mountain, river, forest, scenic drive, Stowe/ Button Bay State Park, bluffs, spectacular views, nature walks, trails, Vergennes.

Nature and Man: Fairbanks Museum and Planetarium, arts, astronomy, history, science, tools, weather station, planetarium, St Johnsbury/ Equinox Sky Line Drive, paved road with spectacular views, Manchester.

History: Old First Church, historic Colonial church, Bennington/ Village of Grafton, restored 19th century village/ Museum of American Fly Fishing, fly fishing memorabilia, famous fisherpeople, Manchester/ Woodstock Historical Society, theme rooms: children's rm, silver, costumes, paintings, farm equip in barn, Woodstock.

Historic Homes: Park-McCullough House, Bennington/ Hawkins House, Bennington/ Historic Hildene, Manchester/ Sheldon Museum, Middlebury/ John Warren House, Middlebury/ Justin Smith Morrill Homestead, Norwich/ President Calvin Coolidge Homestead, Plymouth/ Chester A Arthur Birthplace, St Albans/ John Strong Mansion, Vergennes/ Rokeby, Vergennes.

Art: Bennington Museum, early Vermont eclectic, glass, pottery, Grandma Moses, furniture, sculpture, Bennington/ Brattleboro Museum and Art Center, New England artists, history, Brattleboro/ Robert Hull Fleming Museum, pre-Columbian, European, African, American, Burlington/ Bread & Puppet Museum, puppets, masks, Glover/ Southern Vermont Art Center, painting, sculpture, prints, Manchester/ Vermont State Craft Center at Frog Hollow, Vermont crafts, Middlebury/ Thomas Waterman Wood Art Gallery, 19th century American artists, Montpelier/ Athenaeum Art Gallery, Hudson River artists, St Johnsbury/ Millhouse Bundy Performing & Fine Arts Center, contemporary art, Waitsfield/ Old Mill Museum, craft demonstrations, Weston.

Entertainment: Discovery Museum for Children, participatory exhibits, art, history, science, Burlington/ Pico Alpine Slide, Killington/ Alpine Slide, Stowe/ Lake Champlain Ferries, from Burlington, Charlotte, Grand Isle.

Commercial: Cabot Cooperative Creamery Factory Tour, Cabot/ Crowley Cheese Factory Tours, Healdville/ Morgan Horse Farm Tours, Middlebury/ Plymouth Cheese Corp Factory Tour, Plymouth/ Vermont Marble Co Exhibits, Rutland/ Maple Grove Candy Factory Tours, St Johnsbury/ Cold Hollow Cider Mill, Waterbury.

Seasonal Events and Festivals: Stowe Winter Carnival, Jan, Stowe/ Discover Jazz Festival, June, Burlington/ Fool's Fest, July, Montpelier/ Bread & Puppet

Theater and Domestic Resurrection
Circus, Aug, Glvoer/ Antique &

Classic Car Rally, Aug, Stowe/
Stratton Arts Festival, Sept-Oct,
Stowe.

Virginia

Fame: *Preservation and restoration, a link with the past.*
You must: *drive the Colonial Parkway to Jamestown,
Colonial Williamsburg and Yorktown, visit Mount Vernon or
Monticello, a Civil War battlefield or one of the many other his-
toric preservations.*

Statewide Attractions

•Best Choices:

Mount Vernon
Mt Vernon Memorial Hwy, Fairfax
22121. (703)780-2000.

George Washington lived here,
with his family, before and after his
terms as Commander-in-Chief of
the Colonial Army and as President. Includes mansion, museum,
stables, kitchen, greenhouse, slave
quarters, gardens and tombs of
George and Martha Washington.
**$5/adult; $4/sr citizen; $2/child 6-
11.** 3/1-10/31, daily, 9-5. Rest of
yr, daily, 9-4.

Ash Lawn - Highland
Rte 795, 4 1/4 mi SE of Charlottesville.
(804)293-9539.

Estate owned by James Monroe,
fifth president of U.S. Early 19th
century working plantation. House

has Monroe posessions, boxing,
weaving and spinning demonstrations. Especially interesting are
boxwood gardens, with peacocks,
colonial crafts weekends,
Christmas programs, children's
programs. **$5/adult.** Mar-Oct,
daily, 9-6. Nov-Feb, daily 10-5.
Closed Thanksgiving, 12/25, 1/1.

Appomattox Court House Na-
tional Historical Park
Appomattox 24522. (804)352-8782.

3 mi NE of Appomattox on SR 24.
A village of 27 buildings has been
restored to its appearance in April
9, 1865. On that day the Confederate Army was cut off at Appomattox Court House. Later that
afternoon the surrender terms that
ended the Civil War were drafted
and signed in the McLean House.
$1/car. Daily, 9-5. Closed 1/1, Mar-

tin L. King Day, Presidents' Day, Thanksgiving and 12/25.

Arlington National Cemetery
Arlington Visitors Service, 735 S 18th St, Arlington 22202. (703)521-0772.

Directly across the Potomac from Washington, the best known of the national cemeteries. More than 200,000 men and women who served their country have been interred here, including 2 presidents, William Howard Taft, John F. Kennedy. Significant sights include Arlington House, the Robert E. Lee memorial, Grave of President John F. Kennedy, Confederate Memorial, Tomb of the Unknown Soldier, Marine Corps War Memorial, Mast of the Battleship Maine, Memorial Ampitheater. **Free. Narrated Tourmobile Tour: $2/adult; $1/child 3-11.** 4/1-9/30, daily, 8-7. Rest of yr, daily, 8-5.

Fredericksburg and Spotsylvania National Military Park
Superintendent, Box 679, Fredericksburg 22402. (703)373-4461.

Covers 6,000 acres and includes four major Civil War battlefields: Fredericksburg, Chancellorsville, Wilderness, Spotsylvania Court House. Also includes Old Salem Church, Fredericksburg National Cemetery, Chatham mansion, Stonewall Jackson Memorial Shrine. Visitor Center, Lafayette Blvd and Sunken Rd, has exhibits, movie. Self guided tours begin at center. During summer living his-

tory programs depict camp life. **Free.** 6/15-Labor Day, daily, 8:30-6:30. Rest of yr, daily, 9-5. Closed 1/1, 12/25.

•Good Choices:

Natural Scenery: Blue Ridge Parkway, scenic hwy connecting Shenandoah National Park and Great Smoky Mountains National Park/ Breaks Interstate Park, canyon, mountains, rock formations, caves, springs, Breaks/ Chincoteague National Wildlife Refuge, hundreds of birds, wildlife drive, Chincoteague/ George Washington National Forest, Colonial living farm designed to represent period of Washington's childhood/ Shenandoah National Park, mountains, valley, trees, wildlife sanctuary, scenery, drive, trails/ Skyline Drive, scenic drive runs along the crest of the ridge, Shenandoah National Park/ Prince William Forest Park, wildlife, forest, interpretive program, Triangle.
Nature and Man: Bristol Caverns, Bristol/ Cumberland Gap National Historical Park, natural gap in mountains, forests, animals, drive, trails, museum/ Skyline Caverns, Front Royal/ Thunderbird Museum and Archeological Park, rock formations, caves, trees, archeological dig, museum, slide show, Front Royal/ Bluebird Gap Farm, farm machinery, farm & wild animals, Hampton/ Shenandoah Caverns, New Market/ Virginia Living Museum, animals, plants, marine

animals, boardwalk, planetarium, museum, Newport News/ Lafayette Zoological Park, Norfolk/ Pocahontas Exhibition Coal Mine, tours, Pocahontas.

Gardens: National Memorial Park, gardens, fountains, Falls Church/ Morven Park, estate of Gov W Davis, gardens, restored mansion, working farm, Leesburg/ Norfolk Gardens-By-The-Seas, flowers, early spring to late summer, guided boat tours, Norfolk/ Maymont House and Nature Center, museum, landscaped gardens, Richmond/ Walter H Misenheimer Gardens of Surry, gardens, trails, Spring Grove.

Science and Technology: Wallops Visitor Center, space flight exhibits, Chincoteague/ NASA Visitor Center, air and space museum, Hampton/ North Ana Visitors Center, electrical and nuclear power, Mineral/ Reston, planned community/ Science Museum of Virginia, hands-on exhibits, aquarium, computer games, Richmond/ Roanoke Valley Science Museum, planetarium, exhibits on health, nature, nutrition, energy, Roanoke.

History: Alexandria: Tourist Council walking tours/ Gadsby's Tavern Museum, restored 18th century tavern, hotel/ George Washington's Grist Mill Historical State Park, machine replicas, slide show/ Stabler-Leadbeater Apothecary Shop, store where famous Colonists had perscriptions filled. Fredericksburg: Hugh Mercer Apothecary Shop, preserved pre-Revolutionary War shop/ James Monroe Law Office and Memorial Library, Monroe memorabilia/ Rising Sun Tavern, restored meeting place for patriots. Pentagon, guided tours, film, Arlington/ Booker T Washington National Monument, crops, farm animals, exhibits, slide show, trails/ Historic Michie Tavern, tavern, buildings, colonial furniture, artifacts, Charlottesville/ Colonial Parkway, connects Jamestown, Williamsburg, Yorktown/ George Washington Birthplace National Monument, Colonial living history farm, E of Fredricksburg/ Colvin Run Mill Park, restored working mill, house, barn, exhibits, Great Falls/ Syms-Eaton Museum and Kecoughtan Indian Village, art, artifacts, pre-Colonial to present, Indian village, Hampton/ Jamestown National Historic Site, ruins, paintings of Colonial buildings, Jamestown/ Jamestown Festival Park, reconstruction of 17th century ships, fort and Indian village, Jamestown/ George C Marshall Museum and Library, 20th century US military history, Virginia Military Institute, Lexington/ Natural Bridge Wax Museum, historical figures, Natural Bridge/ Gen Douglas MacArthur Memorial, MacArthur memoribilia, Norfolk/ Capitol, scene of many historical events, Richmond/ Chippokes Plantation State Park, working plantation, Surry/ Yorktown, battlefield & buildings standing after battle of Yorktown/ Yorktown Victory

Center, portrays events leading to Colonists' victory, Yorktown.

Civil War: Manassas National Battlefield Park/ New Market Battlefield Park, New Market/ Petersburg National Battlefield/ Seige Museum, human side of Civil War, Petersburg/ Museum of the Confederacy, Richmond/ Richmond National Battlefield.

The Sea: Mariners' Museum, prints, paintings, photographs, artifacts, ship models, small craft, Newport News/ Hampton Roads Naval Museum, naval history, memorabilia, Norfolk/ Norfolk Naval Station Tours, Norfolk/ Portsmouth Naval Shipyard Museum, naval history, Portsmouth/ Virginia Beach Maritime Historical Museum, area shipwrecks, Virginia Beach/ Virginia Marine Science Museum, marine environment, marine animals, computer, weather, outdoor boardwalk, Virginia Beach.

Historic Churches: Pohick Church, Mount Vernon parish church, Accotink/ Christ Church, church of George Washington, Robert E. Lee, Alexandria/ Old Presbyterian Meeting House, 1774, Alexandria/ Falls Church, 1733, Falls Church/ St George's Church, 1849, Fredericksburg/ St John's Church, 1728, Hampton/ Historic Christ Church, original church built in 1669, Irvington/ Lee Chapel, 1867, Washington and Lee Univ, Lexington/ St Paul's Church, 1739, Norfolk/ Old Blandford Church and Interpretive Center,1734-37 Petersburg/ St John's Episcopal Church, 1741, Richmond/ St Paul's Church, Church of Jefferson Davis, Robert E Lee, Richmond/ Trinity Episcopal Church, Upperville.

Historic Homes: Alexandria: Boyhood Home of Robert E Lee/ Carlyle House/ Lee-Fendall House/ Woodlawn. Fredericksburg: Kenmore/ Mary Washington House. Scotchtown, Ashland/ June Tolliver House, Big Stone Gap/ Smithfield Plantation House, Blacksburg/ Red Hill, Patrick Henry National Memorial, Brookneal/ Brandon Colonial Plantation, Burrowsville/ Sully Plantation, Chantilly/ Edgewood Plantation, Charles City/ Sherwood Forest, Charles City/ Shirley Plantation, Charles City/ Prestwould Plantation, Clarksville/ Belmont - The Gari Melchers Memorial Gallery, Falmouth/ Oatland, 1827 G. Carter estate, Leesburg/ Stonewall Jackson House, Lexington/ Gunston Hall,George Mason residence, Lorton/ Belle Grove, 1794 Maj I Hite estate and working farm, Middletown/ Moses Myers House, Norfolk/ Willoughby-Baylor House, 18th century, Norfolk/ Centre Hill Mansion, 1901, Petersburg/ Trapezium House, Petersburg/ Agecroft Hall, 15th century England, Richmond/ John Marshall House, 1790, Richmond/ Valentine Museum, Richmond/ Maymont House and Nature Center, Richmond/ Birthplace of Woodrow Wilson, Staunton/ Stratford Hall Plantation, working colonial plantation, Stratford/

Bacon's Castle, 1665, Surry/ Adma Thoroughgood House, Virginia Beach.

Art: Torpedo Factory Art Center, watch artists at work, Alexandria/ The College Museum, African, American, Afro-American art, Hampton Univ, Hampton/ Crysler Museum, ancient Greek, Roman, pre-Columbian, European, American paintings, Norfolk/ Virginia Museum of Fine Arts, ancient to contemporary art, Fabrege objects, Richmond/ Roanoke Museum of Fine Arts, Old Masters, local, national, Roanoke/ Abby Aldrich Rockefeller Folk Art Center, 9 permanent galleries of folk art, Williamsburg.

Entertainment: "Trail of the Lonesome Pine," June Tolliver Playhouse, Big Stone Gap/ "The Drama of Creation," Natural Bridge/ The Barns of Wolf Trap, theater, Vienna/ Big Walker Lookout Chairlift, Wytheville.

Children's Museums: Virginia Discovery Museum, for children, Charlottesville/ Richmond Children's Museum, art, humanities, particpatory exhibits, Richmond.

Commercial: Oakencroft Vineyard and Winery Tour, Charlottesville/ Rapidan River Vineyards Tour, Culpeper/ Shenandoah Vineyards Tours, Edinburg/ Mountain Cove Vineyards Tours, Lovingston/ Tri-Mountain Winery and Vineyard Tour, Middletown.

Washington

Fame: *Where sea, mountains and desert meet.*
You must: *drive to the mountains, ride on a ferry, eat freshly caught salmon and home-grown fruit.*

Seattle

Fame: *Northwest Cuisine, Waterfront.*
You must: *get out on the water in a tour boat, ferry etc. and sample Northwest Cuisine.*

•Best Choices:

Pike Place Market
Pike St and First Av. (206)682-7543.

Although Pike Place began as a farmer's market, it has diversified to include not only fresh produce and seafood but arts, crafts, restaurants, shops and street musicians. **Free.** Mon-Sat, 9-6; Sun and holidays, 11-5.

Seattle Center
305 Harrison St, 98109. (206)625-4234.

1 mi from downtown. This is the site of the 1962 World's Fair. The modern architecture of the buildings is exciting and the area now houses a number of attractions, each with a separate, entrance fee. Among the choices are Children's Museum, Fun Forest Amusement Park, Pacific Science Center, Seattle Art Museum Pavilion and the Space Needle. **Admission varies from $2 to $3.50/adult; $2.50 - 1/child.** Most are open 10-5, the Space Needle is open 9 am - midnight.

Bill Speidel's Underground Tours
610 First Av, 98104. (206)682-1511.

Tours begin at Doc Maynard's Public House, Pioneer Building, First Av and James St. After the city burned in 1889, the new city was built on top of the old ruins. Your guide will take you through the old city. Wear comfortable shoes. **$3.75/adult; $3.25/student 13-17; $2.50/sr citizen; $2/child 6-12.** Summer: Mon-Fri, 10, 11, 1, 2, 4, 6; Sat, Sun, 11, 1, 2, 3, 4, 6. Slighly shorter hours Nov - Apr.

Washington State Ferries

Downtown Seattle, Pier 52. (206)464-6400.

These rides provide a spectacular view of the city and give you an opportunity to spend a day or longer exploring another part of Washington. The ride to Winslow takes 30 min, one way, to Bremerton, 60 min, one way. **$3.30/adult; $1.65/sr citizen, child 5-11.** Hours vary with season.

•Good Choices:

Nature and Man: Discovery Park, nature trails, nature walks/ Evergreen Point Floating Bridge/ Lacey V. Murrow Floating Bridge/ Lake Washington Ship Canal and Hiram M. Chittenden Locks, gardens, locks, fish ladder/ Pier 59, see Museum of Ships, Seattle Aquarium/ Puget Sound Vessel Traffic Service Tour, traffic & weather informtion for ships, tours/ Univ of Washington Arboretum, plants from throughout world/ Volunteer Park, gardens, lawns, conservatory/ Woodland Park Zoological Gardens.

Historical and Cultural: Fry Art Museum, 19th century, European, American/ Henry Art Gallery, historical & American art/ Klondike Gold Rush National Historical Park, gold rush history, memorabilia/ Museum of Flight, aviation history/ Nordick Heritage Museum, Scandinavian - Pacific Northwest heritage, textiles, crafts/ Museum of Sea and Ships, Pier 59.

Entertainment: Fire Station No. 5, fire boats, phone ahead for tour/ Omnidome Theater, Pier 59.

Commercial: Chateau Ste Michelle Winery Tour/ Major

Marine Tours/ Pioneer Square Historic District/ Ranier Brewing Co Tour/ Seattle Harbor Tours/ Seattle Times Tour.

Sports: Kingdome Tours/ Longacres Race Track.

Statewide Attractions

•Best Choices:

Riverfront Park
N 507 Howard St, Spokane 99201. (509)456-5512.

I-90, Exit 281, follow Division St to the park. The site of Expo 74, has been turned into a 50 acre city recreational park. A day pass entitles the holder to admission to IMAX theater, Science Center, Carrousel, miniature golf, Pet Palace and Red Baron Ride. **$5/adult; $4/student 13-17; $3/sr citizen, child under 13.** 5/16-9/1, daily, 11-10. 4/10-5/15, 9/1-10/30: Fri, 3-8, Sat, Sun, Noon-8.

Maryhill Museum of Fine Arts
Star Rte 677, Box 23, Maryhill 98620. (509)773-4792.

SR 14, S of Goldendale. Known as the "Castle on the Columbia," this huge building contains American and European art, including a large collection of works by French sculptor Auguste Rodin, possessions donated by Queen Marie of Romania, a collection of miniature fashion designs by French

couturiers. **$3/adult; $1.50/student.** 3/15-11/15, daily, 9-5.

Capitol Group
Capitol Way, Mail Stop AX-22, Olympia 98507. (206)586-TOUR.

I-5, Exit 105A, take 14th Av to the area. Buildings of the legislative, judicial, insurance, gen administrative, Social Security, highway dept, employment security, public lands, library. Of particular interest is the architecture of the capitol bldg, the chance to watch laws being made. There are 55 acres of wooded, landscaped grounds surrounding the bldg, including arboretum, Tivoli fountain, sunken rose garden, Japanese cherry trees, rhododendrons. **Free.** Daily, 8-4:30. Guided tours, Mon-Fri, 9-4:30.

Mount St. Helens National Volcanic Monument
4611 Jackson Hwy, Winlock 98596. (206)274-6644.

I-5, Exit 49, SR 504 to Visitor Center. On May 18, 1980, the volcano erupted with a force 500 times the force of the first atomic bombs. The center will provide views of the mountain, information about the eruption and directions to find other views of the volcano. **Free.** Daily, 9-5.

•Good Choices:

Natural Scenery: Chuckanut Drive, view of Puget Sound, Bellingham/ Coulee Dam National Recreation Area, rock formations, wildflowers, wildlife/ Gifford Pinchot National Forest, caves, mountains, meadows, forest, canyon/ Willapa National Wildlife Refuge, bear, beaver, coyotes, deer, elk, birds, marsh, forests, Ilwaco/ Lake Chelan National Recreation Area, deep lake, waterfalls, forests, trails, nature walks/ San Juan Islands, wildlife refuge, recreation/ Olympia National Park, glaciers, mountains, forest, lakes, wildlife, trails/ Dungeness Spit, wildlife rest stop, Sequim.

Nature and Man: Padilla Bay National Estuarine Research Reserve and Interpretive Center, sanctuary, hands-on simulated environments, Bay View/ Goldendale Observatory, public telescope, Goldendale/ Lower Monumental Lock and Dam, fish ladder, powerhouse overlook, Kahlotus/ Gardner Cave, Metaline Falls/ Mount Baker-Snoqualmie National Forest, mountains, wildlife, fish, scenic drives, trails/ Mount Rainier National Park, volcano, glaciers, forests, meadows, wildlife/ North Cascake Smokejumper Base, tours, Twisp/

Ginko Petrified Forest State Park, 7,000 acres of fossilized trees, trails, Vantage/ Deception Pass State Park, shoreline, lakes, underwater marine park, Whidbey Island.

Arboretums: Sehome Hill Arboretum, Bellingham/ Wind River Nursery and Arboretum, trees, native & exotic, Carson/ John A Finch Arboretum, shrubs, trees, trail, Spokane.

Animals: Northwest Trek, guided tram tour through animal preserve, Eatonville/ Olympic Game Farm, animals used in films, Sequim/ Walk In The Wild zoo, Spokane/ Port Defiance Park, aviary, gardens, zoo, Tacoma.

Gardens: Manito Park, gardens, Spokane/ Ohme Gardens, Alpine gardens, Wenatchee/ Rocky Reach Dam, fish ladder, arts, crafts, history of electricity, steamships, gardens, Wenatchee.

Science and Technology: Wells Dam, hydroelectric generators, fish passages, Azwell/ Grand Coulee Dam, self-guided tours, Coulee Dam/ Hanford Science Center, computers, participatory exhibits tell about energy, US Dept of Energy information center, Richland.

Historical and Cultural: Hoquiam's Castle Mansion, Aberdeen-Hoquiam/ Pioneer Farm Museum, participatory pioneer activities, guided tours, Eatonville/ Port Townsend, Victorian architecture/ Cheney Cowles Memorial Museum, history, geology, natural history, Spokane/ Yakima Nation Cultural Center, history of Yakima

Indians, Toppenish/ Whitman Mission National Historic Site, pioneer buildings, Walla Walla.

Entertainment: Enchanted Village, family entertainment park, after 4 pm, Federal Way/ Wet 'N' Wild, entertainment park, after 4:30, Kennewick/ Puget Sound and Snoqualmie Valley Railroad, operating trains, Snoqualmie/ Yakima Trolley Lines, rides, Yakima.

Commercial: Historic Snohomish, "antique capitol of NW"/ Columbia Winery Tours, Bellevue/ Georgia-Pacific Corp Tours, Bellingham/ Carnation Research Farms Tour, Carnation/ Boeing 747-767 Division Tours, Everett/ Olympia Brewing Co Tour, Olympia/ Chateau Sainte Michelle Winery Tour, Paterson/ ITT Rayonier, pulp mill tours, Port Angeles/ Worden's Washington Winery Tours, Spokane/ Pendleton Woolen Mill, wool processing tour, Washougal/ Chateau Ste Michelle, Woodinville.

West Virginia

Fame: *The Mountain State.*
You must: *attend the Mountain State Arts and Crafts Festival.*

Statewide Attractions

•Best Choices:

Harpers Ferry National Historical Park
Superintendent, Box 65, Harpers Ferry 25425. (304)535-6371.

US 340. Three years before the Civil War began, abolitionist John Brown raided the federal arsenal at Harpers Ferry, planning to arm slaves from the arsenal and incite a rebellion. The town is being restored to 19th century appearance. Film, walking tour, exhibits, interpretive programs. **Free.** Daily, 8-5. Closed 12/25, 1/1.

Blennerhassett Island Historical Park
Parkersburg 26101. (304)428-3000.

Take a sternwheeler to the island, take a free guided tour of the park or a horse-drawn wagon ride, take a hike, visit the old mansion, see the Indian village excavations, have a picnic. **Sternwheeler: $2.50/adult; $1/child 2-12. Horse-drawn wagon: $2/adult; $1/2-12. Park: Free.** June-Aug, Wed-Sun, noon-6. May, Sept, Oct, Sat-Sun, noon-6.

Oglebay Park
Wheeling 26003. (304)242-3000.

SR 88, 2 mi N of jct I-70 and US 40. Municipal park with gardens, greenhouses, miniature golf, skiing, tobogganing, tennis, zoo, mansion museum. **Zoo: $2.75/adult; $2/sr citizen; $1.75/child 2-17. Mansion: $2.50/adult; $2/sr citizen; $1.50/student 13-18. Park: Free.** Open yr around. Closed Thanksgiving, 12/25, 1/1.

State Capitol/Governor's Mansion
1900 Washington St E, Charleston 25305. (304)348-3809.

The State Capitol, designed by architect Cass Gilbert, with golden dome, 180 ft high, and 8 ft, 2 ton rock crystal chandelier hanging from the dome, is said to be one of the most beautiful state capitols. The 20 room mansion is adjacent to the capitol, designed in Georgian Colonial style, with high portico and fluted, white columns. **Free.** Capitol: Mon-Sat, 8:30-4:30. Mansion: Thurs-Fri, 9:30-11:30 am. Closed Thanksgiving, 12/25, 1/1.

•Good Choices:

Natural Scenery: Hawk's Nest State Park and Tramway, museum, lookout point, tram ride, Ansted/ Grandview State Park, scenic gorge, gardens, Beckley/ Blackwater Falls State Park, gorge, falls, Davis/ Monongahela National Forest, mountains, wildlife, plants, forest, trails/ Petersburg Gap, "pictured rocks," cliffs, Petersburg/ Spruce Knob-Seneca Rocks National Recreation Area.

Nature and Man: Beckley Exhibition Coal Mine, working demonstrations, Beckley/ Museums at Sunrise, children's museum, nature center, Charleston/ Highland Scenic Highway, SR 150, Cranberry Glades, to US 219, Edray/ John Brown Wax Museum, Harpers Ferry/ Leetown National Fisheries Center, exhibits, aquariums, library, nature trails, Leetown/ New River Gorge Bridge and Visitors Center, Oak Hill/ Smoke Hole Caverns, Petersburg/ Highland Trace, SR 55, state line, thru Potomac Highlands.

Science and Technology: National Radio Astronomy Observatory Tours, tours, Green Bank.

Historical and Cultural: Historic District, Bramwell/ Museums at Sunrise, fine arts, Charleston/ Glade Creek Grist Mill, Clifftop/ Pricketts Fort State Park, living history museum, Fairmont/ Old Mill, gristmill, looms, Harman/ Huntington Galleries Art Museum, 19th, 20th century art, Huntington/ West Virginia State Farm Museum, historic living farm, Pt Pleasant/ Organ Cave, Ronceverte/ Historic Districts, Wheeling.

186

Buildings: Berkeley Castle, 1/2 scale copy of castle, Berkeley Springs/ Pearl S Buck Birthplace, Hillsboro/ Palace of Gold, "America's Taj Mahal," tours, Moundsville.
Entertainment: Valley Voyager, sternwheeler cruises, Wheeling.
Commercial: Pilgrim Glass Corporation, observation area, Huntington/ Blenko Glass Co, observation of glassblowingmuseum, Milton/ Homer Laughlin China Co. Tour, Newell/ Viking Glass Co Tour, New Martinsville/ West Virginia Glass Specialty Co, tours, Weston/ Fenton Art Glass Co, tours, museum, Williamstown.
Seasonal Events and Festivals: Mountain State Arts and Crafts Fair, July, Ripley/ Festival of Lights, Nov-Jan, Oglebay Park, Wheeling.

Wisconsin

Fame: *Lakes and forests, a place to relax.*
You must: *sample some of the regional foods: Cornish pasty, Wisconsin cheese, bratwurst, cranberries, fish boils.*

Statewide Attractions

•Best Choices:

Milwaukee County Zoo
10001 W Bluemound Rd, Milwaukee 53226. (414)771-3040.

The zoo has one of the world's most comprehensive collections of animals displayed in natural habitat. Daily tours in zoomobiles. **$3.50/adult; $1.50/sr citizen, child 3-15. Zoomobile: $1.** Memorial Day - Labor Day, Mon-Sat, 9-5; Sun and holidays, 9-6. Rest of yr, 9-4:30. Closed Thanksgiving, 12/25, 1/1.

Heritage Hill State Park

2640 S Webster, Green Bay 54301. (414)497-4368.

40 acre site with 22 buildings grouped in four theme areas to illustrate the historic development of the area. Customed guides conduct tours and portray life of early pioneers. **$4/adult; $3/sr citizen; $2/student 6-12.** Jun-Aug, Tues-Sun, 10-5. May and Sept, Sat-Sun, 10-5. Also open day after Thanksgiving, 2nd wknd in Dec.

Milwaukee Public Museum
800 W Wells St, Milwaukee 53233. (414)278-2700.

A unique museum that allow visitors to enter imaginative environmental exhibits that vary from Streets of Milwaukee to Old Delhi. Life-sized replicas of dinosaurs; Wizard Wing Discovery Center. **$3/adult; $1.50/child 4-17.** Daily, 9-5. Closed Thanksgiving, 12/25, 1/1.

Manitowoc Maritime Museum
75 Maritime Dr, Manitowoc 54220. (414)684-0218.

The largest maritime museum on the Great Lakes, it features 3-dimensional exhibits depicting 19th century riverfront, extensive displays of models and maritime aritifacts. Moored adjacent to the museum is WW II submarine, U.S.S. Cobia. **$2/adult; $1/child 6-12. Combination ticket with Cobia: $4/adult; $2/child.** 5/1-10/31: Daily, 9-5. Rest of yr: Mon-Fri, 9-5; Sat-Sun, 10-4.

•Good Choices:

Natural Scenery: Devil's Lake State Park, mountains ring lake, cliffs, rock formations, nature hikes, trails, Baraboo/ Apostle Islands National Lakeshore, 20 islands with wilderness, trails, Bayfield/ Grandad Bluff, scenic view of city, LaCrosse/ Copper Falls State Park, waterfalls, Mellen.
Nature and Man: Madeline Island/ University Arboretum, Madison/ Mitchell Park, gardens and conservatory, Milwaukee/ Schlitz Audubon Center, Milwaukee/ Alfred L Boerner Botanical Gardens, Univ of WI, Milwaukee/ Wehr Nature Center, Univ of WI, Milwaukee/ Honey Acres Museum, beekeeping, hive, nature walk, Oconomowoc/ Mackenzie Environmental Education Center, wildlife, arboretum, firetower, Poynette/ Crystal Cave, Spring Valley/ The Farm, animals, milking demonstrations, gardens, Sturgeon Bay/ Green Meadows Farm, working farm, Waterford/ Lost Canyon, Wisconsin Dells.
Zoos, animal parks Aqualand Wildlife Park, Wisconsin wildlife, Boulder Junction/ Irvine Park, zoo and recreation, Chippewa Falls/ Wilderness Walk, animals in natural habitats, Hayward/ Henry Vilas Park Zoo, Madison/ Jim Peck's Wildwood Live Tame Wildlife, Minocqua/ Racine Zoological Park, Racine.
Science and Technology: U.S. Forest Products Laboratory, use of wood and wood products, Madison/ Point Beach Energy Information Center, electricity production, Two Rivers.
History: The Hideout, Al Capone's hideout, Courderay/ Paul Bunyan Camp, 1890's logging camp, Eau Claire/ Old Wade House, living history stagecoach inn, Greenbush/ State Capitol Tours, Madison/ St Joan of Arc Chapel, restored 15th Century French Chapel, Milwaukee/ Chalet of the Golden Fleece, Swiss

museum, New Glarus/ Fairlawn Mansion and Museum, Victorian mansion and museum, Superior/ Whaleback Carrier Meteor, ship, Superior/ Winnebago Indian Museum, Wisconsin Dells.

Historic Houses: Little Norway, 1856 Norwegian homestead, Blue Mounds/ Octagon House, Hudson/ Tallman Restorations, restored 19th century houses, Janesville/ Pabst Mansion, Milwaukee/ Pendarvis, Cornish lead miners' homes, Mineral Point/ Beyer Home Museum, Victorian mansion, museum, Oconto/ Villa Louis, Victorian mansion, decorative arts, museum, fur house, Prairie du Chien/ Octagon House, Watertown.

Historic Villages: Stonefield Village and State Farm Museum, restored village, mansion, farm tools, Cassville/ Galloway House and Village, restored mansion, village, gristmill, museum, Fond du Lac/ Aztalan Museum, pioneer village, Aztalan and Woodland Indian artifacts, Lake Mills/ Pinecrest Historical Village, Manitowoc/ Swiss Historical Village, New Glarus.

Special Interest Museums: Uihlein Antique Racing Car Museum, Cedarburg/ Nature's Miracle Museum, rocks and minerals, Dodgeville/ Rail America, railroad museum and ride, Green Bay/ EAA Air Museum, aircraft, Oshkosh.

Art: Madison Art Center, changing exhibits, Madison/ Elvehjem Museum of Art, 2300 BC to present, Univ of WI, Madison/ Rahr-West Museum and Civic Center, Victorian house, artifacts, American art, art collection, Manitowoc/ Milwaukee County War Memorial, including Charles Allis Art Museum, 600 BC to early 1900s, Milwaukee Art Museum, Old Masters, American, contemporary art, Villa Terrace, Milwaukee/ Paine Art Center and Arboretum, French, Oriental art, arboretum, English garden, Oshkosh/ Charles A Wustum Museum of Fine Arts, painting, graphics, crafts, sculpture, Racine/ Museum of Norman Rockwell, prints, magazine covers, Reedsburg.

Entertainment: Emerald Isle Boat Line, harbor cruise, Milwaukee/ Chief Waupaca Sternwheeler Cruise, Waupaca.

Commercial: Dard Hunter Paper Museum, Appleton/ Door Peninsula Winery Tour, Carlsville/ Stone Mill Winery and Cedar Creek Settlement, Cedarburg/ General Motors Assembly Division Tour, Janesville/ Kohler Visitor Center, factory tours, Kohler/ Christina Wine Cellars Tours, LaCrosse/ Swiss Miss Textile Mart factory tour, embroideried fabric, New Glarus/ Stallman's Cheese Factory tours, Oconomowoc/ Rhinelander Paper Co Tour, Rhinelander/ Scott Paper Co Tour, Oconto Falls/ Badger Paper Mills Tour, Peshtigo/ The Mining Museum, museum, mine, train ride, Platteville/ Wollersheim Winery Tour, Prairie du Sac/ Johnson Wax Administration and Research Center, offices by Frank Lloyd Wright, research, film, Racine.

Brewery Tours: Leinenkugel Brewery Tours and Museum, Chippewa Falls/ Hibernia Brewing Tour, Eau Claire/ G Heileman Brewing Co. tours, LaCrosse/ Miller Brewing Co Tour, Milwaukee/ Pabst Brwery Tour, Mil

waukee.

Sports: Green Bay Packer Hall of Fame, Green Bay/ National Fresh Water Fishing Hall of Fame, Hayward.

Seasonal Events and Festivals: Scheer's Lumberjack Show, 6/1- 9/1, Hayward.

Wyoming

Fame: *Cowboy State; Yellowstone Park; Grand Teton Park.*
You must: *visit Yellowstone and Grand Teton; see a rodeo.*

Statewide Attractions

•Best Choices:

Yellowstone National Park
Superintendent, Box 168, Yellowstone National Park 82190. (307)344-7381.

Famed for its thermal wonders, including geysers, fumaroles, bubbling mud pots and hot pools. Elk, buffalo, moose, coyotes, mule deer, pronghorn antelope, bighorn sheep and many birds can be seen. **One wk pass, Yellowstone and Grand Teton: $5/car.** Open to vehicle traffic 5/1-10/31. Rest of yr open to snowmobile or snow coach.

Grand Teton National Park
Drawer 170, Moose 83012. (307)733-2880.

Noted for the beauty of the magnificent Teton mountains rising to heights of more than 13,000 ft, it

also has alpine lakes, sagebrush flats, pine forests and abundant wildlife. Grand Teton is just north of Yellowstone. **One wk pass, Grand Teton and Yellowstone: $5/car.** Open to vehicle traffic 5/1-10/31. Rest of yr open to snowmobile or snow coach.

Buffalo Bill Historical Center
Box 1000, Cody 82414. (307)587-4771.

This four-museum complex has over 160,000 ft of exhibition space and has been called the "Smithsonian of the West." The four main exhibit areas are Buffalo Bill Museum, representing the great showman; Whitney Gallery of Western Art, with art from the early 1880's; Plains Indian Museum, representing the Plains' tribes; Winchester Arms Museum, with firearms displays. Also includes garden areas. **$5/adult; $4.25/sr citizen; $3.25/student; $2/child.** Jun-Aug, daily, 7-10. May, Sept, daily, 8-5. Mar-Apr, Oct-Nov, Tues-Sun, 10-3. Closed Dec-Feb.

Fort Laramie National Historic Site

Superintendent, Ft Laramie 82212. (307)837-2221.

---

20 mi NW of Torrington. This area has a colorful history, from fur trading post to army post, situated on the Oregon Trail and in the path west to the California gold rush. It contains 22 original buiidings, many have been restored and furnished. Summer guides participate in a living history program. **$1/adult.** 6/15 - Labor Day, 8-8. Rest of yr, 8-4:30. Closed Thanksgiving, 12/25, 1/1.

•Good Choices:

Natural Scenery: Devils Tower National Monument, rock formation from movie "Close Encounters," Devils Tower/ Bridger-Teton National Forest, mountains, forest, lake, trails, surrounds Jackson/ Sinks Canyon State Park, canyon, pool, wildlife, Lander/ Bighorn Canyon National Recreation Area, canyon, mountains, Lovell/ Pryor Mountain Wild Horse Range, wild horse sanctuary, Lovell/ Skyline Scenic Drives, Pinedale/ Bighorn National Forest, canyon, mountains, lake, canyon, Sheridan/ Hot Springs State Park, mineral hot spring, pool, bathhouses, Thermopolis.

Nature and Man: Trout Creek Buffalo Preserve, bison herd, Cody/ Jackalope Warm Springs Plunge, 84 degree artesian water, Douglas/ National Elk Refuge, winter home for elk, Jackson.

Historical and Cultural: National First Day Cover Museum, for stamp collectors, Cheyenne/ Governor's Mansion, Cheyenne/ State Museum and Art Gallery, Cheyenne/ Old Trail Town, frontier restorations, Cody/ Fort Bridger State Museum, pioneer history, craft demos, Evanston/ South Pass City, ghost city, Lander/ Fine Arts Museum, 16th century to present, Laramie/ Wyoming Frontier Prison, tours, Rawlins/ Remember When Auto Museum, Riverton/ Bradford Brinton Memorial Ranch Museum, Western art and history, Sheridan/ Trail End Historic Center, mansion, Sheridan.

Commercial: Accident Oil Co, tour, Newcastle.

Seasonal Events and Festivals: Cheyenne Frontier Days, July.

Canada

All rates in Canadian dollars unless otherwise indicated

Alberta

Fame: *Mountains, prairies, lakes, glaciers.*
You must *visit Banff National Park, Jasper National Park and Lake Louise.*

Provincewide Attractions

•Best Choices:

Banff National Park
Chamber of Commerce, Box 1298, Banff T0L 0C0. (403)762-3777.

Some of the world's most awe-inspiring mountain scenery with range after range of tall rocky peaks, wooded valleys, crystal clear waters, narrow canyons, slow-moving glaciers, dazzling white ice fields. **4 days Banff and Jasper: $2/vehicle.** Open yr around but part of park may be closed 10/1 - 4/15.

Jasper National Park
Chamber of Commerce, Box 98, Jasper T0E 1E0. (403)852-3858.

More majestic mountains, alpine meadows, jeweled lakes, rugged glaciers. Although it is under separate management, it's really a part of the same scenery found in Banff. **4 days Jasper and Banff: $2/vehicle.** Open yr around but part of park may be closed 10/1 - 4/15.

Head-Smashed-In Buffalo Jump
16 km (11 mi) W of Hwy 2 on secondary Hwy 785, Ft Macleod. (403)553-2731.

The largest and best preserved buffalo jump in N America. Designated a World Heritage Site by UNESCO in 1981. Interpretive guides, five display galleries, audio-visual presentations. **Free.** Early May to Early Sept, 9-8. Rest of yr, 10-5.

Polar Park
14 km SE of the Sherwood Park Frwy on Hwy 14.

A reserve for cold climate animals, the park features over 100 species of animals from Canada, Northern China, Russia and other cold climate countries. **$4/adult; $2/sr citizen, student 7-16.** Daily, 8 am - dark.

Nikko Yuko Japanese Gardens
8 Av S and Mayor Magrath Dr, Lethbridge. (403)328-3511.

A symbol of Japanese-Canadian friendship, these are gardens of meditation, revolving around water, rocks and green shrubs. The buildings and bridges were built in 1967 in Japan and reassembled in Lethbridge. **$2/adult; $1/sr citizen, student.** Open 5/15-10/15.

•Good Choices:

Natural Scenery: Icefields Parkway, streams, waterfalls, Lake Louise to Jasper/ Lake Louise, glacier, lake/ Sheep Region Wildlife Sanctuary, view Bighorn sheep, Sheep River/ White Goat Wilderness, wildlife, mountains, glacier, trail, eastern border of Jasper and Banff National Parks. **Nature and Man:** Alberta Wildlife Park, 100 species of animals, Bon Accord/ Alberta Horticultural Research Centre, flower and shrub gardens, Brooks/ Waterton Lakes National Park, international peace park with Glacier National Park in U.S./ Calgary Zoo, Calgary/ Devonian Gardens, indoor sub-tropical garden, pools, waterfall, Calgary/ Sam Livingston Fish Hatchery and Rearing Station, aquariums, self-guided tours, Calgary/ Cochrane Ranche, historic site, wildflowers, wildlife, Cochrane/ Univ of Alberta Devonian Botanic Garden, scenic gardens, nature trail, Devon/ Waskasoo Park, historic areas, nature centre, recreation, Red Deer/ Sleepy Valley Game Farm, native

and exotic animals, petting zoo, tours, Rocky Mountain House/ John Janzen Nature Centre, plants, animals, exhibits, nature walks, Edmonton/ Muttart Conservatory, arid, tropical, temperate plants, Edmonton/ Valley Zoo, Edmonton/ Elk Island National Park, elk, plains & wood bison, meadows, forests, trails, Edmonton. **Science and Technology:** Centennial Planetarium and Science Centre, observatory, hands-on science displays, Calgary/ Energeum, hands-on energy displays, Calgary/ Edmonton Space Sciences Centre, planetarium, IMAX Theatre, science exhibits, Edmonton/ Strathcona Science Park, including Natural Resources Centre and Archaeological Centre, computers, audio visual shows, excavation, hands-on displays, Edmonton/ Oil Sands Interpretive Centre, displays, multi-media and hands-on mining exhibits, Fort McMurray. **Historical and Cultural:** Dinosaur Provincial Park, fossil fields, interpretive programs, walks, NE of Brooks/ Heritage Park, restored prairie railroad town, Calgary/ Tyrell Museum of Paleontology, fossils, garden, computers, videos, Drumheller/ Alberta Legislative Building, Edmonton/ Fort Edmonton Park, train, street car rides, replica villages, fort, Edmonton/ John Walter Historic Site, 1875-1900 houses, Edmonton/ Rutherford House, 1911-1915, Edmonton/ Ukrainian Cultural Heritage Village, recreated village, demonstrations, Hwy 16 50 km E

of Edmonton/ Fort Whoop-Up, notorious whiskey trading post, Lethbridge/ Rocky Mountain House National Historic Park, history of fur trading post, nature trails, buffalo, Rocky Mountain House/ Historical Village and Pioneer Museum, Shandro.
Art: Alberta College of Art Gallery, contemporary art, Calgary.
Transportation Museums: Calgary Aerospace Museum, restored aircraft, Calgary/ Remington's Carriage Collection, Cardston/ Canada's Aviation Hall of Fame, Edmonton/ Reynolds Museum, antique vehicles, Wetaskiwin.
Commercial: Canadian Salt Company Tours, Lindbergh/ United Oilseed Products Tour, Lloydminster/ Andrew Wolf Wine Cellars Tour, Stony Plain.
Sports: Alberta Sports Hall of Fame and Museum, Calgary.

British Columbia

Fame: *Pacific coastal province; Vancouver, Vancouver Island and Victoria.*
You must *visit one of the two major cities, Victoria or Vancouver.*

Provincewide Attractions

•Best Choices:

Stanley Park
West Georgia St, Vancouver.

1,000 acres of gardens, beaches, nature trails, lakes. Includes tennis courts, miniature golf courses, seawall, midget railroad, lawn bowling greens, giant checkerboard and many other things to see and do. Small zoo and large aquarium. **Aquarium: $5/adult; $2.75/child. Zoo: Free.**

Provincial Museum
675 Belleville St, Victoria V8V 1X4.
(604)387-3014, 387-3701.

Natural and human history, guided tours. Here you'll find a steam railway station, a model T Ford, prehistoric Indian artifacts and extinct animals. A well-organized, diverse, fascinating museum. Free. Daily, 10-5:30. Closed 12/25, 1/1.

Pacific Undersea Gardens
490 Belleville St, Victoria V8V 1W9.
(604)382-5717.

Inner Harbour across from the Parliament Bldgs. Underwater windows enable the viewer to see over 5,000 marine specimens from the local area. Scuba diver shows starring Armstrong, the Pacific Octopus. **$4.75/adult; $3.50/student; $2/child 5-11.** May-Sept, 9-dusk. Rest of yr, 10-dusk.

Burnaby Village Museum
4900 Deer Lake Av, Burnaby V5G 3T6. (604)294-1233.

Costumed attendants provide living history in town restored to the period between 1890 and 1925. Sniff bakery aromas, watch a blacksmith work. **$3/adult; $2/sr citizen, student.** 3/1-12/31, Tues-Sun.

Maritime Museum
28 Bastion Square, Victoria V8W 1H9. (604)385-4222.

Galleries include those devoted to Captain Cook, sail boats, tow boats, Royal and Canadian Navy. Home of Tilikum and Trekka, two famous small boats that sailed around the world. Outstanding presentation of British Columbia maritime heritage from early explorers to recent past. **$3/adult; $2/sr citizen; $1/child over 6.** 7/1-Labour Day, daily, 10-6. Rest of yr, Mon-Sat, 10-4; Sun, noon-4.

•Good Choices:
Nature and Man: Vancouver Game Farm, 85 species of animals viewed from roadway, Aldergrove/ Bowen Park, gardens, animal farm, recreation, Nanaimo/ Okanagan Game Farm, wild animals in natural setting, Penticton/ Agriculture Canada Research Station, flower gardens, Penticton. Vancouver: VanDusen Botanical Garden, exotic, native plants/ Queen Elizabeth Park, conservatory, view. Victoria: Beacon Hill Park, lakes, gardens, waterfowl/ Crystal Garden, waterfall, gardens, fish, reptile house/ Sealand, underwater views, trained seals, whale shows.

Science and Technology: Dominion Radio Astrophysical Observatory, tours, Penticton. Vancouver: Arts, Sciences and Technology Centre, hands-on exhibits/ Planetarium.

Historical and Cultural: Barkerville, restored gold rush town/ Burnaby Art Gallery, Burnaby/ Fort Langley National Historic Park, restored Hudson's Bay post, Ft Langley/ Centennial Museum, coal mine, dioramas, historic shops, Nanaimo/ Beardale Castle Miniatureland, handcrafted miniatures, animated toys, Revelstoke. Vancouver: Maritime Museum, restored schooner, model ships, artifacts/ Univ of BC Museum of Anthropology, NW Indian artifacts/ Samson V Maritime Museum, paddlewheeler floating museum/ Vancouver Museum, Vancouver history, NW Indian culture. Victoria: Art Gallery of Greater Victoria, Japanese, European, Canadian art/ BC Forest Museum, logging artifacts, train ride/ Classic Car Museum/ Craigdarroch Castle,

1889/ Craigflower Manor National Historic Site, 1856 colonial/ Fort Rodd Hill National Historic Site, 1895-1956 artillery fort, tours/ Hatley Castle, 1908 estate/ Helmcken House, 1852, original furnishings/ Legislative Building.
Entertainment: Ferry: Nainamo,

Vancouver, Victoria/ Fable Cottage Estate, gardens, storybook characters, mansion, Victoria/ Miniature World, models, doll house, railway, sawmill, circus, Victoria.
Commercial: Vancouver areas: Granville Island/ Gastown/ Chinatown.

Manitoba

Fame: *The Heartland Province.*
You must *visit the Museum of Man and Nature.*

Provincewide Attractions

•Best Choices:

Museum of Man and Nature
190 Rupert Av, Winnipeg R3B 0N2. (204)956-2830.

Travel from the beginning of the earth to 1920 Winnipeg in one afternoon. Along the way visit the Arctic, the Inuit and Chipewyan Indians, the Boreal Forest, the Grasslands and a 17th century sailing ship. It's a way to personally discover Manitoba. **$2.50/adult; $1.50/sr citizen, student, child.** 5/15-9/15, Mon-Sat, 10-9; Sun, 12-9. 9/16-5/14, 10-5; Sun, noon-6.

Lower Fort Garry National Historic Park
Box 37, Group 343, RR 3, Selkirk R1A 2A8. (204)983-3600.

20 mi N of Winnipeg on Hwy 9. Lower Ft Garry has been restored to its 1850's appearance as a busy fur-trading post for the Hudson's Bay Co. The original buildings are staffed with costumed personnel, who recreate the post by carrying out the daily duties of the fur traders and settler of Red River. **$3/adult; $1.50/child 5-16.** Mid May - Labor Day, daily, 9:30-6.

Assiniboine Park and Zoo
2355 Corydon Av, Winnipeg R3P 0R5. (204)888-3634.

The park has 303 acres which includes a miniature railway, English garden, conservatory, Aunt Sally's Farm, zoo and many recreational facilities. The 100 acre zoo has 300 species, including a large collection of rare and endangered animals, with emphasis on nearctic species. **Free.** Daily, 10 am to 1/2 hr before sunset -- mid summer to 9 pm; mid winter to 4 pm.

Riding Mountain National Park

Wasagaming R0J 2H0. (204)848-2811.

---

65 mi N of Brandon, about 175 mi NW of Winnipeg. 1150 sq miles of rolling forested plateau, native prairie grasslands, boreal vegetation and prairie marshes. The park has black bears, Manitoba elk, moose, coyotes, bison and over 260 species of birds. Interpretive centre, trails and exhibits. $3/car. Open yr around.

•Good Choices:

Natural Scenery: Spirit Sands of Spruce Woods Provincial Heritage Park, drifting dunes, trails, Carberry/ Whiteshell Provincial Park, lakes, rock, grassland, fishing, Rennie.

Nature and Man: Winnipeg: Fort Whyte Centre for Environmental Education, interpretive program, trail/ Oak Hammock Marsh Wildlife Management Area, interpretive tours, visitor centre.

Science and Technology: Winnipeg: Manitoba Planetarium, wide variety of shows/ Touch the Universe Science Gallery, hands-on exhibits.

Historical and Cultural: Commonwealth Air Training Plan Museum, WWII aircraft, Air Force mementos, Brandon/ Dugald Costume Museum, fashions of the past, Dugald. Winnipeg: Dalnavert, McDonald House Museum, 1895/ Grant's Old Mill, reconstructed 1829 mill/ Legislative Building, tours/ Royal Canadian Mint, tour/ Ukrainian Cultural and Educational Centre, art, history, books/ Western Canada Aviation Museum/ Winnipeg Art Gallery, Inuit art, changing exhibits of Canadian, European, U.S. art/ Winnipeg Commodity Exchange, gallery, guides.

Commercial: Old Market Square, open air market, Winnipeg.

Sports: Assiniboin Downs Racetrack, Winnipeg.

Seasonal Events and Festivals: Red River Exhibition, June, Winnipeg/ Ukranian Festival, Aug, Dauphin/ Folklorama, Aug, Winnipeg.

New Brunswick

Fame: *Seashore: from the cool, rugged Bay of Fundy to the warmer beaches of the Northumberland Strait.*
You must *eat fresh New Brunswick seafood, sample dulse (seaweed) or fiddleheads (fern tops).*

Provincewide Attractions

•Best Choices:

Kings Landing Historical Settlement
Box 522, Fredericton E3B 5A6.
(506)363-3081.

34 km W of Fredericton off Trans-Canada Hwy, Exit 259. Recreated Loyalist village depicting life in New Brunswick in the 19th century. A costumed staff of more than 100 in 60 buildings recalls the sights, sounds, smells and pace of the Loyalist lifestyle of the time. **$5/adult; $4.50/sr citizen; $2/child 6-8.** Jun-Jul, Sept-mid Oct: daily, 10-5. Jul-Aug: daily, 10-6.

Acadian Historic Village
Box 820, Caraquet E0B 1K0. (506)727-3467.

Rte 11, between Caraquet and Grand-Anse, 10 km W of Carquet. The simple life in this recreated village is a sharp contrast to the comfortable life in Kings Landing. Houses are devoid of ornamentation, illustrating the times of poverty and hardship experienced by Acadians returning to their homeland. The revival of the traditional trades such as blacksmithing, cartwriting, weaving and the making of shingles by hand enabled the settlers to survive. The unique diking system used to reclaim the marshlands, traditional Acadian foods, the old trades, costumes and traditions are demonstrated by guides. **$5/adult; $2/child 6-18.** June-Aug, daily 10-6; Sept, daily 10-4.

Grand Falls Gorge
Grand Falls.

The Saint John River drops a dramatic 70 ft creating one of the largest cataracts E of Niagara Falls. The gorge is 1 mi long and has fascinating wells-in-the-rocks. Interpretative displays, stairs, walking trails offer a variety of vantage points from which to view the natural phenomenon. **Free.**

Roosevelt Campobello International Park
Campobello Island. (506)752-2922.

On Rte 774, Campobello Island, 1 1/2 mi from Canadian Customs. The Franklin Delano Roosevelt summer cottage and estate. Beautiful gardens, guided tours, film presentations. **Free.** Open every year from Sat before Memorial Day for 20 weeks. Approx mid May - early Oct.

•Good Choices:

Natural Scenery: Fundy National Park, cliffs, beaches, woods, Alma/ Flowerpot Rocks, rock formations, Hopewell Cape/ Kouchibouguac National Park, salt marshes, warm salt water beaches, sand dunes, Kent County/ Reversing Falls Rapids, Saint John.

Nature and Man: Magnetic Hill Game Farm, wild animal park and petting zoo, Moncton/ New Brunswick Mining and Mineral Interpretation Center, history, geology, mine shaft, Petit-Rocher/ Huntsman Marine Laboratory Museum and Aquarium, St Andrews/ Marine Center, aquarium, fishing industry, Shippagan. **Historical and Cultural:** Beaverbrook Art Gallery, Canadian art, English porcelain, Fredericton/ Ross Memorial Museum, house filled with antiques, paintings, St Andrew/ Loyalist House, Saint John/ New Brunswick Museum, Canadian history, ships, shipbuilding, natural science, oriental art, Saint John.
Commercial: City Market, Mon-Sat, Saint John.
Seasonal Events and Festivals: Festival by the Sea, Aug, Saint John.

Newfoundland and Labrador

Fame: *Remote, dramatic scenery, glacial lakes and streams, sparse population.*
You must *try codjigging, feast on native treats such as cod tongues, fish and brewis, cod and scrunchions or bake-apple berries.*

Provincewide Attractions

•Best Choices:

Gros Morne National Park
Hwy 430, Wiltondale.

In a province that has exciting scenery, this park has spectacular scenery. Look for steep cliff walls, fjords, lakes, rugged mountains, bogs and wild flowers. **$2/car.**

•Good Choices:

Natural Scenery: Terra Nova National Park, lakes, streams, forest, bays, trails, Bonavista Bay/ Auto Tours, contact Department of Tourism, St Johns.
Historical and Cultural: Cape Bonavista Lighthouse, Bonavista/ Mockbeggar Property, merchant residence, carpenter's shop, fish store, Bonavista/ Mary March Museum, history of Beothuck Indians, Grand Falls/ Cable Station, history of cable telegraphy, Heart's Content/ Commissariat House, St John's/ Newfoundland Museum, exhibits on native Newfoundlanders, St John's/ Quidi Vidi Battery, reconstructed to War of 1812, St John's/ Hiscock House, small business household, Trinity.

Northwest Territories

Fame: *A land of the midnight sun, northern lights, the taiga and the tundra.*

You must *find an example of art or craft, produced by a local artist, to take home with you.*

Provincewide Attractions

•Best Choices:

Prince of Wales Northern Heritage Centre
Government of the NW Territories, Yellowknife X1A 2L9. (403)873-7551.

Collection includes Inuit, Dene and Metis history and artifacts, together with early mining and aviation history, presented through dioramas, artifacts, slide presentations. Lookout platform with panoramic view. Free.

•Good Choices:

Natural Scenery: Nahanni National Park, a UNESCO World Heritage Site, spectacular scenery, Fort Simpson/ Wood Buffalo National Park, herd of wood bison, Fort Smith/ Alexandra Falls, Hay River/ Auyuittuq National Park, Arctic plants, animals, spectacular scenery, visitors centre, Pangnirtung.

Historical and Cultural: Nunuuta Museum, Arctic arts and crafts, Frobisher Bay/ Northern Life Museum and National Exhibition Centre, history and culture, Fort Smith.

Commercial: West Baffin Eskimo Cooperative, arts and crafts, Cape Dorset/ Giant Yellowknife Mines, gold mine tour, Yellowknife/ Nerco Con Mine, gold mine tour, Yellowknife.

Seasonal Events and Festivals: Caribou Carnival, March, Yellowknife/ Midnight Golf Tournament, June, Yellowknife.

Nova Scotia

Fame: *Scottish culture and traditions, early French settlements and the setting for the poem "Evangeline," fishing villages nestled in picturesque coves.*

You must *see the Highland Games, visit Grand Pre National Park, follow the Lighthouse Route from Halifax to Yarmouth.*

Provincewide Attractions

•Best Choices:

Grand Pre National Historic Park
near Wolfville, on the Evangeline Trail.

This is the site of the French settlement memorized by Henry Wadsworth Longfellow's poem, Evangeline. The Acadians could not bring themselves to give up their French heritage during the fight between the British and French forces for Nova Scotia. The Acadians were deported by the British without giving them an alternative destination, families were often torn apart and tragedies were common. Here you'll find the Acadian Memorial Church, displays, and formal landscaped gardens. **Free.** Open yr around. Tours mid May - Mid Oct, daily.

Cape Breton Highlands National Park
Igonish Beach B0C 1L0. (902)285-2270.

Northern Cape Breton Island. A spectacularly beautiful park, well worth visiting. Most of the park is blanketed with Acadian forest while heath bogs cover the interior. The mountains provide magnificent contrast to the rocky eastern shore or the natural sand beaches. Many diverse hiking trails. Information centers at Cheticamp and Igonish Beach. **$3/car.** Open yr around. Best access is Jun-Aug.

Fortress of Louisbourg National Historic park
Box 160, Louisbourg B0A 1M0. (902)733-2280.

Reconstruction of a prosperous 1744 French fort. People in period costumes fill the streets and shops, recreating 18th century life in the fort. Visit the Governor's home, soldier's barracks, guardhouses, private dwellings, storehouses, buy bread at the bakery or eat 18th century food at an inn. **$6/adult; $1.50/child. *Canadian dollars.**

Jun, Sept, daily, 10-6. Jul-Aug, daily, 9-7.

•Good Choices:

Natural Scenery: Kejimkujik National Park, Liverpool/ Victoria Park, Truro.
Nature and Man: Annapolis Royal Historic Gardens, historic botanic gardens, Annapolis/ Ross Farm, 19th century working farm, Hwy 12 N of Chester/ Public Gardens, Halifax/ Shubenacadie Wildlife Park, Nova Scotia animals, Hwy 102, Exit 10, 38 km S of Truro/ Lighthouse Route, SW coast, Hwy 103, Halifax to Yarmouth/ Fisheries Museum of the Atlantic and Aquarium of Native Fish, Lunenburg.
Science and Technology: Annapolis Tidal Power Project, harnessing the tides, Annapolis/ Alexander Graham Bell National Historic Park, displays of Bell's scientific work, Baddeck.
Historical and Cultural: Champlain's Habitation, 1605 settlement, Annapolis/ Lower St George St, 19th century historic buildings, Annapolis/ Sherburne Village, 19th century living history, Antigonish/ Great Hall of Clans and Craft Centre, Gaelic College,

Baddeck/ Barrington Woolen Mill, historic water powered mill, Barrington/ Quaker Whaler's House, 1785 house, Dartmouth/ Port Royal National Historic Park, reconstructed 17th century fur trading post, Digby/ Halifax: Citadel National Historic Park, contains 19th century fort, art gallery, army museum, Nova Scotia museum; Maritime Museum of the Atlantic, nautical history; Nova Scotia Museum, natural and human history; Province House; St Paul's Church, 18th century/ Ross-Thompson House, 1780s store, Shelburne/ Shelburne County Museum, Shelburne/ Nova Scotia Museum, mansion, antiques, gardens, Windsor/ Firefighters Museum of Nova Scotia, 1863 to present, Yarmouth.
Entertainment: Ferryboat, Dartmouth to Halifax/ Sightseeing tours, Tourist Centre, Dartmouth/ Fisherman's Wharf, fishing fleet, Digby.
Commercial: Musee' Acadien, museum, crafts cooperative, cafe, Cheticamp/ Bonda Inc Industrial Tour, clothing, Yarmouth.
Seasonal Events and Festivals: Highland Games, July, Antigonish/ Nova Scotia Provincial Exhibition, Aug, Truro.

Ontario

Fame: *Incredible Ontario: wilderness, major cities, farms, industries.*
You must *visit Old Fort William for historic perspective; visit Niagara Falls for a scenic view.*

Ottawa

Fame: *The capital city of Canada, one of Canada's most beautiful cities.*
You must *visit the Parliment Buildings.*

•Best Choices:

Parliment Buildings
Parlimentary Guide Program, House of Commons, Rm 607-B, La Promenade Bldg, 151 Sparks St, Ottawa K1P 5R3. (613)996-0896.

Wellington St on Parliment Hill. The seat of government for all of Canada, the Parliament Bldgs comprise three buildings, the House of Commons, the Seante Chamber, the Speaker's Chamber, offices, and the Parliamentary Library. **Free.** Tours: Jul-Aug, daily, 8-8:30. Rest of yr, daily, 9-4:30.

Central Experimental Farm
Queen Elizabeth Driveway. (613)995-5222.

A 1,200 acre farm in the center of the suburbs, with a horse-drawn wagon tour, Agriculture Museum, gardens, arboretum, fields, herds of cattle, sheep, pigs and horses.
Free. Museum, barns, greenhouse, daily, 9-4. Wagon rides, May-Sept, Mon-Fri, 10-11:30, 2-3:30.

•Good Choices:

Nature and Man: Gatineau Park, woodland, lakes, animals/ National Museum of Natural Sciences, audiovisual, models/ Rideau Canal, locks, interpretive programs, scenic walks.
Science and Technology: National Museum of Science and Technology, particpatory exhibits.
Historical and Cultural: Laurier House, former residence of prime ministers/ National Aviation Museum/ National Gallery of Canada, paintings, prints, photographs, Old Masters, contemporary/ National Museum of Man, story of mankind prehistoricto today/ National Postal Museum, North American stamps, postal artifacts/ Royal Canadian Mint, coin

and medal collections, tours of production/ Supreme Court.
Entertainment: Rent a boat or take a cruise on the Rideau Canal.
Commercial: Byward Market, farmers' market, arts, crafts.
Seasonal Events and Festivals: Winterlude, Feb/ Festival of Spring, May/ Changing the Guard, Jul-Aug, 10-6, hourly, Rideau Hall.

Toronto

Fame: *A "city for all ages," CN Tower.*
You must *ride to the top of the CN Tower, tour the Harbourfront.*

•Best Choices:

CN Tower
301 Front St W, M5V 2T6. (416)360-8500.

World's tallest free-standing structure at 1,815 ft, 5 in. Ride a glass-faced elevator to the top in 58 seconds. Panoramic view of Toronto, Lake Ontario and the Toronto Islands. **$6*/adult; $4/sr citizen, student; $3.50/child.** Daily, 10-11:30, 1-4, 6-9.

Harbourfront and Queen's Quary Terminal
410 Queen's Quay W, Suite 500, M5V 2Z3. (416)364-7127.

Unique new waterfront centre. Shop in Queen's Quay Terminal, visit Antique Market, stroll the water's edge walkways, through parks or relax in a waterfront cafe. Dance theatres and art exhibits. **Free entrance.** Yr around, Mon-Sat.

Toronto Eaton Centre
220 Yonge St, M5B 2H1. (416)979-3300.

An indoor shopping complex, covered by a translucent dome, with over 300 shops and services. **Free entrance.** Mon-Fri, 10-9; Sat, 10-6.

•Good Choices:

Nature and Man: Colborne Lodge, High Park, gardens, zoo/ Metropolitan Toronto Zoo/ Toronto Islands Park and Ferry, park, farm animals, amusement park.
Science and Technology: Mc-Laughlin Planetarium/ Ontario Science Centre, particpatory exhibits, Don Mills.
Historical and Cultural: Art Gallery of Ontario, Old Masters to Contemporary/ Black Creek Pioneer Village, recreated rural 19th century village/ Casa Loma, medieval castle/ Historic Fort York, restored original bldgs, demonstrations/ Mackenzie House, restored 19th century house/ Redpath Sugar Museum, memorabilia related to sugar/ Marine Museum

of Upper Canada, shipping memorabilia, tugboat/ Royal Ontario Museum, art, archaeology, natural science/ Spadina, restored home, gardens/ Toronto's First Post Office, living history, tours/ Black Creek Pioneer Village, 19th century living history, Downsview.
 Entertainment: Ontario Place, entertainment complex: theatre, IMAX, music, children's theatre, all for admission
 Commercial: Toronto Stock Exchange/ Yorkville, trendy shopping area.
 Sports: Greenwood Race Track/ Hockey Hall of Fame/ Woobine Race Track.
 Seasonal Events and Festivals: Canadian National Exhibition, Aug/ Royal Agricultural Winter Fair, Nov.

Provincewide Attractions

•Best Choices:

Old Fort William
Thunder Bay P0T 2Z0. (807)577-8461.

An authentic reconstruction of the original fort as it was from 1816 to 1821. The largest of its kind in North America. Historical interpretive activities include visiting a doctor's house, apothecary, a cooper, carpenter, blacksmith, tinsmith, armourer, boat builder, bakery, loading and unloading canoes, fiddling, dancing. There are Indian and voyageur encampments, a fully operational farm, living quarters, 19th century dining hall, a Great Hall and many other buildings. **High Season: $4.20/adult; $2.10/sr citizen, student. Low Season: $3.20/adult; $1.60/sr citizen, student.** July-Aug: daily, 10-6. 5/16-6/30, 8/30-9/30: Mon-Fri, 10-4; Sat-Sun, 10-5. Oct-May, daily walking tours, 11, 1:30, 3.

Niagara Falls
Box 150, Niagara Falls L2E 6T2. (416)356-2241, Ext 39.

South of Rainbow Bridge on Niagara Pkwy. Two cataracts separated by Goat Island. The U.S. Falls are 184 ft high and 1,060 ft wide. The Horseshoe Falls are 176 ft high and form a 2,200 ft curve. The falls are illuminated by colored spotlights at night and present an unforgettable scene. **Free.**

Upper Canada Village
Box 740, Morrisburg K0C 1X0. (613)543-2911.

Crysler Farm Battlefield Park, about 11 km E of Morrisburg on Hwy 2. Typical early Canadian village in the 1800s. Includes homes, churches, mills, tavern, general store, bakery and cheese factory, hotel, horse-drawn carryalls, and bateau, miniature train. Costumed guides recreate the period. 19th century meals served at the hotel. **$5.25*/adult; $3.90/student; $3.25/sr citizen; $1.25/child 6-12.** Jul-Aug, daily, 9:30-6. 5/15-6/30, 9/1-10/15, daily, 9:30-5. Off-season, Mon-Fri, 9-4; Sat-Sun, 9-5.

•Good Choices:

Nature and Man: Royal Botanical Gardens, gardens, arboretum, wildlife sanctuary, Hamilton/ Thunder Bay Amethyst Mine Panorama, mine, museum, tour, Thunder Bay.

Science and Technology: Ontario Science Centre, participatory exhibits, Don Mills/ Science North, participatory science exhbits, Sudbury.

Historical and Cultural: Bell Homestead, home of Alexander Graham Bell, Brantford/ Dundurn Castle, 19th century mansion, Hamilton/ Old Fort Henry, historic miliary uniforms, precision drill unit, Kingston/ McMichael Canadian Collection, Canadian art, Indian artists, Kleinburg/ Museum of Indian Archaeology & Lawson Prehistoric Indian Village, ongoing reconstruction of village, London/ Sainte-Marie Among the Hurons, reconstruction of first inland missionary settlement, Midland/ Ontario Electric Railway Museum, historic electric railcars, trolley rides, Rockwood/ The Meeting Place, Mennonite history, St Jacobs.

Entertainment: Maid of the Mist, boat trip in front of falls, Niagara Falls.

Commercial: Seagram Museum, history of wine and liquor industry, Waterloo.

Prince Edward Island

Fame: *The island province, Canada's smallest and most densely populated province.*
You must *go to the beaches, have a lobster supper.*

Provincewide Attractions

•Best Choices:

Prince Edward Island National Park
PO Box 487, Charlottetown C1A 7L1. (902)672-2211.

Blue Heron Drive. The park has 25 miles of the best sandy beaches with warm salt waters. Also includes Green Gables House, beach walks, camping, interpretation progrms, campfires, puppet shows, tennis, golf, lawn bowling. **$3/car.**

•Good Choices:

Nature and Man: PEI Marine Aquarium and Manor of Birds, Cavendish/ Moore's Migratory Bird Sanctuary, King's Byway.
 Science and Technology: Planetarium of Univ of PEI, Charlottetown.
 Historical and Cultural: Orwell Corner Rural Life Museum, Charlottetown/ Province House, Charlottetown/ Acadian Museum, Lady Slipper Drive/ Green Park Historic Park, shipbuilding, Lady Slipper Drive/ Green Gables House, PEI National Park.
 Entertainment: Rainbow Valley, amusement park, Blue Heron Drive.

Quebec

Fame: *A French province, with the atmosphere of the European country.*
You must *visit the Laurentians, enjoy the wonderful French food.*

Montreal

Fame: *A sophisticated city, the largest city in Canada and the second largest French speaking city in the world.*
 You must *visit Old Montreal and underground Montreal*

•Best Choices:

Old Montreal
bounded by the St Lawrence River, McGill, Berri and Notre-Dame Sts.

This is the city that grew from the original settlement, founded by Paul de Chomedey in 1642. The city grew within this area until the 1800s. It now has one of the largest concentrations of 17th, 18th and 19th century buildings to be found in North America. First stop here should be at the Tourist Information Centre, 174 Notre Dame St E, to learn more about the area and to get maps for a walking tour.

Underground City
any underground station of the Metro.

When Montreal's city planners were planning for the Metro, they decided to allot room for walkways between stations and for shops along the walkways. Many large buildings may have entrances below ground as well as above the street level. It's possible to spend a day shopping or doing business without ever having to go outside.

•Good Choices:

Nature and Man: Angrignon Park, children's zoo, Winter Wonderland/ Aquarium de Montreal/ Floral Park, permanent displays throughout summer/ Garden of Wonders, summer zoo/ Grandby Zoo/ Ile Notre-Dame, recreation, exhibitions/ Jardin botanique de Montreal, 3rd largest botanical garden in world/ La-Fontaine, Garden of Wonders, children's zoo, children's theatre in Aug/ Maisonnauve, botannical garden/ Mount Royal, look out over the city, folk dances, interpretation centre/ Winter quarters, winter zoo.

Science and Technology: Planetarium de Montreal.

Historic: Battle of Chateauguay National Historic Park, site of 1812 battle between U.S. and Canadians/ Fort Chambly, 1709 restored French fort/ Fort Lennox, 1819 British fort/ Montreal History Centre, history of Montreal/ Pointe-du-Moulin, historic mill/ Ile des Moulins, 19th century buildings, mill.

Historic Houses: Chateau Ramezay, residence of former French governors/ Sir George-Etienne Cartier Museum, two historic houses.

Art: Montreal Museum of Fine Arts, Egyptian statues to 20th century abstracts/ Musee des arts decoratifs, decorative arts/ Musee du Cinema, history of film making/ Palais de la Civilisation, summer museum for major exhibition.

Churches: Mary Queen of the World Cathedral, small replica of St Peter's Bascilica/ Notre Dame Basilica, 1829, neo-Gothic art and architecture/ Notre-Dame-de-Bonsecours Chapel, the sailors church/ St Patrick's Church, 1847 Gothic built to serve English speaking catholics.

Commercial: Canadian Guild of Crafts, objects created by Canadian craftspeople.

Quebec City

Fame: *the center of French national feeling in Canada, a split-level city with Upper Town and Lower Town.*

You must *explore the city on foot.*

•Best Choices:

Lower Town

The oldest part of the city had, for awhile, been allowed to deteriorate while the city built new buildings in Upper Town. Today restoration is underway and Lower Town is beginning to look very much like it did in the 17th and 18th centuries. Head for Place Royale, the center of activity today, just as it was in the old days. Look for the Information Centre, 29 rue Notre Dame, where you'll be able to learn about the restoration process, guided and self tours.

Musee du Fort
10 rue Sainte-Anne, G1R 3X1.
(418)692-2175.

See and hear the six assaults upon the city of Quebec recreated using a model of the 18th century city, with multi-vision, sound and light effects. **$2.75/adult; $1.50/sr citizen, student.** Spring, summer, Mon-Fri, 10-6; Sat-Sun, 10-5. Fall, Mon-Fri, 10-5, Sat-Sun, noon-5. Winter, Mon-Sat, 11-4, Sun, 1-5. Closed 12/1-12/20.

Citadel and Musee Militaire
Cote de la Citadelle, G1R 4V7.
(418)648-5234.

At the summit of Cape Diamond, the Citadel forms the southern boundary of the Quebec defensive system. It is made up of 25 buildings, built in a star-shaped plan, including the Governor-General's residence, officers' mess, the Cape Diamond Redoubt and several bastions. The Regimental Museum (Musee Militaire) is located in a 1750 powder house and accessible as part of a guided tour of the Citadel. Exhibitions include original arms displays, uniforms, documents, decorations from the 17th century to the present. **$2.75/adult; $1/child.** 6/15-Labor day, daily, 9-7. May - 6/15, Oct, daily, 9-5. Sept, daily 9-7. Mar-Apr, Mon-Fri, 9-4. Nov, Mon-Fri, 9-noon. Dec, Jan, Feb, by reservation.

•Good Choices:
Nature and Man: Battlefield Park, gardens, monuments, fountains/ Quebec Aquarium/ Quebec Zoo.

Historic: Artillery Park, 17th century defensive site/ Cartier-Brebeuf Park, commemorates Jacques Cartier and Jean de Brebeuf, ship replica, interpretive center, tours/ La Maison des Vins, guided tours of underground wine vaults/ Musee Historique, wax museum/ Port of Quebec in the 19th century, National Historic Site/ Musee L'Empire de Madame Belley, see unique, unusual clothes.

Historic Houses: Villa Bagatelle, 19th century neo-Gothic, gardens.

Churches: Basilica of Notre-Dame, historic and ornate/ Basilica of Sainte-Anne-de-Beaupre, Romanesque style, vaults, story of Jesus' life/ Church of Notre-Dame-des-Victoires, 1688, oldest stone church in Quebec/ Quebec Seminary, museum, tour/ St Andrew's Church, oldest congregation of Scottish origin.

Art: Galerie du Musee du Quebec, exhibits by Canadian and foreign artists/ Quebec Museum, ancient to contemporary art.

Entertainment: Funicular, elevator between Lower and Upper Town/ Gondola ride, Parc du Mont Ste-Anne, summer.

Seasonal Events and Festivals: Carnaval, pre lent/ Exposition Provinciale de Quebec, Aug.

Provincewide Attractions

•Best Choices:

Seaphin Village
Ste Adele. (514)229-4777.

1 mi N of Ste Adele on Hwy 117.
A village, in a forest, of log cabins
and shops like those found in the
Laurentians about 100 yrs ago. Includes an amusement park and a
miniature train ride. **$1.50/car and
$3.50/adult; $1.75/child 5-17.**
6/15-9/15, daily, 10-5. 5/15-6/15,
9/15-10/15, Sat-Wed, 10-5.

Metis Park
Route 132, Grand Metis G0J 1W0.
(418)775-2221.

The last private owner of this estate was Elsie Stephen Meighan
Reford, a talented gardener. She
was able to cultivate magnificent
English gardens, with 100,000
plants and flowers that are seldom
grown in the Gaspe peninsula.
**Gardens: $2/car. Mansion:
$1/adult; $.50/sr citizen, student
8-18.** 6/15-9/15, daily, 8:30-8.

•Good Choices:

Natural Scenery: Forillon Na-
tional Park, varied plants, animals,
geological formations, Gaspe/
Muricie National Park, Laurentides
Mountains/ Parc national de la
Gaspesie, Gaspe Penninsula/ Perce
Rock, unusual rock formation,
Perce/ Waterfalls, Riviere-du-
Loup.

Nature and Man: Jardin zoologique, Bonaventure/ Granby Zoological Garden, Granby/ Lake Boivin
Nature Interpretation Centre, woodland, marsh, waterfowl, exhibits,
tours, Grandby/ Jardin zoologique,
Saint-Felicien/ Mount Tremblant
Provincial Park, wilderness,
wildlife, plants, 300 lakes, 3 rivers,
waterfalls, mountains, recreation,
spectacular fall foilage, Saint-
Jovite.

Science and Technology:
Nuclear Power Station, Gentilly.

Historical and Cultural: Moulin
de Beaumont, restored mill,
Beaumont/ Manoir et Domaine
Trent, period home, tours, Drum-
mondville/ Centre national
de'exposition, art center, Jon-
quiere/ Musee maritime Bernier,
maritime museum, L'Islet-sur-
Mer/Moulin La Pierre, shingle
mill, flour mill, wool carding mill,
Norbertville/ Musee du Bas-St-
Laurent, art and ethnology, Riviere-
du-Loup/ Le Moulin des Arts,
visual arts gallery, Saint-Etienne/
La Seigneurie des Auinales, manor
mill, house gardens, Saint-Roch-
des-Aulnaies/ Domaine Joly De
Lotbiniere, manor house, Sainte-
Croix/ Maison Dumulon, pioneer
family home, store, post office,
Sainte-Germaine-Boule/ De Ton-
nancour House, oldest house, Trois
Rivieres.

Entertainment: Village de securite routiere, made for children, rules of the road, Chicoutimi.
Commercial: Compagnie de Papier Q.N.S. Ltee, paper mill tour, Baie-Comeau/ Societe Canadienne de Meaux Reynolds Limitee, Reynolds Aluminum tour, Baie-Comeau/ Pates Domtar, paper company tour, Lebel-sur-Quevillon.

Saskatchewan

Fame: *Breadbasket of Canada, a prairie province.*
You must *visit Western Development Museum in North Battleford, see the "Trial of Louis Riel."*

Provincewide Attractions

•Best Choices:

Royal Canadian Mounted Police Cetennial Museum
RCMP Depot Division, Dewdney Av W, Regina. (306)780-5838.

Offical museum of RCMP, portrays history of the force with displays of equipment, weapons, photos, archival material, personal belongings and memorabilia. Seargeant Major's drill parade, 1 pm wkdays. **Free.** 6/1-9/15, daily, 8-8:45. 9/16-5/31, daily 8-4:45. Tours, Mon-Fri, 9, 10, 11, 1:30, 2:30, 3:30.

Wascana Centre
Center of City, Regina.

2300 acre park combining natural scenery and attractions. Among the highlights are: CBC Regina Broadcast Centre; Diefenbacker Homestead, boyhood home of former P.M. J. G. Diefenbaker; Legislative Building; Museum of Natural History; Waterfowl Park. Take a 50 min double decker bus tour of the Centre which departs from the headquarters building and the Legislative Landing. **Bus Tour: $2/adult; $1/child under 16. Other listed attractions are free.** Most open daily, 10-8.

•Good Choices:

Natural Scenery: Cypress Hills Provincial Park, hills, pines, wildflowers, animals, SW corner of SK/ Duck Mountain Provincial Park, lake, forests, Manitoba border 25 km E of Kamsack/ Good Spirit Lake Provincial Park, sand dunes, lake, 34 km NW of Yorkton/ Pike Lake Provincial Park, grass, trees, beach, animals, SW corner of SK.

Nature and Man: Forest Nursery, Big River/ Saskatchewan Minerals, Sodium Sulphate, recovery plant tour, Chaplin/ Estevan Brick Wildlife Display, life native animals, Estevan/ Bird Haven Game Bird and Animal Farm, Halbrite/ PFRA Tree Nursery, Indian Head/ Buffalo Pound Provincial Park, herd of plains bison, NE of Moose Jaw/ Wild Animal Park, native to SK, Moose Jaw/ Floodwood Gardens, show gardens, ice cream and drink, Rouleau/ Forestry Farm Zoo, animals and birds native to SK, Saskatoon.

History: Western Development Museum, transportation, Moose Jaw/ Western Development Museum, transportation, North Battleford/ Diefenbaker House, Prince Albert/ Government House, historic residence of Lieutenant Governor, Regina/ Rt Hon J G Diefenbaker Centre, archives and museum, Saskatoon.

Historic Parks: Motherwell Homestead National Historic Park, 1912 homestead, Abernethy/ Batoche National Historic Park, remains of Louis Riel headquarters village, Batoche/ Battleford National Historic Park, original NWMP post, Battleford/ Cumberland House Historic Park, HBC fur trade post, Cumberland House/ Cannington Manor Historic Park, 1896 English settlement, Manor/ Wood Mountain Post Historic Park, NW Mounted Police and Sioux Indians displays, Wood Mountain.

Art: Art Museum & National Exhibition Centre, permanent and traveling exhibitions of art, history, science, Moose Jaw/ Dunlop Art Gallery, local, regional, international art, Regina/ Gallery on the Roof, art and view of city, Regina. Saskatoon: Memorial Library and Art Gallery, Canadian artists/ Mendel Art Gallery, regional, national, international art/ Museum of Ukranian Culture/ Ukrainian Museum of Canada, Ukranian culture in Canada.

Entertainment: "Trial of Louis Riel" theatre production, Government House, Regina.

Commercial: Taylors Honey Farm, guided tour, Nipawin/ Saskatchewan Indian Arts and Crafts, Midtown Village Mall, Saskatoon/ Sifto Salt Plant Tours, Unity.

Yukon

Fame: *The Klondike Gold Rush, Robert W. Service poetry.*
You must *try panning for gold.*

Provincewide Attractions

•Good Choices:

Natural Scenery: Kluane National Park, glaciers, mountains.
Nature and Man: Yukon Gardens, 22-acre botanical gardens, Whitehorse.
Historical and Cultural: Dawson City Museum, gold rush artifacts, Dawson City/ Discovery Claim, site of first four gold claims, Bonanza Creek, Dawson City/ Minto Park, antique locomotives, Dawson City/ Robert Service Cabin, Dawson City/ Klondike Gold Rush National Historical Park, Skagway/ Alaska Highway Interpretive Centre, Watson Lake/ MacBride Museum, gold rush artifacts, Whitehorse/ S.S. Klondike, restored paddlewheeler, Whitehorse.
Entertainment: Diamond Tooth Gertie's, Canada's only legal gambling casino, Dawson City/ Klondike Era Films, antique films about gold rush, Dawson City.

Chambers of Commerce

United States

Alabama
State of Alabama
Bureau of Tourism & Travel
532 S. Perry St.
Montgomery, AL 36130

Alaska
Anchorage Convention & Visitors
Bureau
201 E. Third Av.
Anchorage, AK 99501

Arizona
Arizona Office of tourism
1480 East Bethany Home road
Phoenix, AZ 85014

Arkansas
Arkansas Dept. of Parks & Tourism
1 Capitol Mall
Little Rock, AR 77201

California
California Office of Tourism
Dept. of Commerce
1121 L St., Suite 102
Sacramento, CA 95814

Colorado
Colorado Tourism Bureau
State of Colorado
1625 Broadway
Suite 1700
Denver, CO 80202

Connecticut
Connecticut Dept. of Economic
Development
Tourism Division
210 Washington St.
Hartford, CT 06106

Delaware
Tourism Department
Delaware Development Office
99 Kings Highway
PO Box 1401
Dover, DE 19903

District of Columbia
Washington D.C. Convention &
Visitors Assn.
1575 Eye St. NW
Washington, D.C. 20005

Florida
Florida Division of Tourism
Visitor Inquiry
126 Van Buren St.
Tallahassee, FL 32301

Georgia
Georgia Dept. of Industry & Trade,
Tourist Division
PO Box 1776
Atlanta, GA 30301

Hawaii
Hawaii Visitors Bureau
2270 Kalakaua Av., Suite 801
Honolulu, Hawaii 96815

Idaho
Department of Commerce
State of Idaho
State Capitol Bldg, Room 108
Boise, Idaho 83720

Illinois
Chicago Tourism Council
Historic Water Tower In-The-Park
806 N. Michigan Av.
Chicago, IL 60611

Illinois Office of Tourism
State of Illinois Center
310 S. Michigan, 1st Fl.
Chicago, IL 60604

Indiana
Indiana Tourism Development Div.
Indiana Commerce Center
1 North Capitol Av.
Indianapolis, IN 46204-7288

Iowa
Tourism Bureau
Iowa Department of Economic
Development
State of Iowa
200 East Grand
Des Moines, IA 50309

Kansas
Kansas Dept. of Commerce
Travel & Tourism Div.
400 West 8th, Suite 500
Topeka, KS 66603

Kentucky
Kentucky Dept. of Travel Development
ment
Capital Plaza Tower
Frankfort, KY 40601

Louisiana
Louisiana Dept. of Transportation
and Development
Box 94245
Capitol Station
Baton Rouge, LA 70804-9245

Maine
Maine Publicity Bureau
State of Maine
94 Winthrop St.
Hallowell, ME 04347

Maryland
Maryland Office of Tourism
Development
45 Calvert St.
Annapolis, MD 21401

Massachusetts
Massachusetts Dept. of Tourism &
Development
100 Cambridge St.
Boston, MA 02202

Boston Chamber of Commerce
125 High St.
Boston, MA 02110

Michigan
Michigan Travel Bureau
Department of Commerce
Town Center Building
333 S. Capitol Av.
Lansing, MI 48933

Minnesota
Minnesota Office of Tourism
375 Jackson St., 250 Skyway Level
St. Paul, MN 55101

Mississippi
Mississippi Dept. of Economic
Development
Division of Tourism
PO Box 849
Jackson, MS 39205-0849

Missouri
Missouri Div. of Tourism
Truman State Office Bldg.
PO Box 1055
Jefferson City, MO 65102

Montana
Travel Montana
Department of Commerce
1424 Ninth Av.
Helena, Mont 59620

Nebraska
Nebraska Dept. of Economic
Development
Division of Travel and Tourism
301 Centennial Mall S.
PO Box 94666
Lincoln, NE 68509-4666

Nevada
Nevada Commission on Tourism
Capitol Complex
Carson City, NV 89710

New Hampshire
State of New Hampshire
Office of Vacation Travel
PO Box 856
Concord, NH 03301

New Jersey
State of New Jersey
Department of Commerce and
Economic Development
Division of Travel & Tourism

CN 826
Trenton, NJ 08625-0826

New Mexico
New Mexico Tourism & Travel
Division
Economic Development &
Tourism Dept.
Joseph Montoya Bldg.
1100 St. Francis Dr.
Sante Fe, NM 87503

New York
State of New York
Department of Commerce, Div. of
Tourism
135 Delaware Av.
Buffalo, NY 14202

New York Convention & Visitors
Bureau
Two Columbus Circle
New York, NY 10019

North Carolina
Travel and Tourism Division
430 N. Salisbury St.
Raleigh, NC 27611

North Dakota
North Dakota Tourism
Liberty memorial building
600 E. Boulevard
Bismarck, ND 58505

Ohio
Ohio Division of Travel & Tourism
PO Box 1001
Columbus, OH 43266-0101

Oklahoma
Oklahoma Tourism & Recreation
Dept.
Literature Distribution Center
215 NE 28th
Oklahoma City, OK 73105

Oregon
Tourism Bureau
State of Oregon
643 Union St. Se
Salem, OR 97310

Pennsylvania
Pennsylvania Bureau of Travel
Development
Dept. PR, 426 Forum Bldg.
Harrisburg, PA 17120

Rhode Island
Rhode Island Tourism Div.
Seven Jackson Walkway
Providence, RI 02903

South Carolina
Tourism Division
South Carolina
1205 Pendleton St.
Columbia, SC 29201

South Dakota
South Dakota Tourism
Box 1000
Pierre, SD 57501

Tennessee
Department of Tourist Develop-
ment
State of Tennessee
320 6th Av. N., PO Box 23170
Nashville, TN 37202

Texas
Texas Dept. of Highways & Public
Transportation
Travel & Information Division
11th & Brazos Sts.
Austin, TX 78701

Utah
Utah Travel Council
Council Hall
Capitol Hill
Salt Lake City, UT 84114

Vermont
State of Vermont
Travel Division
Montpelier, VT 05602

Virginia
Virginia Div. of tourism
Bell Tower on Capitol Square
101 N. 9th St.
Richmond, VA 23219

Washington
State of Washington
Dept. of Trade and Economic Dev.
General Administration Bldg.
Olympia, WA 98504-0613

West Virginia
Department of Commerce
State of West Virginia
Charleston, WV 25305

Wisconsin
Wisconsin Div. of Tourism
Development
123 West Washington Av.
PO box 7970
Madison, WI 53707

Wyoming
Wyoming Travel Commission

I-25 at College Dr.
Cheyenne, WY 82002-0660

Canada

Alberta
Travel Alberta
Dept. E
Box 2500
Edmonton, Alberta
Canada T5J 2Z4

British Columbia
Ministry of Tourism
Recreation and Culture
1117 Wharf St.
Victoria, British Columbia
Canada V8W 2Z2

Manitoba
Manitoba Business Development
and Tourism
Winnipeg, Manitoba
Canada R3C 3H8

New Brunswick
Tourism, Recreation & Heritage
New Brunswick
CP Box 12345,
Fredericton, NB
Canada E3B 5C3

Newfoundland
Newfoundland and Labrador Dept.
of Development
Tourism Branch
Box 2016
St. John's, Newfoundland
Canada AIC 5R8

Northwest Territories
Travel Arctic FB
Government of the Northwest Ter-
ritories
Yellowknife, NWT
Canada X1A 2L9

Nova Scotia
Nova Scotia Dept. of Tourism
5151 Terminal Rd., 3rd Floor
Box 456
Halifax, NS
Canada B3J 2R5

Ontario
Tourism Marketing Branch
Ontario
77 Floor St. W., 9th Floor
Toronto, Ontario
Canada M7A 2R9

Prince Edward Island
Visitor Services Div.
Dept. of Finance & Tourism
Box 2000
Charlottetown, PEI
Canada CIA 7N8

Quebec
Gouvernement du Quebec
Ministere du Tourisme
Reseignements Touristiques
Tourisme Quebec
C P 20000
Quebec, Canada
G1K 7X2

Saskatchewan
Saskatchewan Tourism & Small
Business
2103 - 11th Av.
Regina, Saskatchewan
Canada S4P 3V7

Yukon Territory
Yukon Tourism
Box 2703
Whitehorse, Yukon
Canada, Y1A 2C6

Notes

Travel Books

London guidebook with theme tours

Now an independent traveler can make the most of London with step-by-step routes through the best of London's castles, royal residences, museums, or fascinating tourism hot spots. Ruth Humleker's tours are complete with special maps, timetables, and transportation instructions---all you'll need to see the best of this fabulous city in limited time. **London for the Independent Traveler.** 210 pages, maps. $13.50 postpaid (PP).

Find the best in New York

If you have only a few days to sightsee New York, here's the perfect guidebook. Complete with step-by-step maps, Ruth Humleker's guide has day-long self-guided tours of the best and most interesting things in Manhattan. Theme tours range from Romantic New York, Art Lover's New York, and Shopper's New York (and lots of others) to the Basic Three Days in New York in which the author takes independent travelers on a whirlwind tour of the "Big Apple" utilizing easy-to-follow timetables, routes and special maps. **New York for the Independent Traveler.** 210 pages, maps. $10.50 PP.

Budget Motel Guide selects under $40 nightly lodgings

"Helps save money while providing useful information on the best of the least costly."---Bookviews

More than 3,500 selected motels and inns that offer rooms for $40 or less for two persons overnight in the U.S. and Canada are listed in the **State by State Guide to Budget Motels.** It's the perfect travel companion for vacations, getaways or business travel to give you the basic information you need to travel comfortably for less. Why pay those high prices when you can check out the listing, price description of quality budget motels in every state. It's the largest directory of its kind in what consumer-oriented magazines call today's best lodging bargains. **State by State Guide to Budget Motels.**   300 pages, $9.50 PP.

National guide to unique B &B's under $40

Now you can find charming, historic lodges, beds & breakfasts and country inns at moderate prices. Great for low-cost getaways or vacations in the U.S. and Canada, with special emphasis on popular vacation areas. At $40 a night for two, these B&Bs and country inns not only have charm and character but offer a terrific bargain in today's high-priced travel world. Listings itemize prices, tell special features, attractions (such as special breakfasts), give addresses, telephone numbers. **Affordable Bed & Breakfasts.** 210 pages, $10.50 PP

Best low-cost things to see and do

Plan a fun-filled, *affordable* family vacation with this value-minded guide to thousands of the best attractions in the U.S. and Canada that are free or charge no more than $5 admission. You can find many memorable experiences without straining the family budget. Choose from live performances, regional happenings, special attractions, historic sites, scenic wonders and more. It's fun just reading about where you can go and what you can do with this basic guidebook. **Best Low Cost Things to See and Do.** 224 pages, $10.50 PP.

Kids Trip Diary

An all-in-one journal and activity for kids age 6 through 12. Here's a terrific book designed to entertain youngsters while traveling and at the same time to spark

their imaginations and enhance their enjoyment of new places and impressions. A child can record his or her own memories, take part in "getting ready to go," find many hours of fun games, and record favorite experiences. It's a wonderful souvenir and memory book parents can treasure for years. **Kid's Trip Diary.** 80 pages, $5.50.PP

Complete Trip Diary

A traveler's own memories are the most precious souvenirs of any trip and this vacation journal helps record important facts, places, and impressions of daily sights and activities. Not a blank book, but an easy-to-use structured diary that lets anyone keep a smart travel journal. **MarLor's Complete Trip Diary** also helps organize a trip, keep track of important dates and schedules, maintain a firm grip on expenses (never get caught short again!) and keep a useful "to do" checklist. A very handy working book to use before as well as during vacations. And when vacation is over, you can put it on the bookshelf for many happy memories ahead. **Complete Trip Diary.** 80 pages, $5. PP

Order Form

Please send me the following books:

Total amount enclosed:

My name:

Address

City   *State*   *Zip*

MarLor Press / 4304 Brigadoon Dr./ Saint Paul, MN 55126
Your satisfaction guaranteed---or you may return your book in 30 days for full refund